Mastery of Keys

A Comprehensive Guide of Scales, Arpeggios, and Chords

A book for every pianist: student, teacher, and professional

ISBN: 979-8-9890167-0-9

Copyright © 2023 Bill Walker Music Publishing
Do not share, trade or distribute any portion of this book without the author's written permission. Making copies of individual exercises for personal use is permitted.
All Rights Reserved.

www.billwalkercomposer.com

Published by
Bill Walker Music Publishing

8227 S 70th Dr
Laveen, AZ 85339

All interior information and layout as well as front and back cover designs by Bill Walker.
Artwork for the cover is licensed through Adobe Stock

Printed in the United States of America

Mastery of Keys: A Comprehensive Guide of Scales, Arpeggios, and Chords

Welcome to a musical journey that unlocks the hidden treasures of the piano world! You're about to embark on a unique adventure that will not only deepen your understanding of scales, arpeggios, and chords but also revolutionize the way you approach the piano. Whether you're a beginner taking your first steps or an experienced pianist seeking to broaden your horizons, this book is designed with you in mind.

Have you ever wished for a comprehensive guide that explored the vast landscape of keys, scales, and chords beyond the conventional limits? Look no further, for this book is the answer to that very aspiration. It emerged from a desire to create the resource that I wished I had during my own piano journey. Traditional methods often confine their teachings to just keys representing the twelve tones, neglecting the fact that there are indeed fifteen major and fifteen minor keys.

Within these pages, you'll find an approach that embraces the fifteen major and fifteen minor keys, illuminating the keyboard in its entirety. I acknowledge that some keys may seem less trodden in the world of music composition, but their existence justifies the learning of them. Playing in all keys isn't just about mastering notes; it's about enhancing your versatility, sharpening your musical ear, and empowering you to tackle any piece of music that comes your way.

This book's essence lies in its comprehensive yet accessible presentation of scales, arpeggios, and chords. For scales, I've crafted an array of exercises suitable for all piano learners, beginners through advanced. Explore scales in various iterations, from 5 finger scales to scales in 3rds, octaves, and even venture into the realm of chromatic scales. Fingering is thoughtfully provided, guiding you from the early stages where every note counts, to a level where your fingers instinctively dance across the keys.

Speaking of arpeggios, the complexity of fingerings across exercises can be baffling, yet I've got you covered. This book offers a helping hand with fingering throughout your arpeggio journey, ensuring that you confidently navigate the intricate patterns and transitions.

Have you ever found yourself wondering about the multitude of chords that can be created from a single root note? I have! So, in this book, I've expanded the horizon beyond the basic major and minor chords, delving into augmented, diminished, and seventh chords. For jazz enthusiasts, I've presented a spectrum of chords that align with the essence of each key signature. While the entire spectrum of jazz chords is beyond the scope of this book, it certainly takes you steps closer.

The Circle of Fifths, that mystical wheel of musical harmony, awaits you at the book's conclusion. It's more than just a diagram, it's your guide to modulating between keys, a compass for understanding sharps and flats, and a treasure map to navigate the vast landscape of music theory.

As you reach the end of these pages, you'll discover a glossary of common musical terms and tempos, demystifying the language of music. Each section has been crafted with your learning in mind.

This book is an ode to the passion and dedication that every pianist pours into their craft. It's an invitation to embrace the full spectrum of keys, scales, and chords, transcending limitations and unlocking boundless potential. Whether you're a novice, an enthusiast, or a seasoned performer, I invite you to dive in, explore, and find the immense value that awaits within these pages.

So, let your fingers dance across the keyboard, let the notes resonate within your heart, and let this book be a guiding star on your musical voyage. May you discover new realms of expression, ignite your creativity, and embark on a journey that will forever transform your relationship with the piano.

Happy playing!

Bill Walker

This book is dedicated to my wife, Angie, whose
love and support made this book possible.

Table of Contents

Section 1: Scales

Five Finger Scales 1
Major Scales: One Octave 3
Major Scales: Two Octaves 7
Major Scales: Three Octaves 14
Major Scales: Four Octaves 29
Minor Scales: Natural, Melodic, and Harmonic 44
Major & Harmonic Minor Scales in 3rds 59
Major & Harmonic Minor Scales in 6ths 74
Major & Harmonic Minor Scales in 10ths 89
Major & Harmonic Minor Scales in Octaves 104
Chromatic Scales 134

Section 2: Arpeggios

Major, Minor, Dominant 7th, and Diminished 7th 139

Section 3: Chords

Scale-Tone Triads, Cadences, and Inversions 154
24 Chords Beginning on Each Root Note 169

Section 4: Appendices

Appendix A: The Circle of Fifths Diagram .... *i*
Appendix B: Glossary .... *ii*

Mastery of Keys
A Comprehensive Guide of Scales, Arpeggios, and Chords

Practice each scale and arpeggio exercise until mastery is achieved.
Begin by practicing each hand separately. Then practice hands together.
Metronome mark provided as a guide.

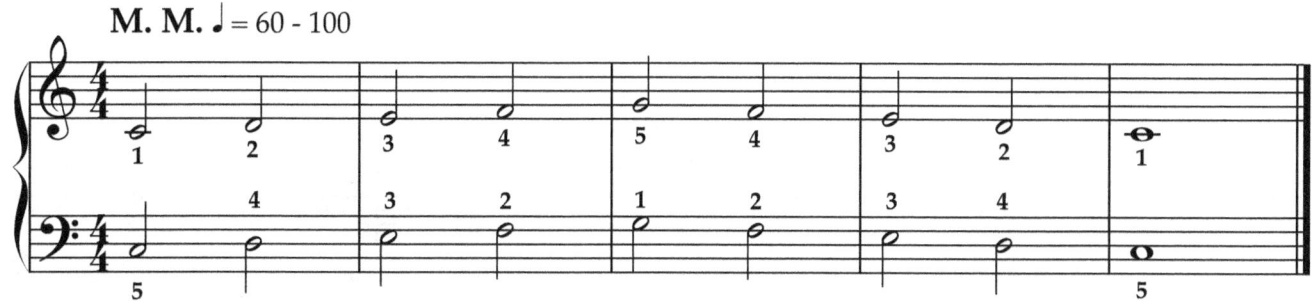

Five finger scale beginning on C: each note played twice

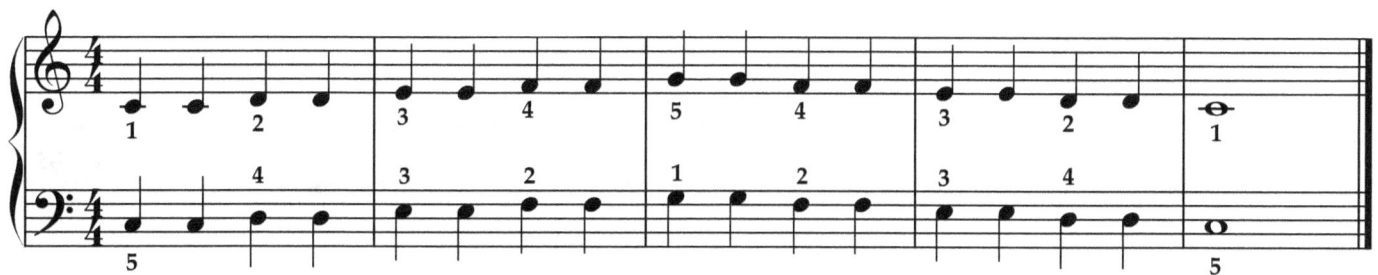

Five finger scale beginning on C: ascending one octave

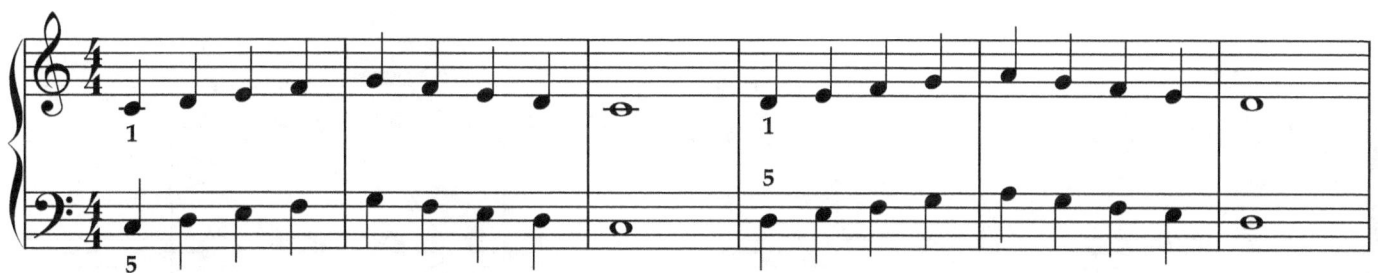

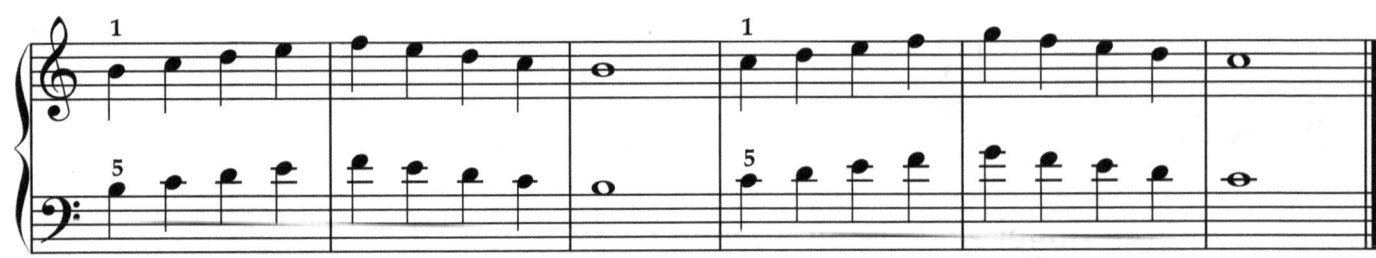

Five finger scale beginning on C
Each note played twice ascending one octave

C major scale: one octave

G major scale: one octave

D major scale: one octave

Note: For an explanation of scales, see *Appendix B*, pages *viii - x*

A major scale: one octave

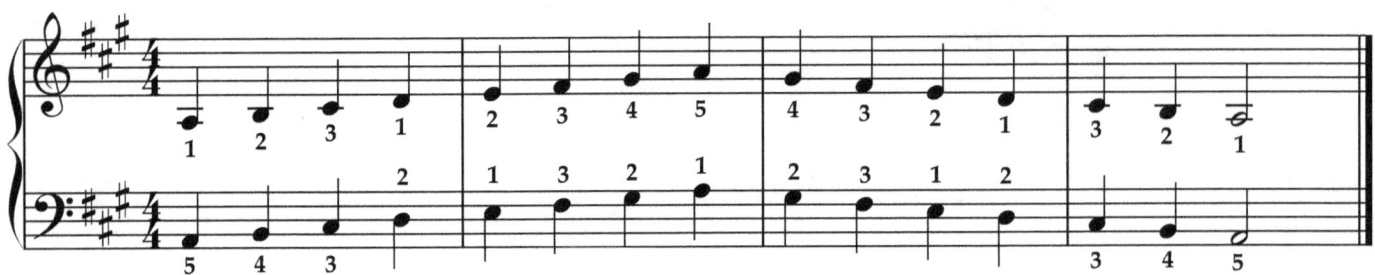

E major scale: one octave

B major scale: one octave

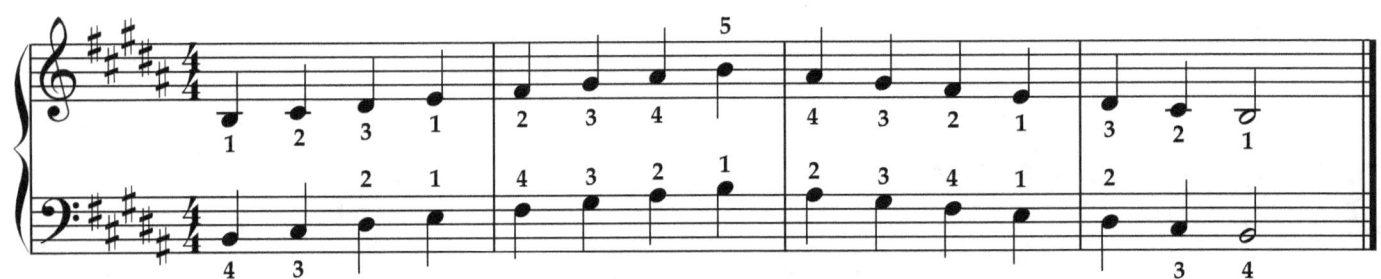

F-sharp major scale: one octave

C-sharp major scale: one octave

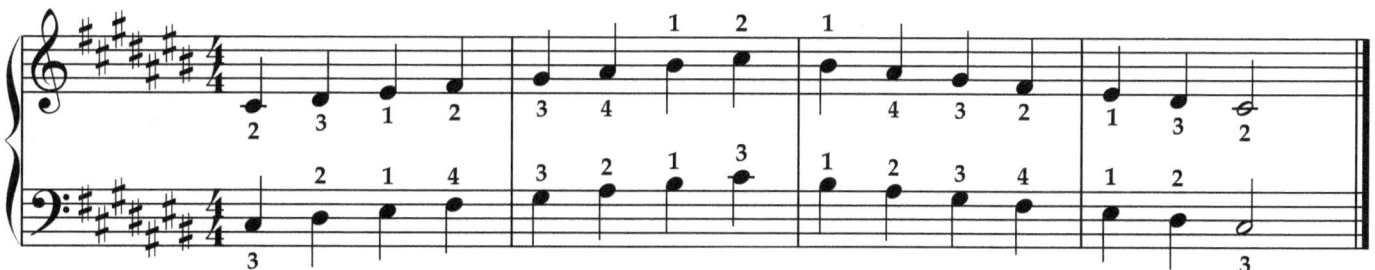

F major scale: one octave

B-flat major scale: one octave

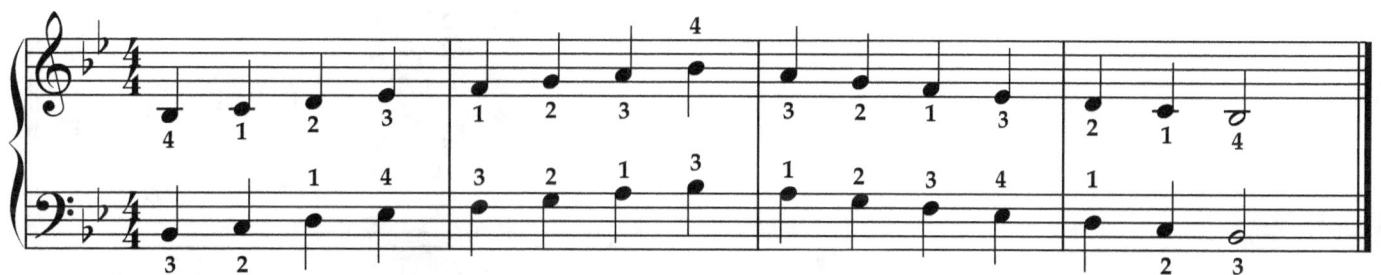

E-flat major scale: one octave

A-flat major scale: one octave

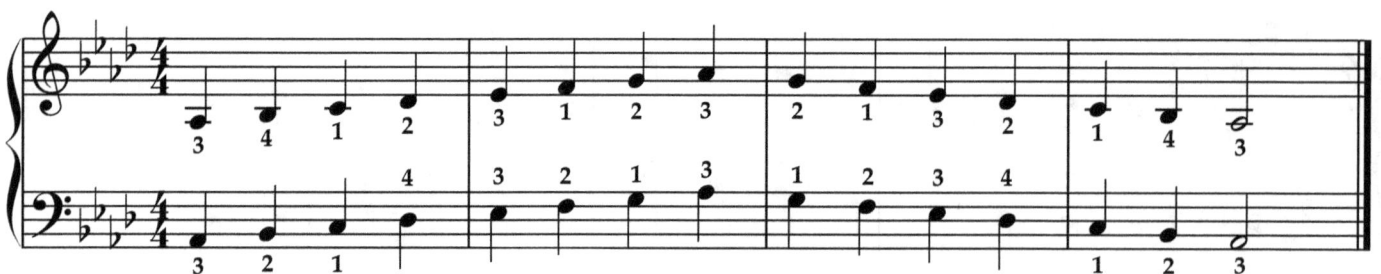

D-flat major scale: one octave

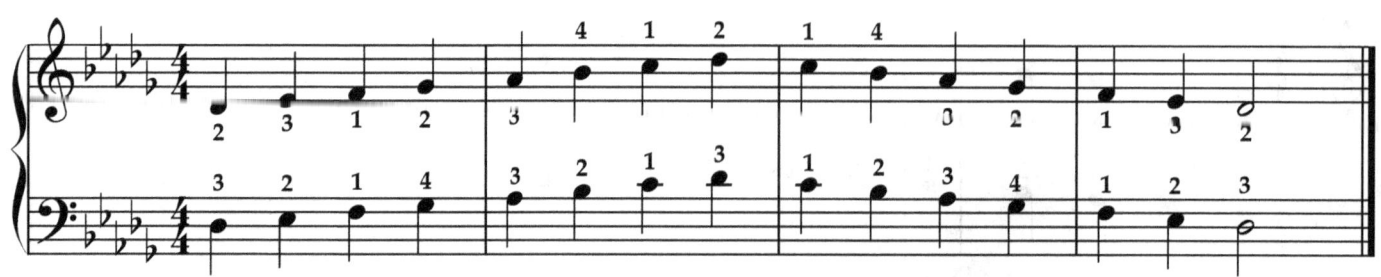

G-flat major scale: one octave

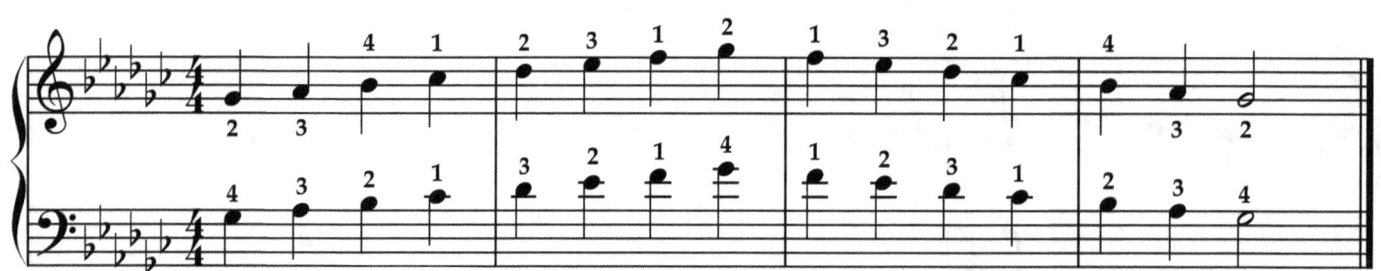

C-flat major scale: one octave

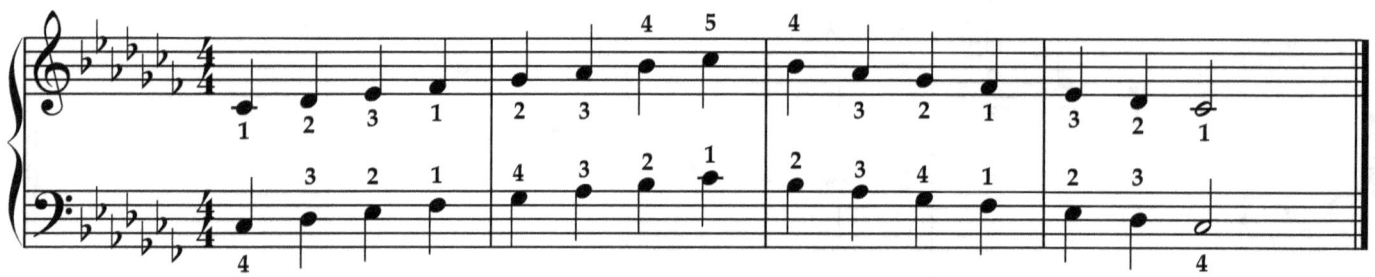

C major scale: two octaves

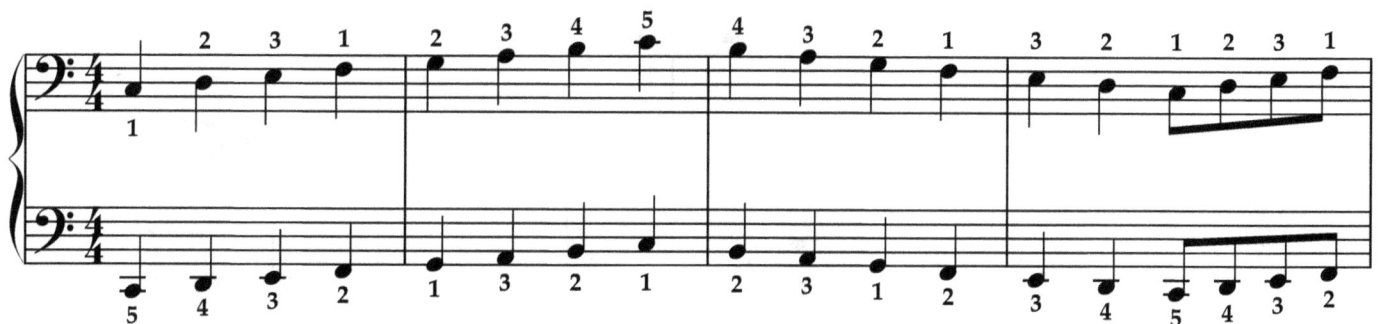
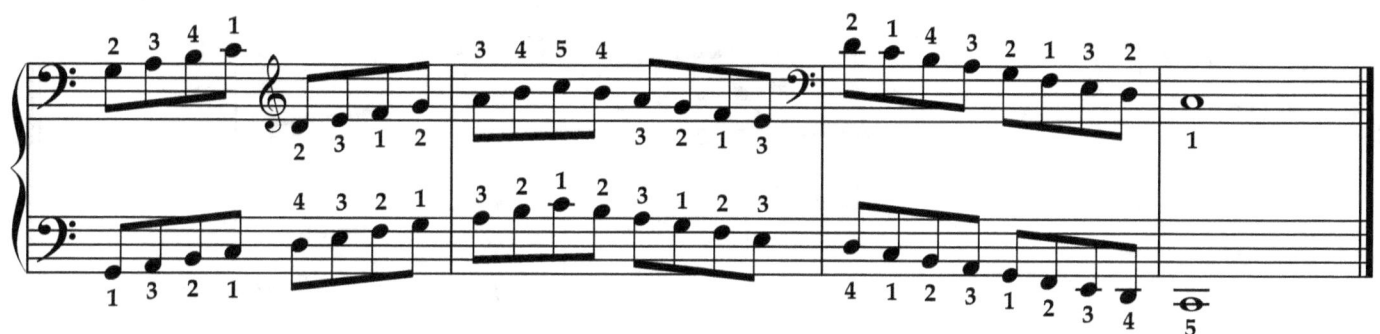

G major scale: two octaves

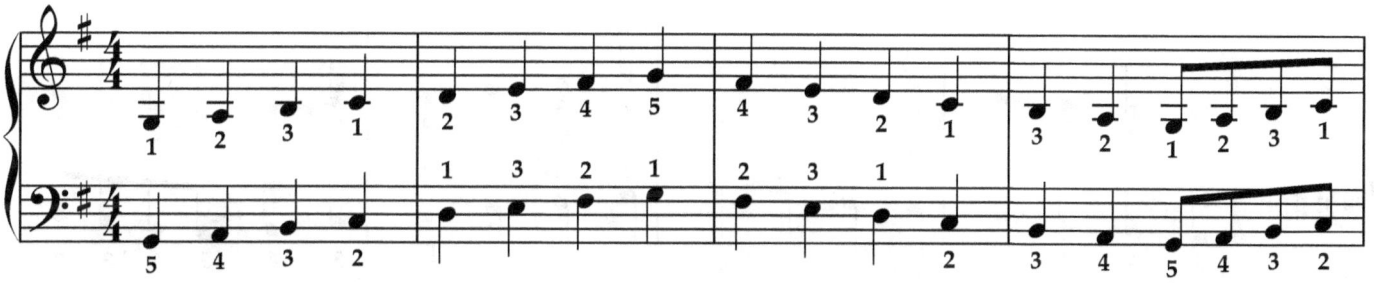

D major scale: two octaves

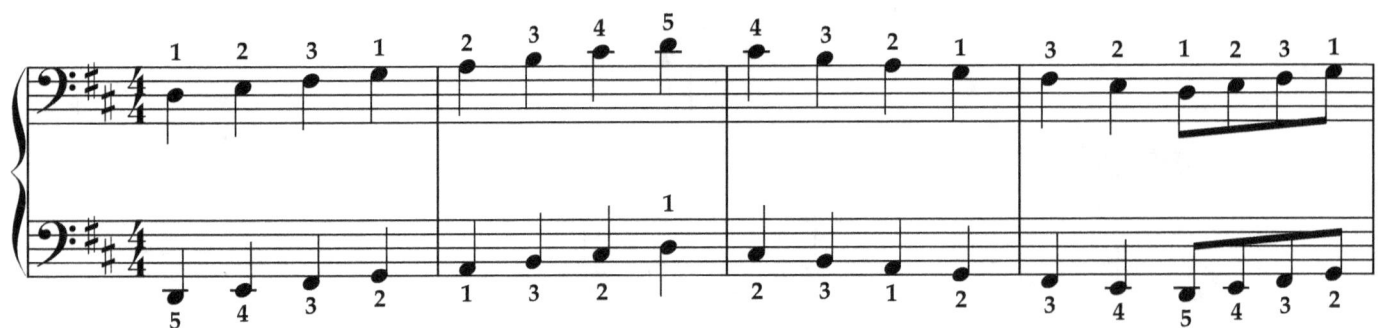
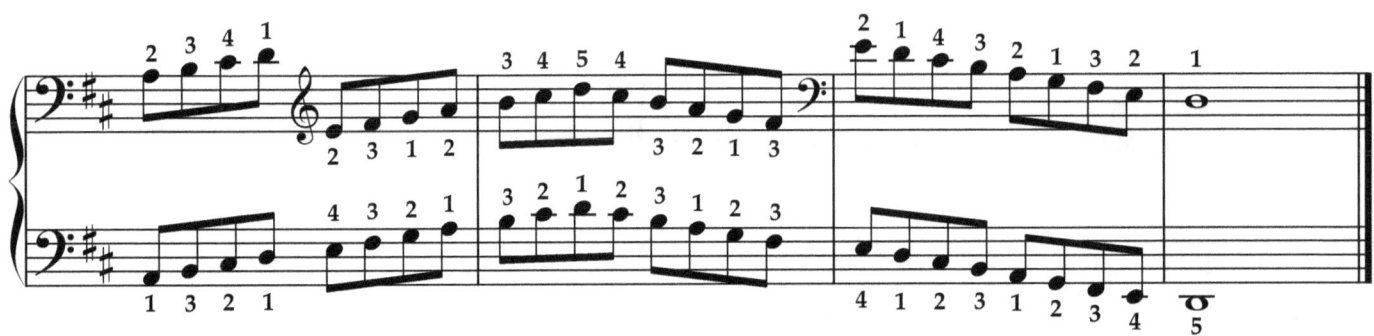

A major scale: two octaves

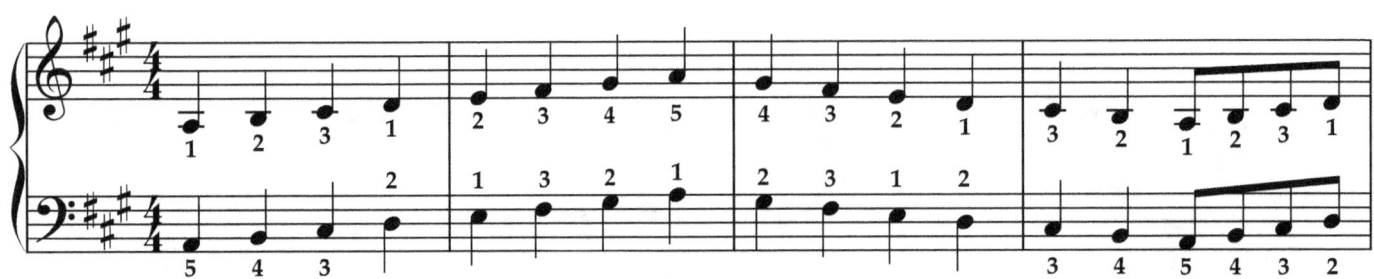
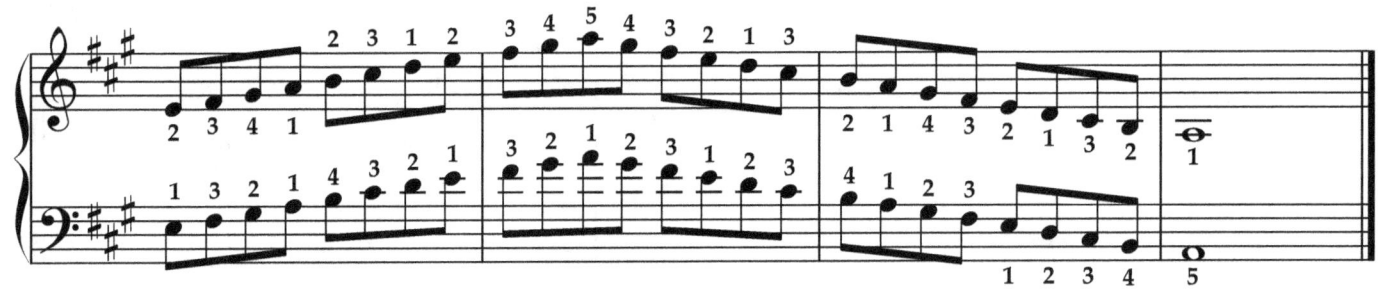

E major scale: two octaves

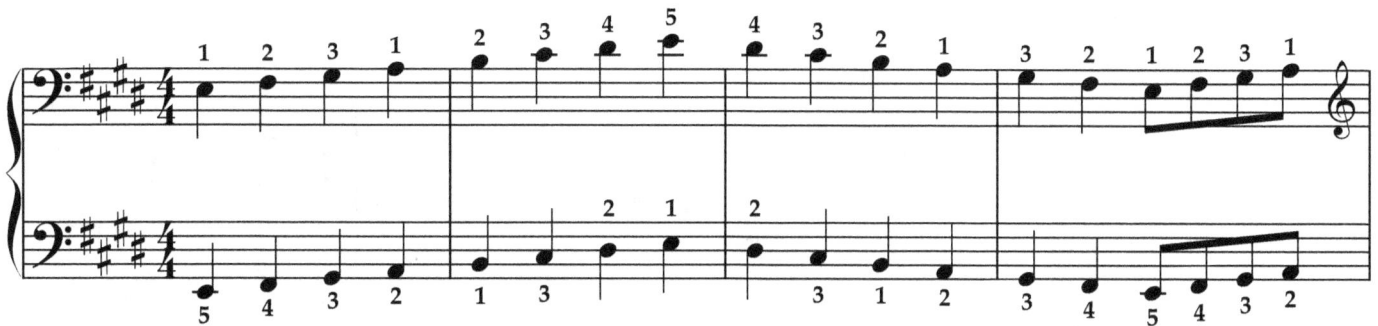

B major scale: two octaves

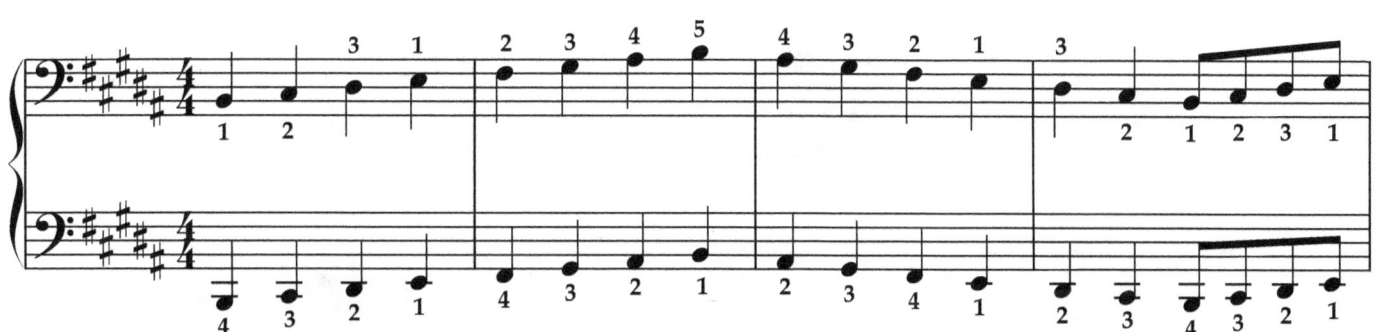
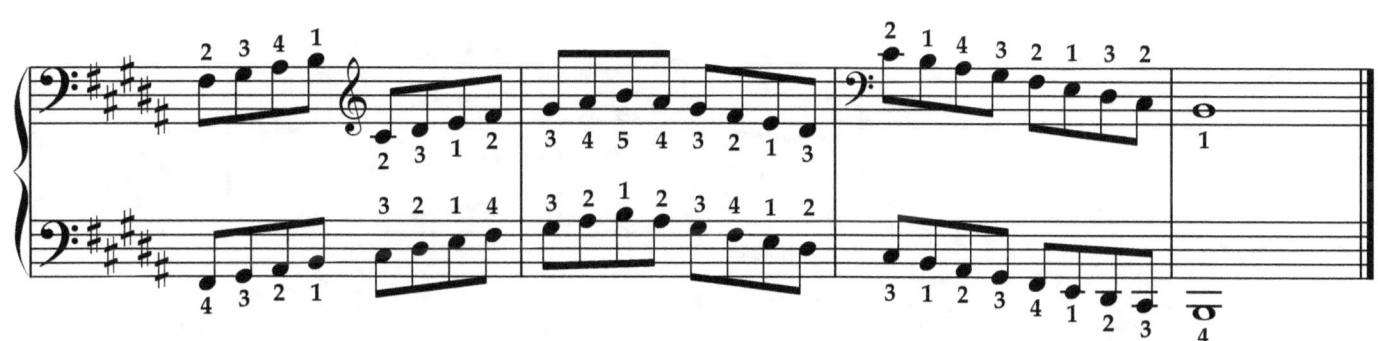

F-sharp major scale: two octaves

C-sharp major scale: two octaves

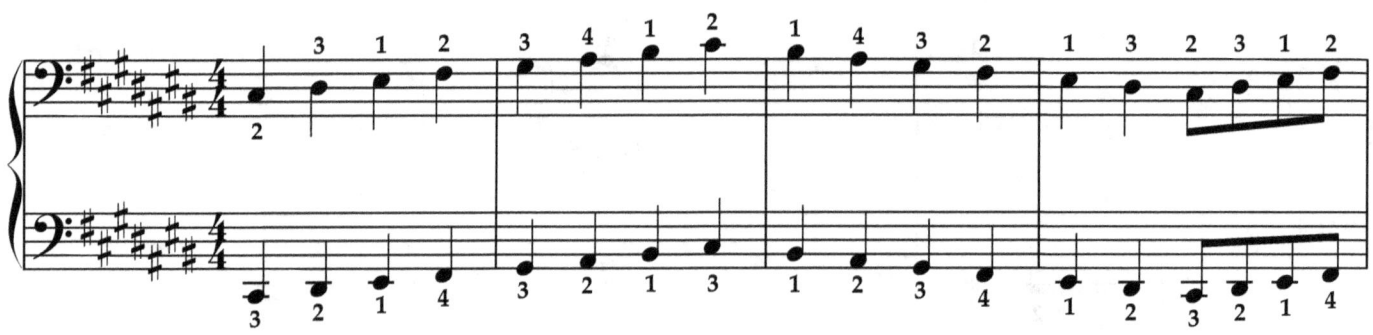

F major scale: two octaves

B-flat major scale: two octaves

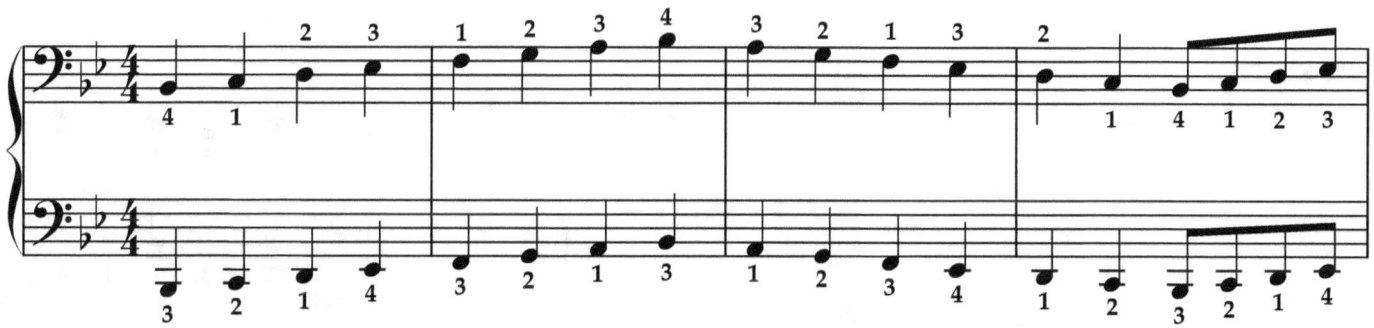

E-flat major scale: two octaves

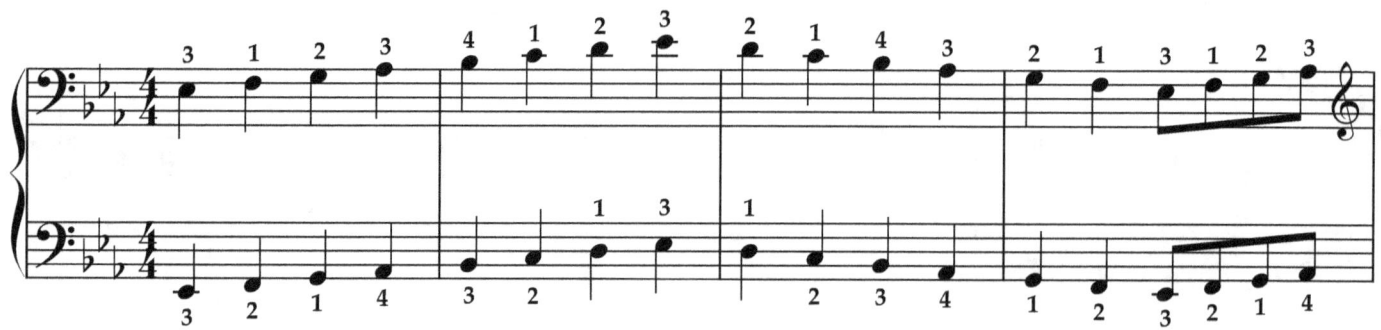
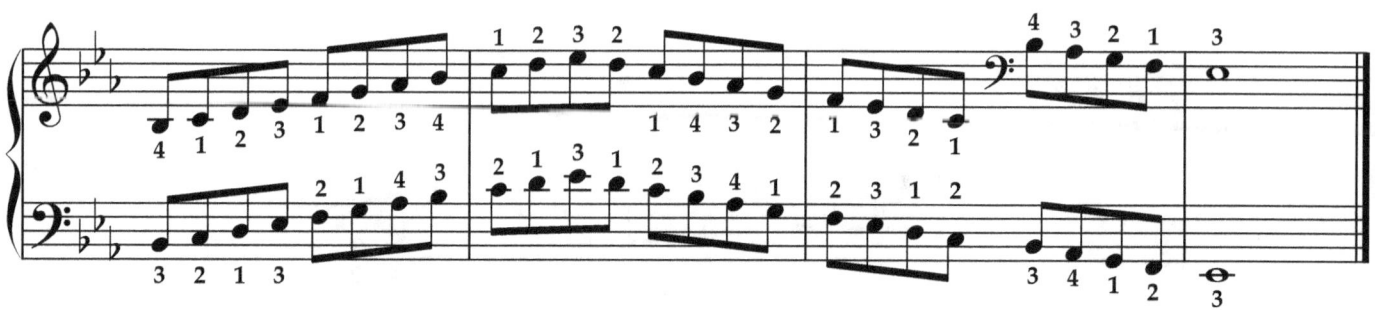

A-flat major scale: two octaves

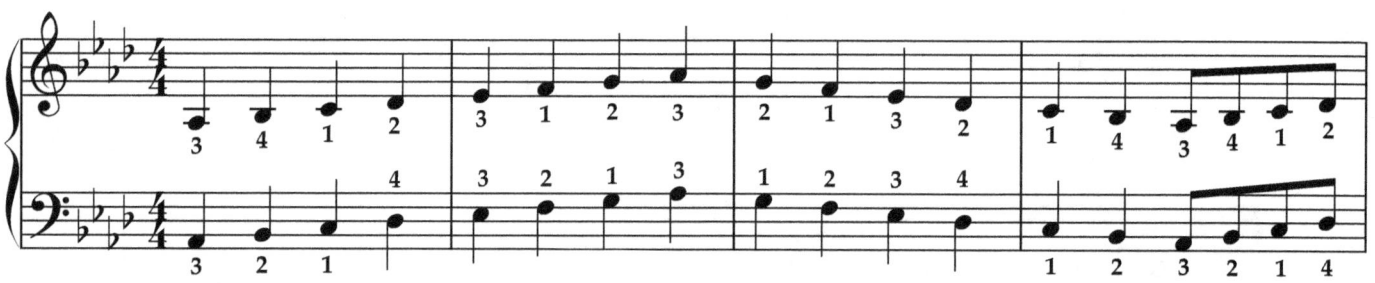

D-flat major scale: two octaves

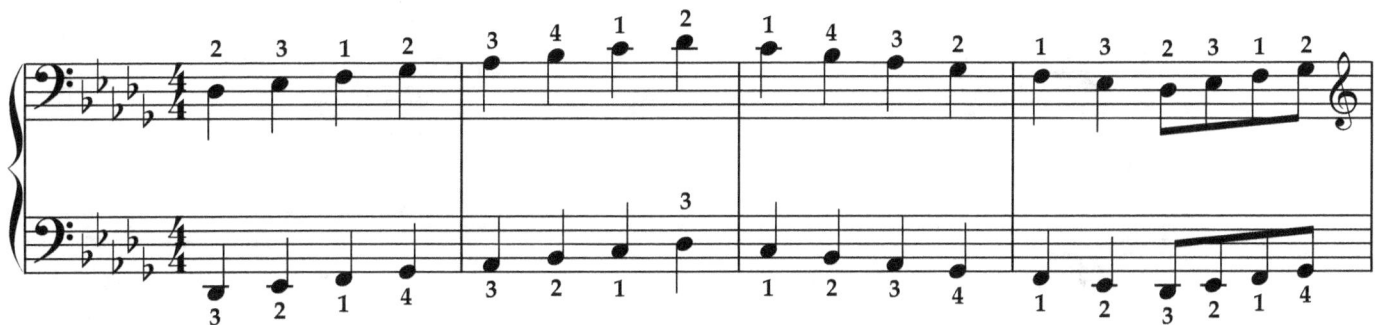

G-flat major scale: two octaves

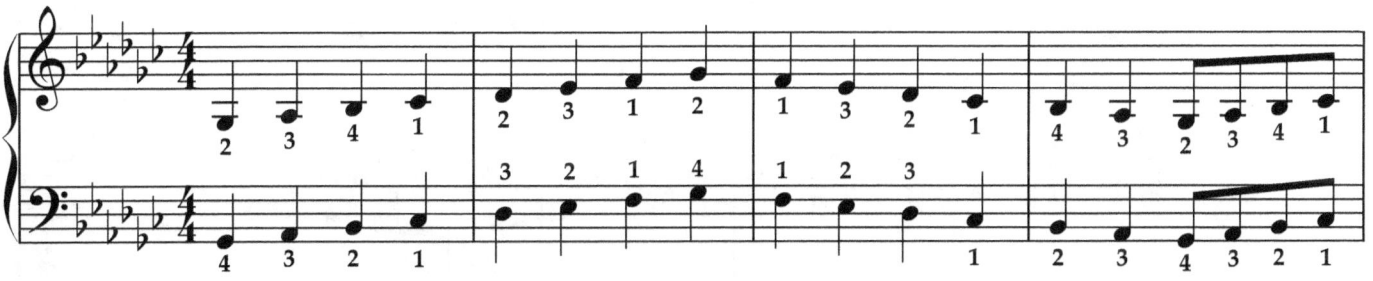

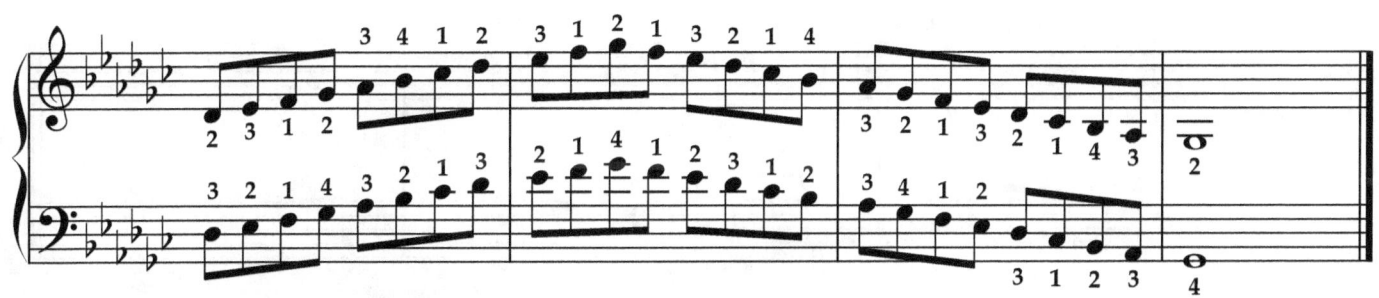

C-flat major scale: two octaves

C major scale: three octaves

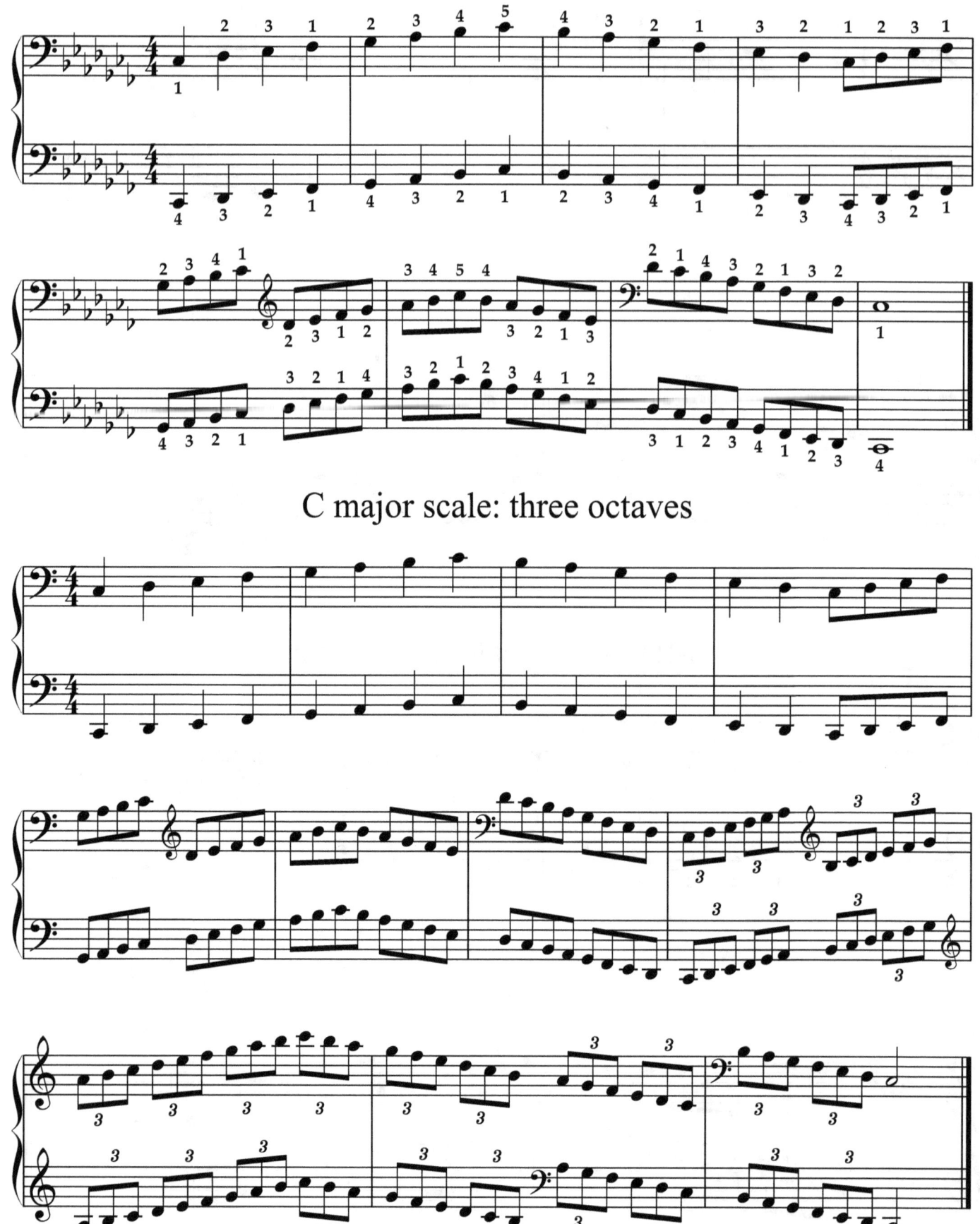

G major scale: three octaves

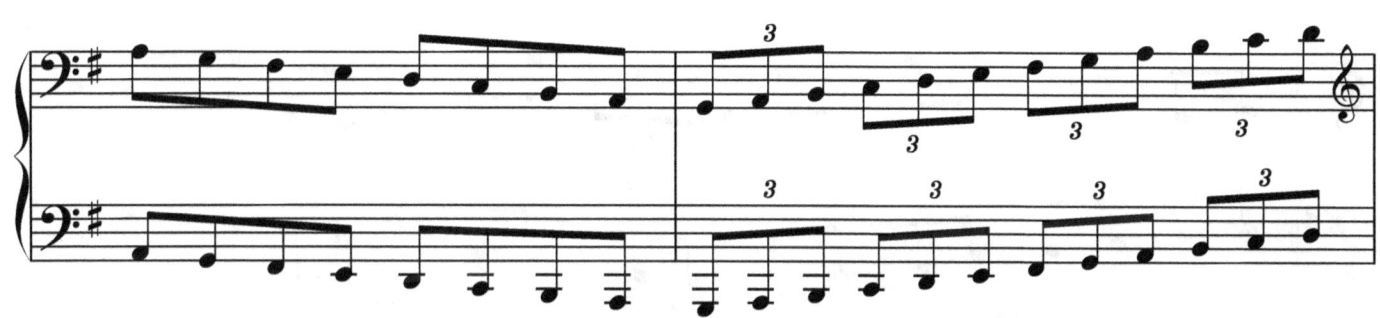

D major scale: three octaves

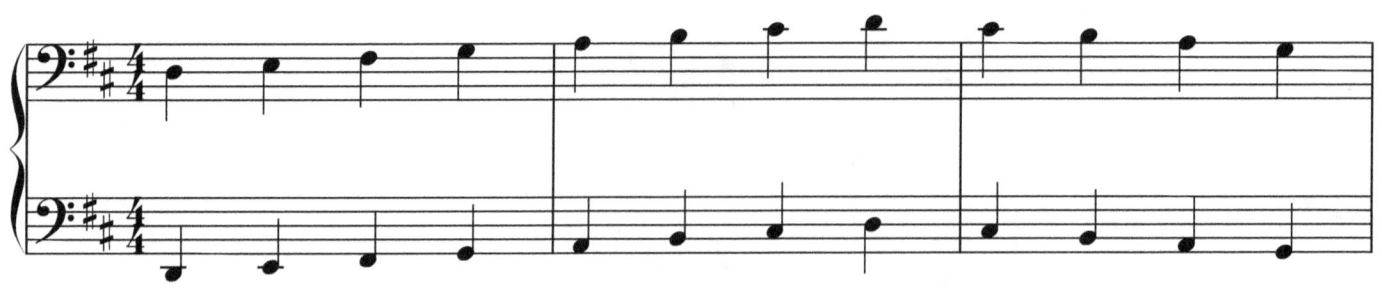

A major scale: three octaves

E major scale: three octaves

B major scale: three octaves

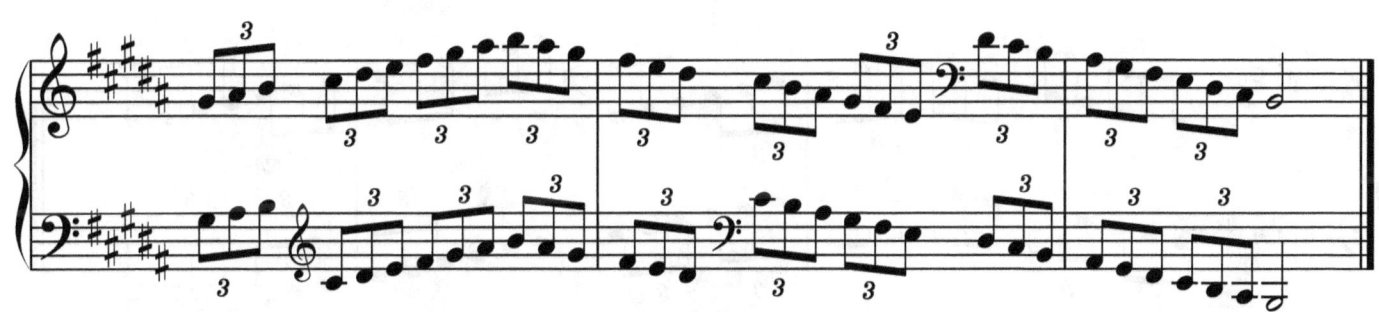

F-sharp major scale: three octaves

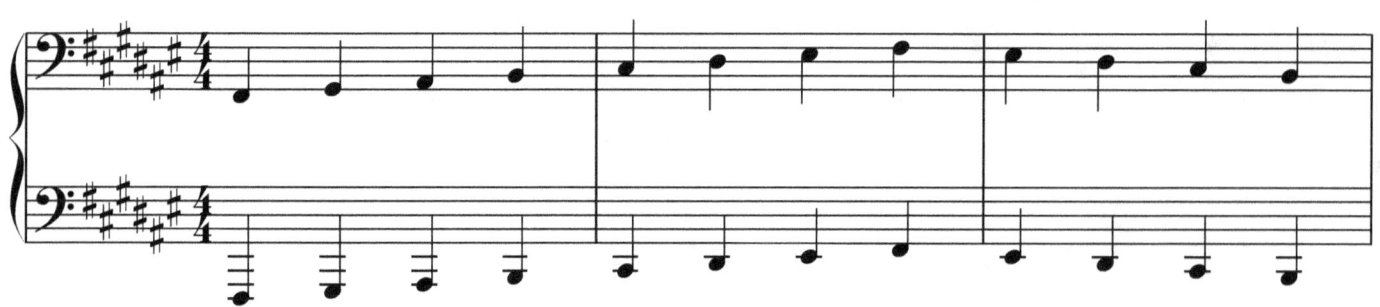

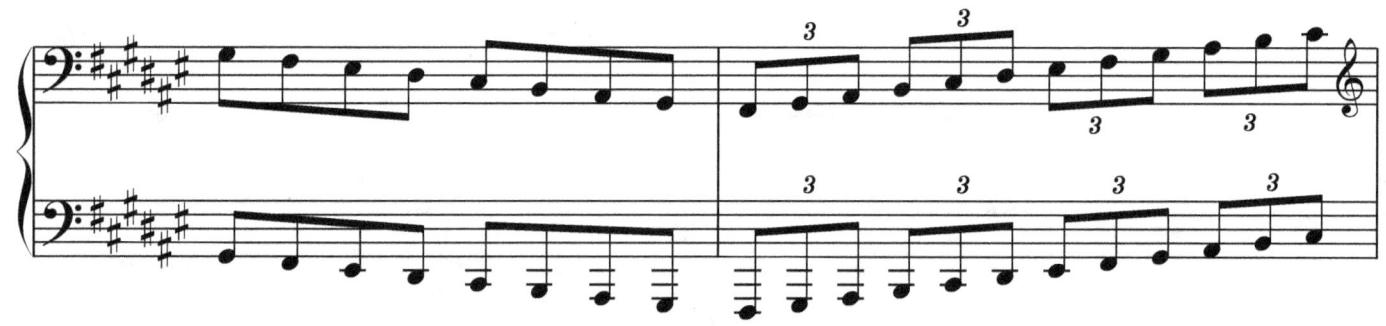
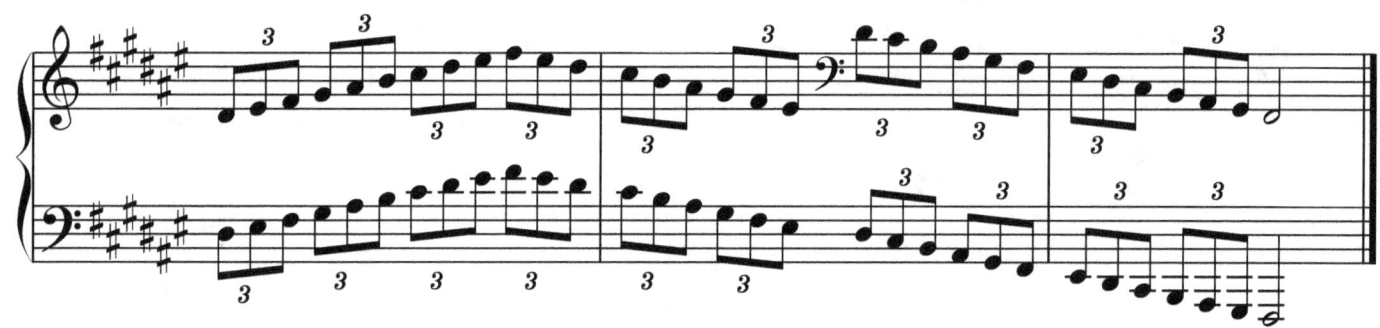

C-sharp major scale: three octaves

F major scale: three octaves

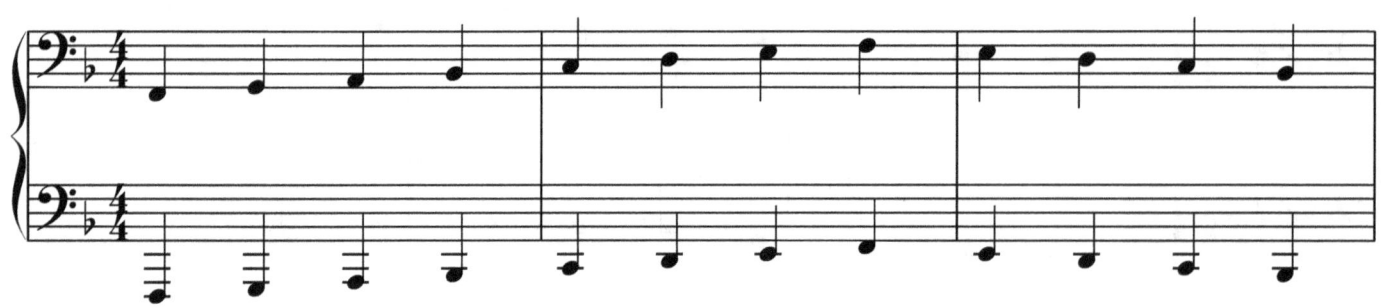

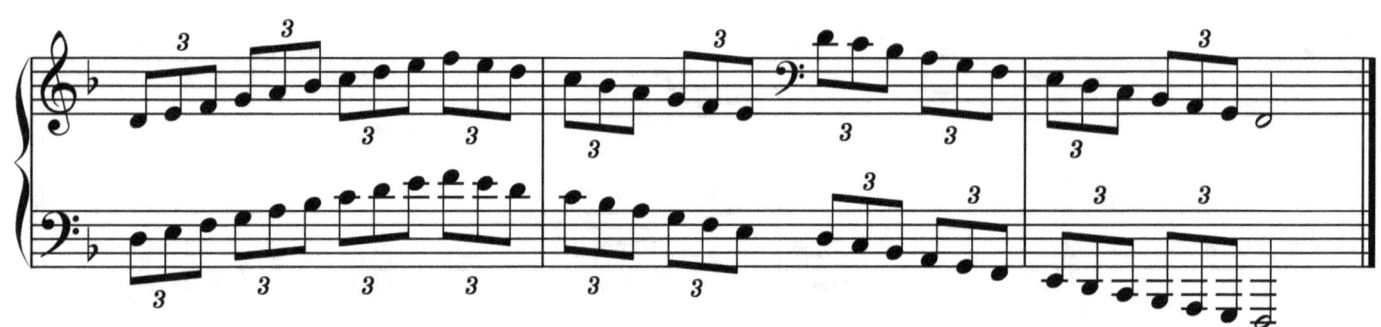

B-flat major scale: three octaves

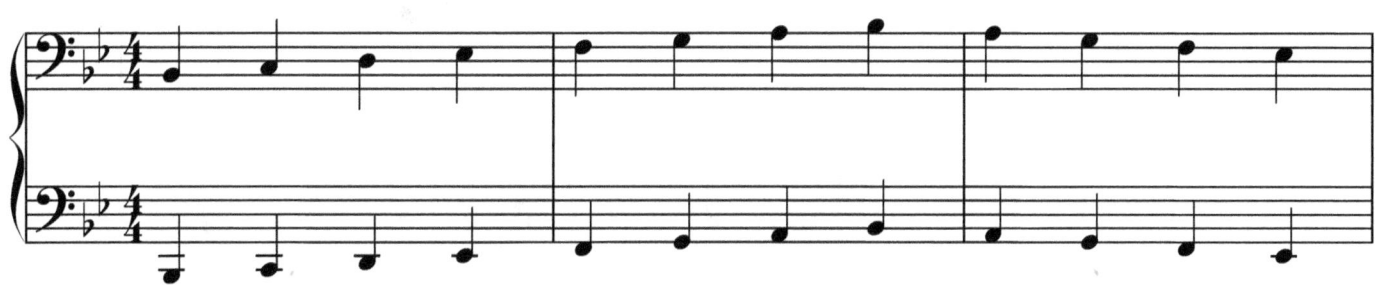

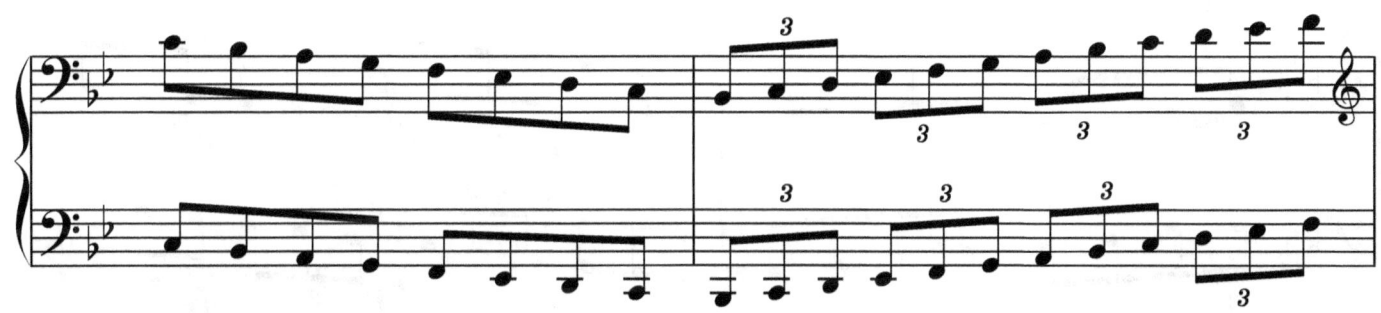

E-flat major scale: three octaves

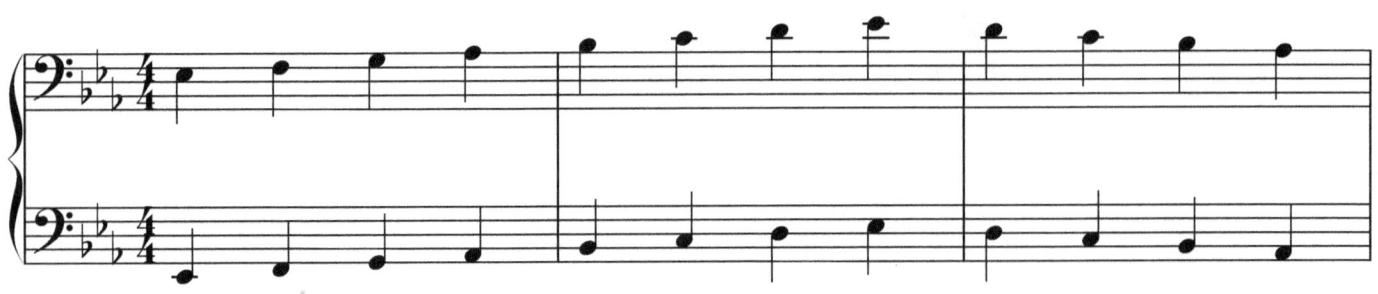

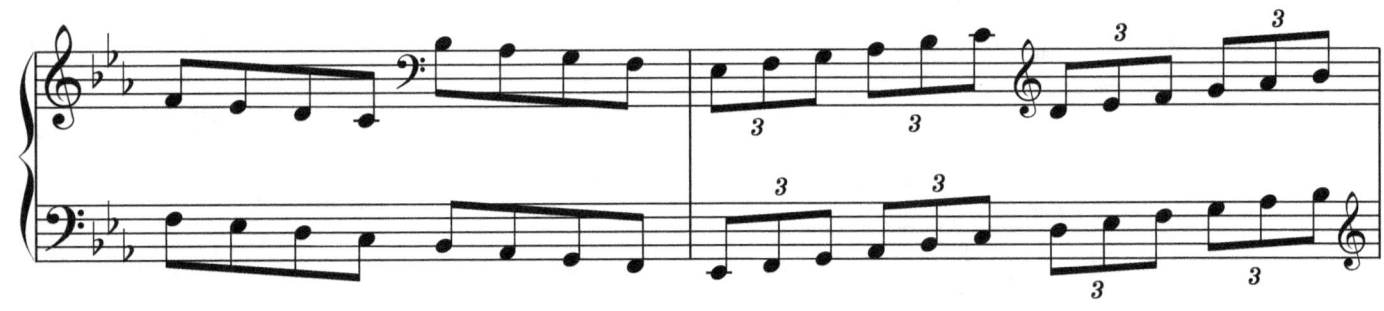

A-flat major scale: three octaves

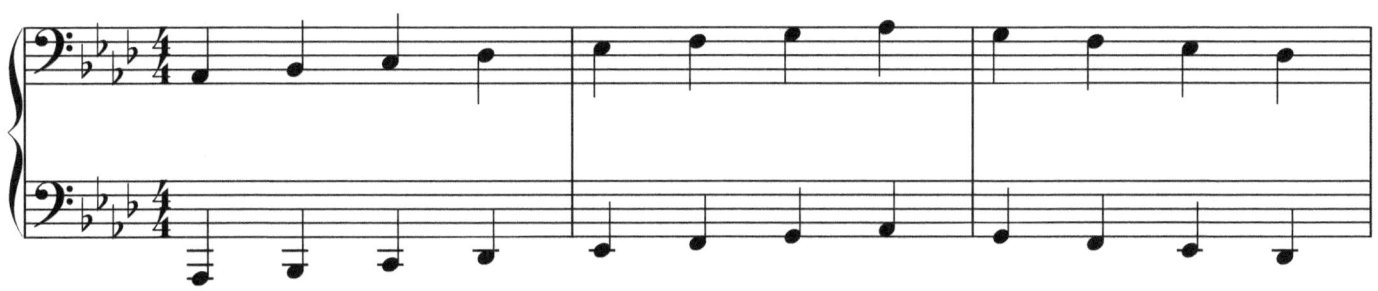

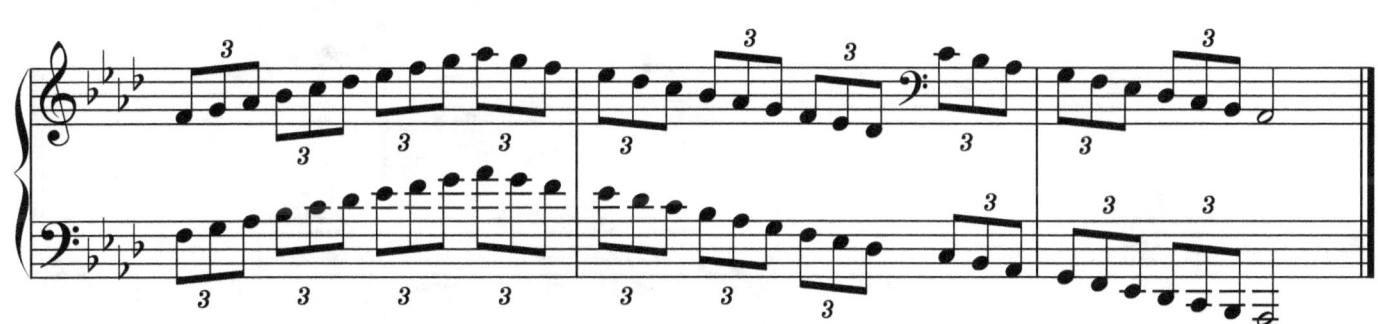

D-flat major scale: three octaves

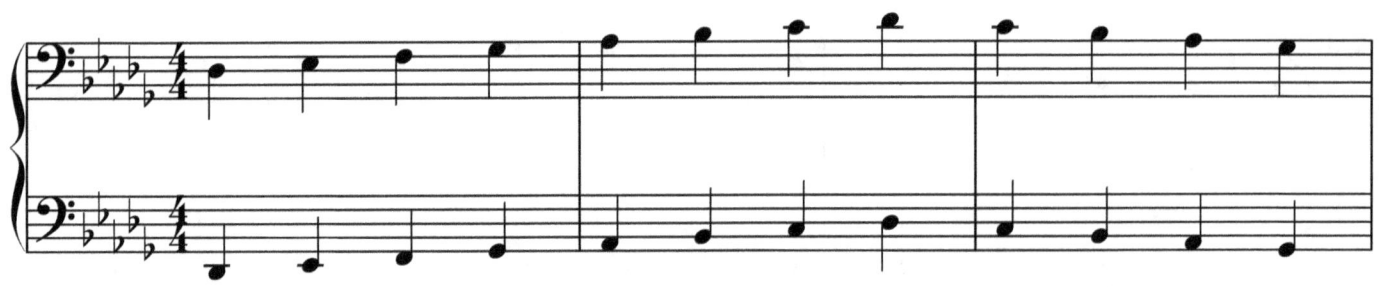

G-flat major scale: three octaves

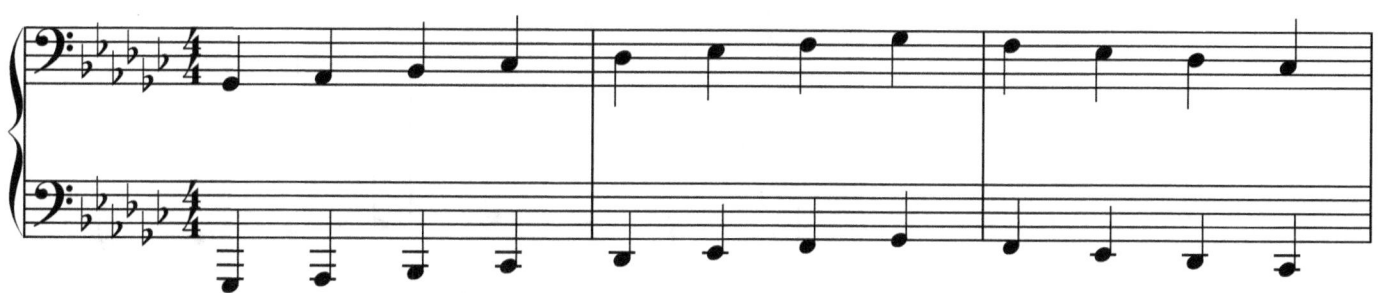

C-flat major scale: three octaves

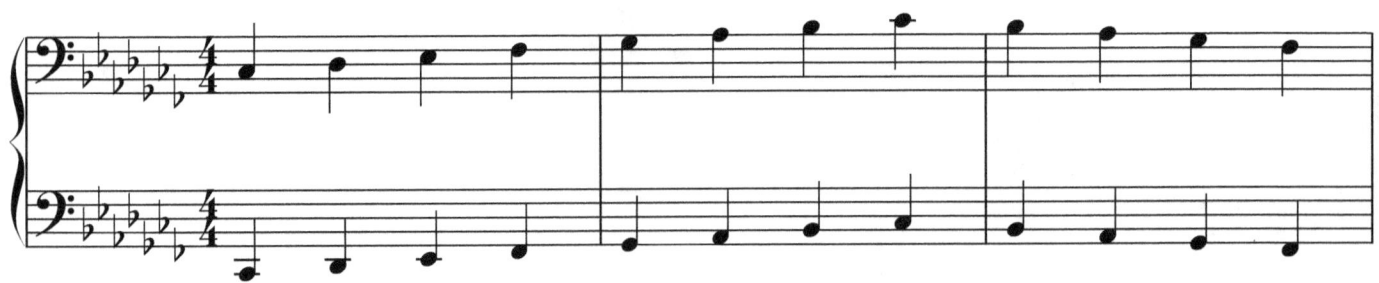

C major scale: four octaves

G major scale: four octaves

D major scale: four octaves

A major scale: four octaves

E major scale: four octaves

B major scale: four octaves

F-sharp major scale: four octaves

C-sharp major scale: four octaves

F major scale: four octaves

B-flat major scale: four octaves

E-flat major scale: four octaves

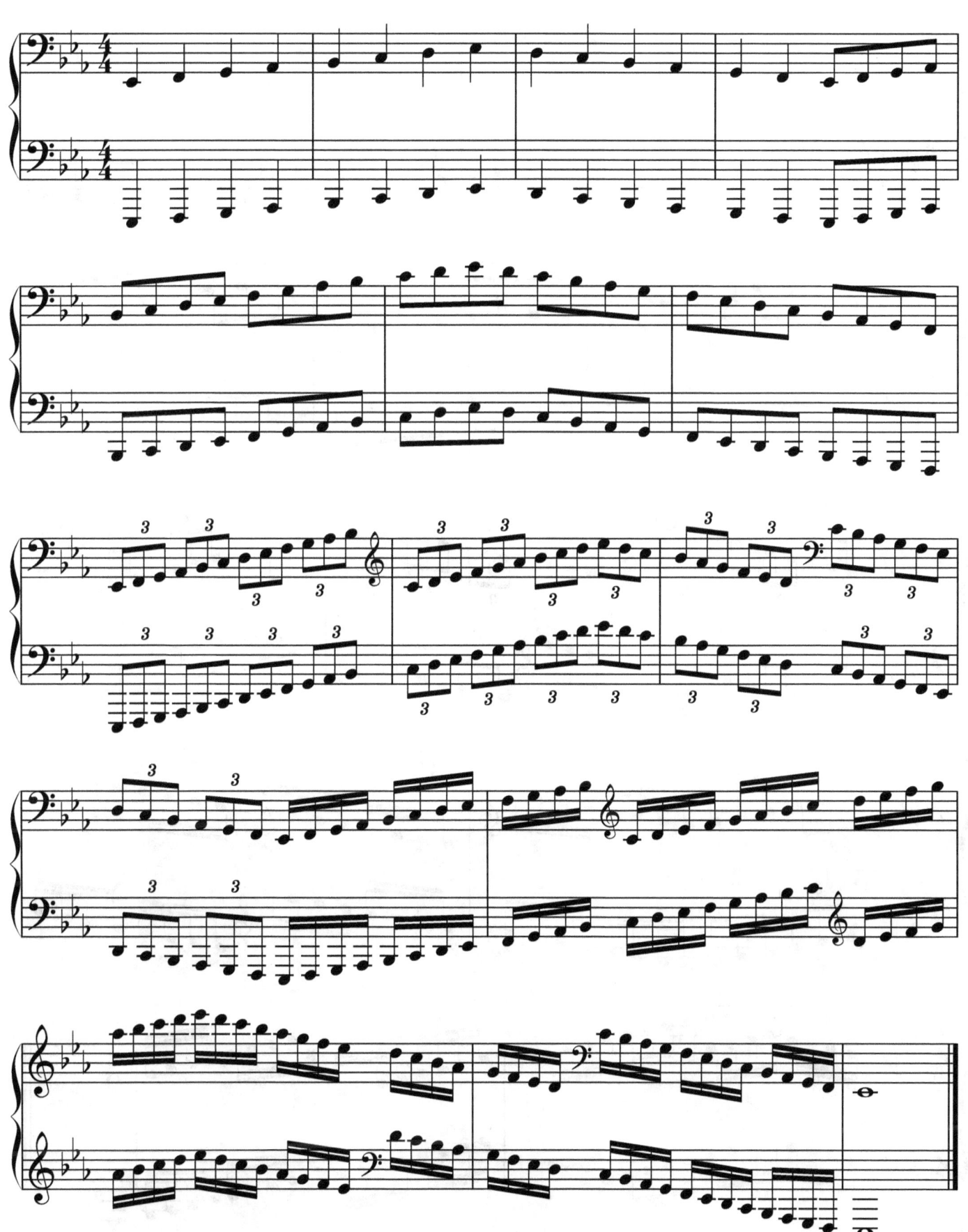

A-flat major scale: four octaves

D-flat major scale: four octaves

G-flat major scale: four octaves

C-flat major scale: four octaves

C major
(Relative major of A minor)

A minor
(Relative minor of C major)

natural minor

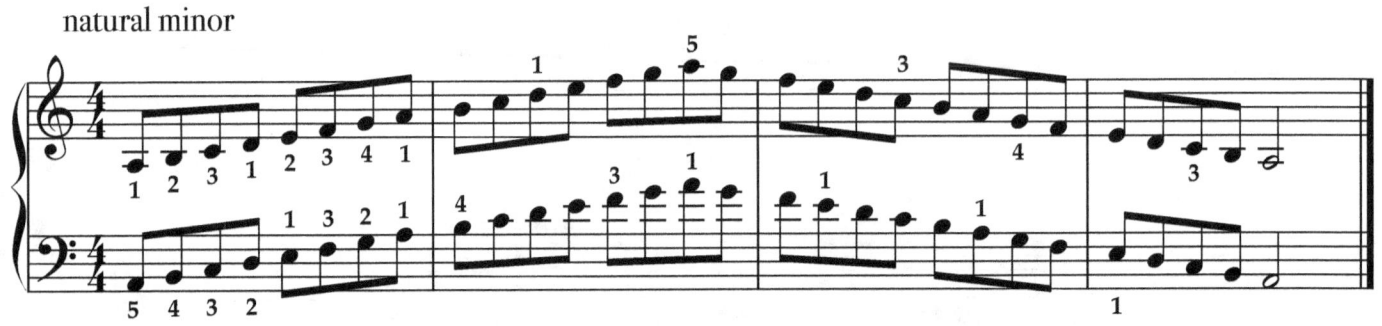

melodic minor

harmonic minor

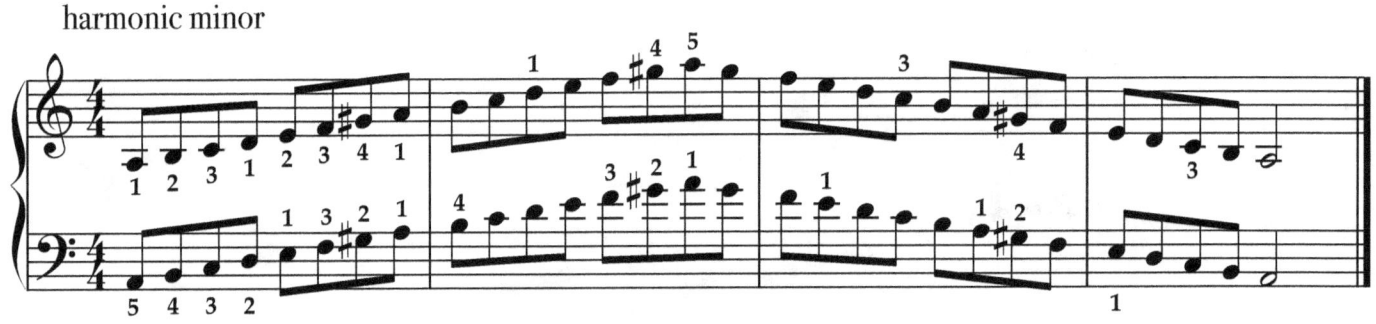

G major
(Relative major of E minor)

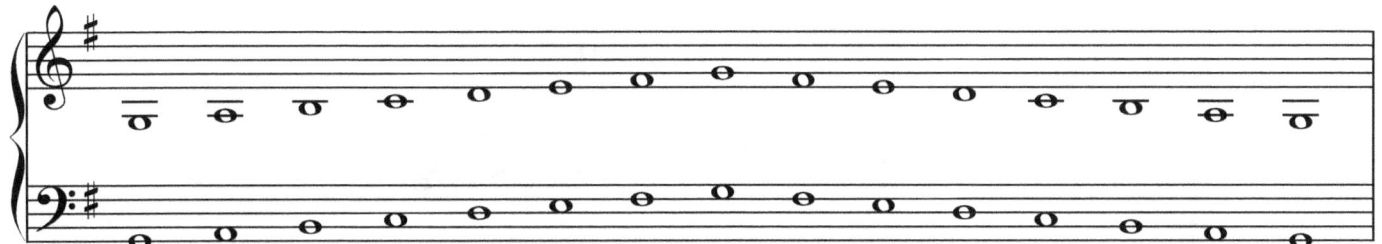

E minor
(Relative minor of G major)

natural minor

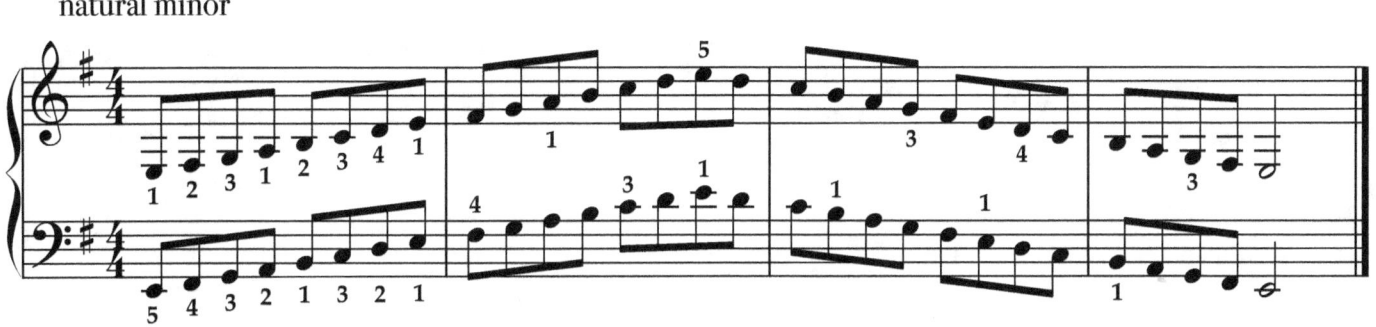

melodic minor

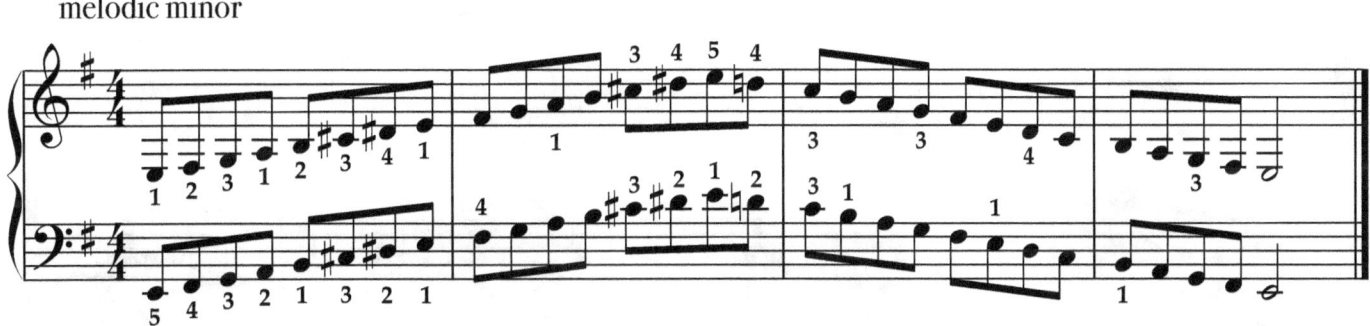

harmonic minor

D major
(Relative major of B minor)

B minor
(Relative minor of D major)

natural minor

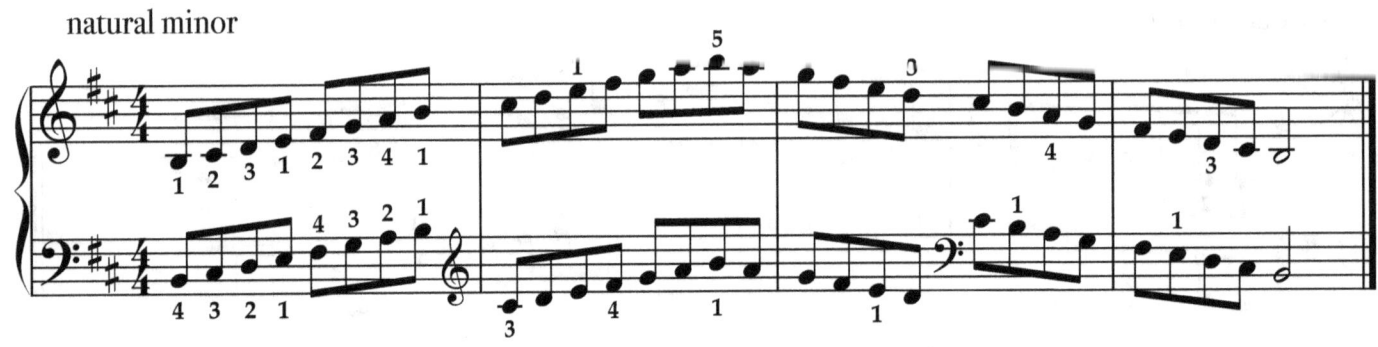

melodic minor

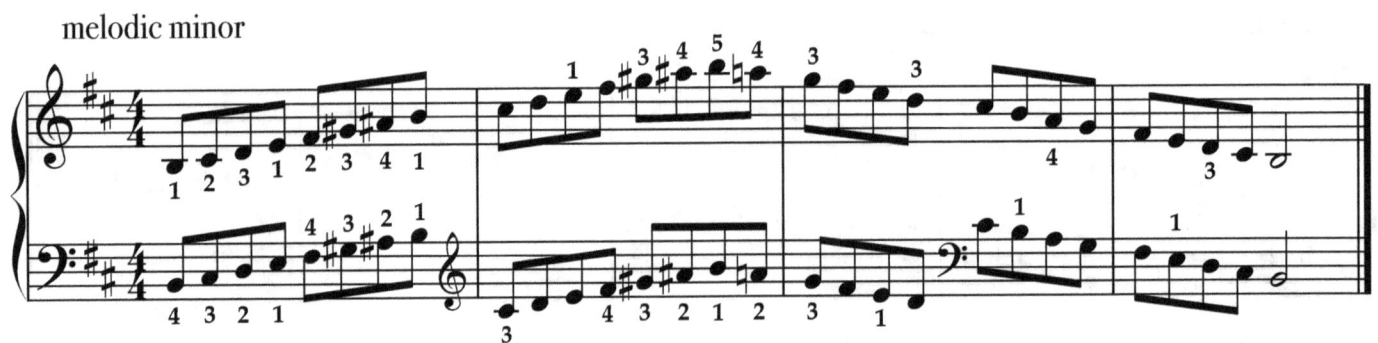

harmonic minor

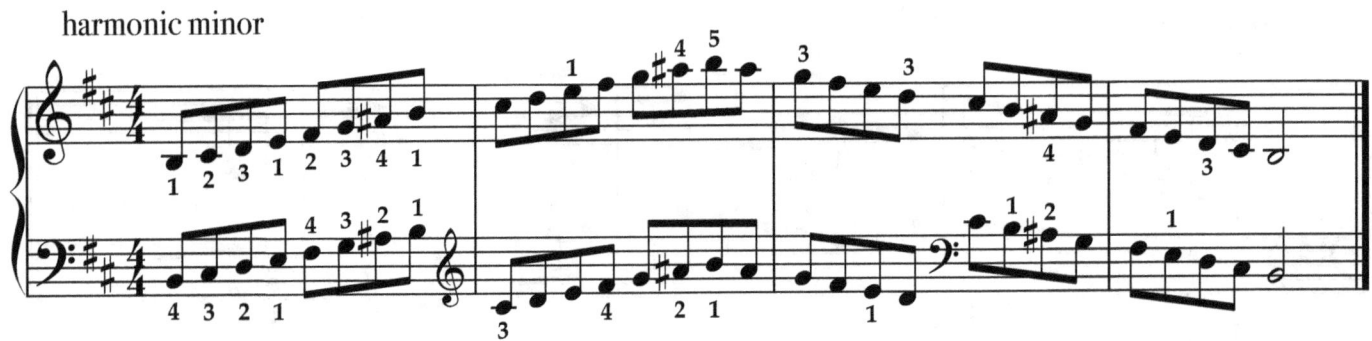

A major
(Relative major of F-sharp minor)

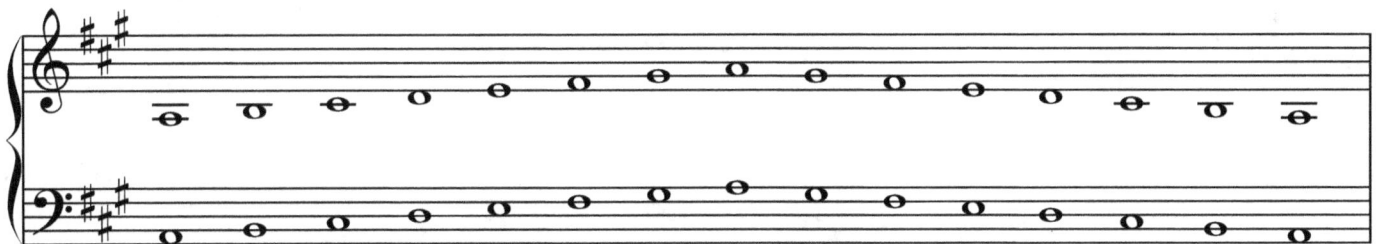

F-sharp minor
(Relative minor of A major)

natural minor

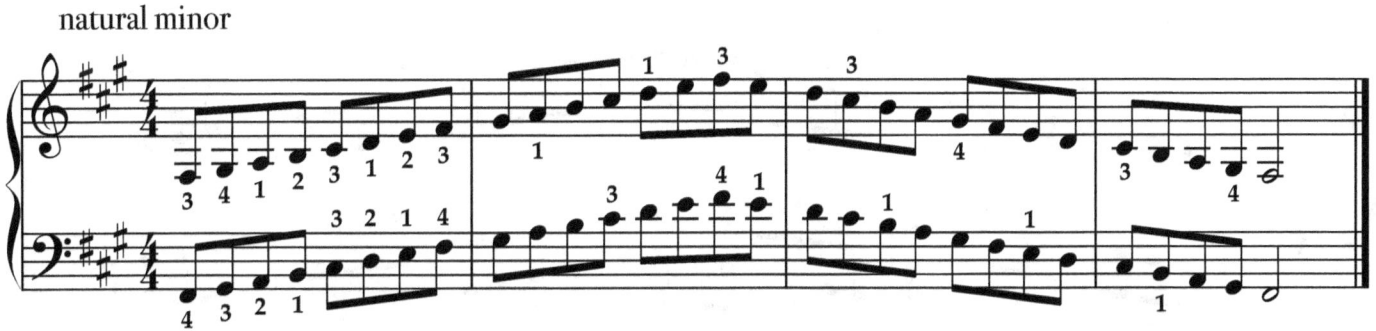

melodic minor

harmonic minor

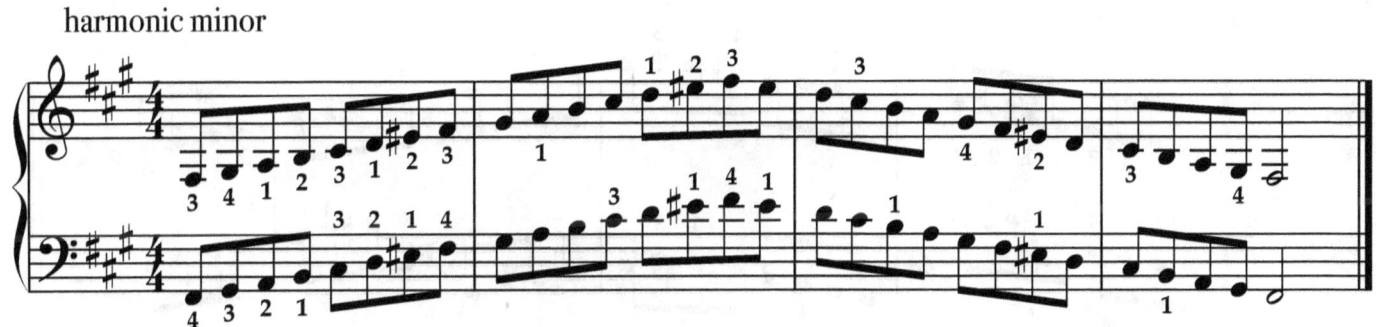

E major
(Relative major of C-sharp minor)

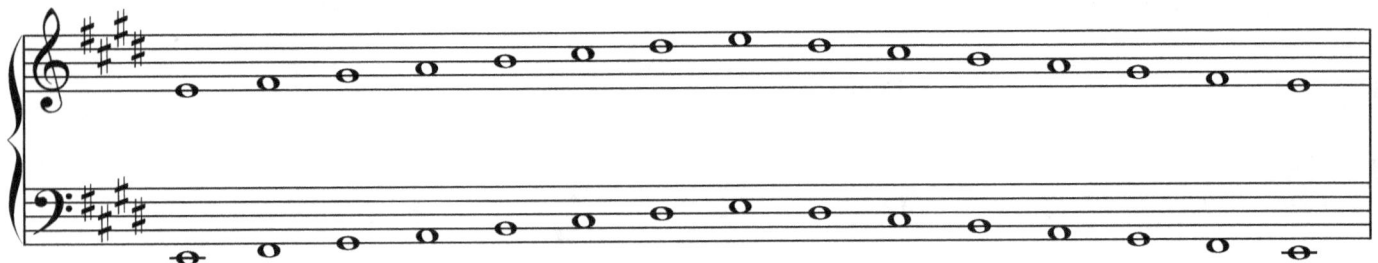

C-sharp minor
(Relative minor of E major)

natural minor

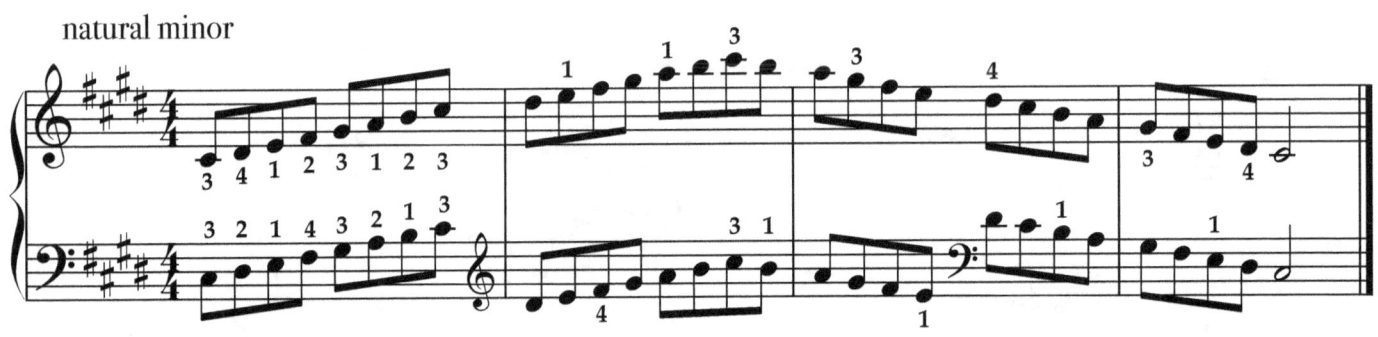

melodic minor

harmonic minor

B major
(Relative major of G-sharp minor)

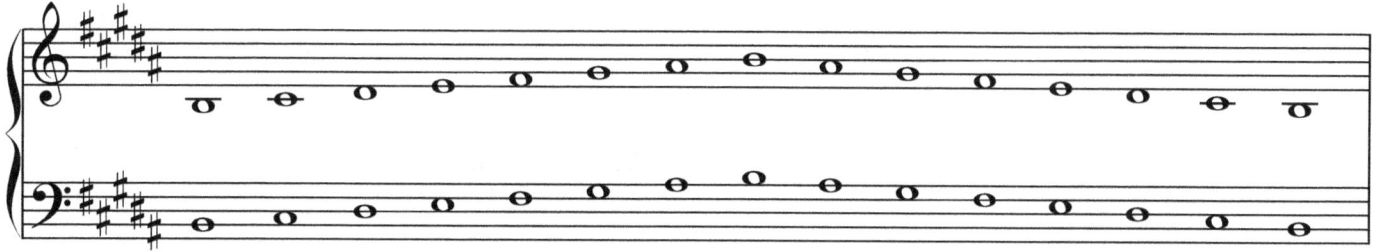

G-sharp minor
(Relative minor of B major)

natural minor

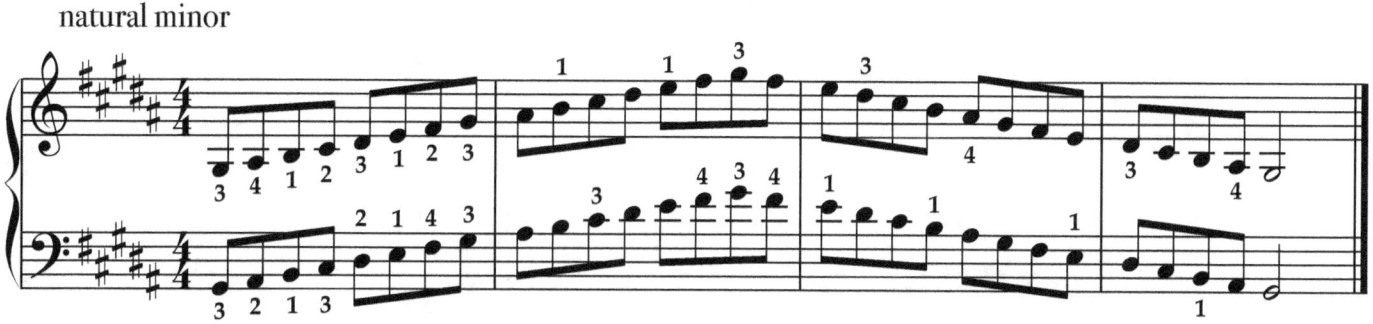

melodic minor

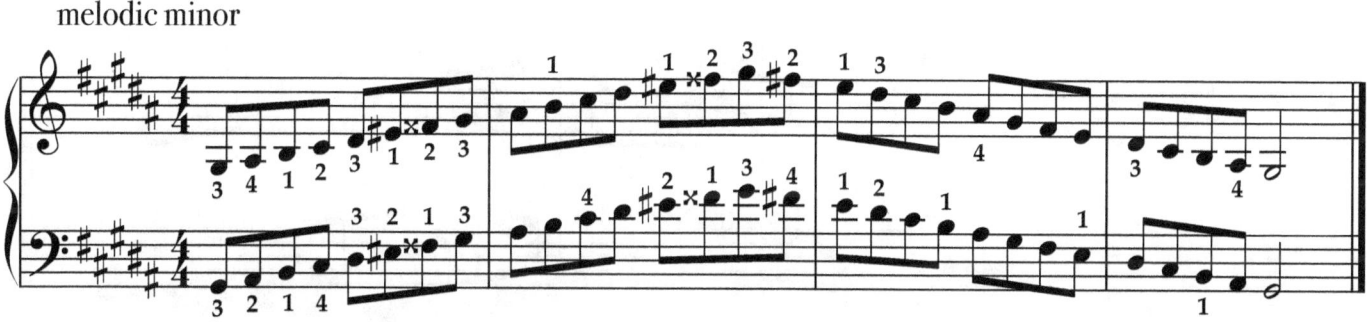

harmonic minor

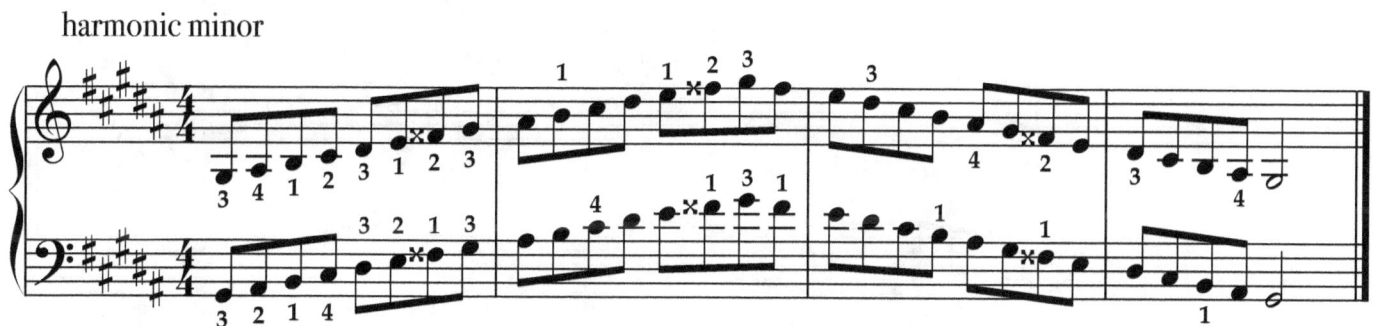

F-sharp major
(Relative major of D-sharp minor)

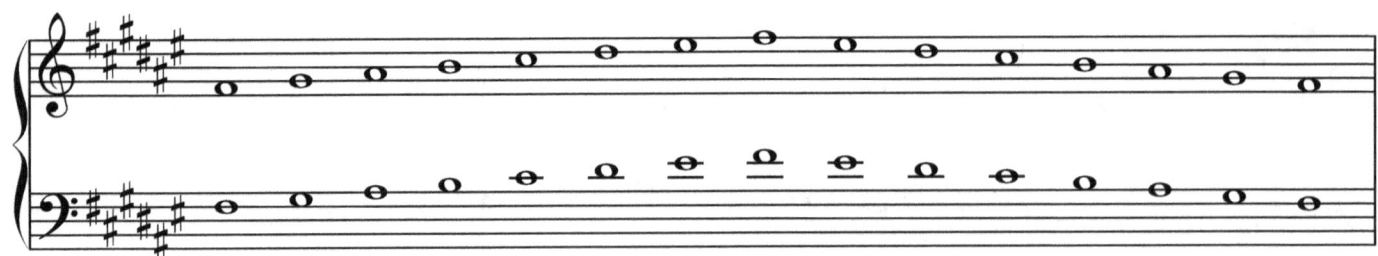

D-sharp minor
(Relative minor of F-sharp major)

natural minor

melodic minor

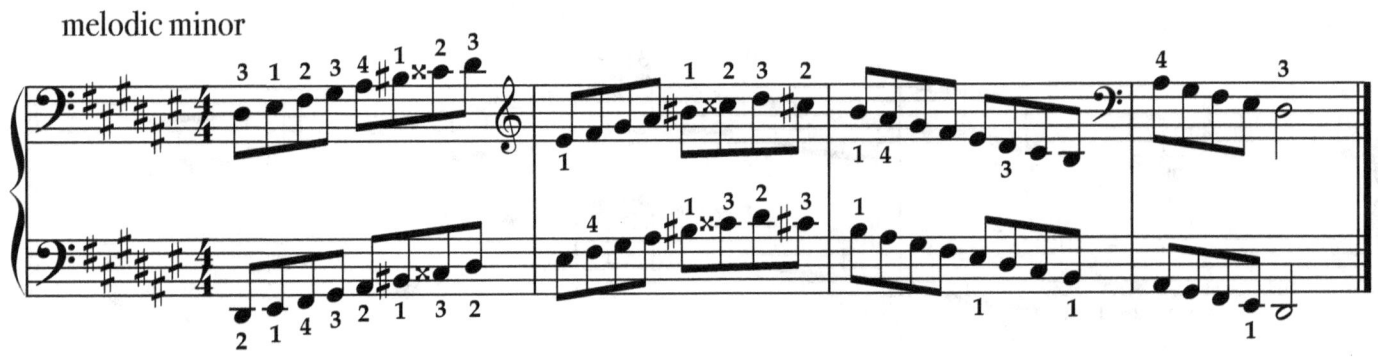

harmonic minor

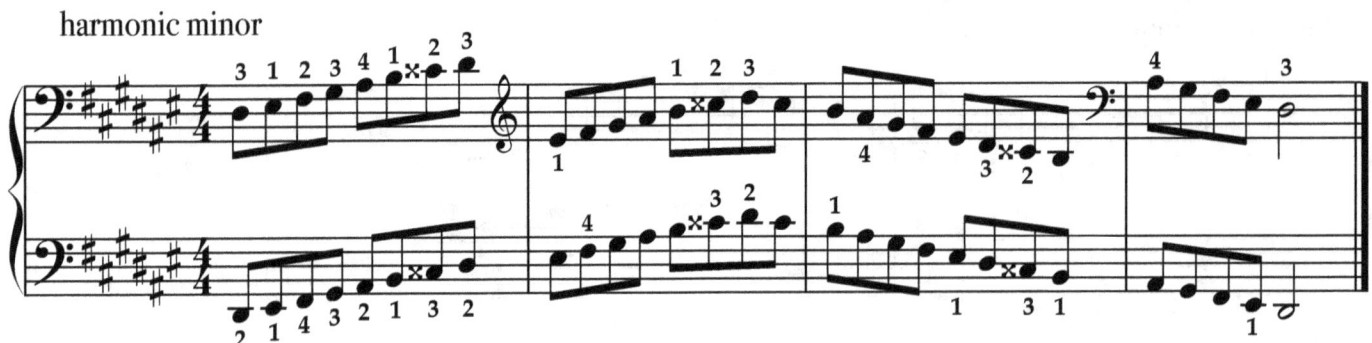

C-sharp major
(Relative major of A-sharp minor)

A-sharp minor
(Relative minor of C-sharp major)

natural minor

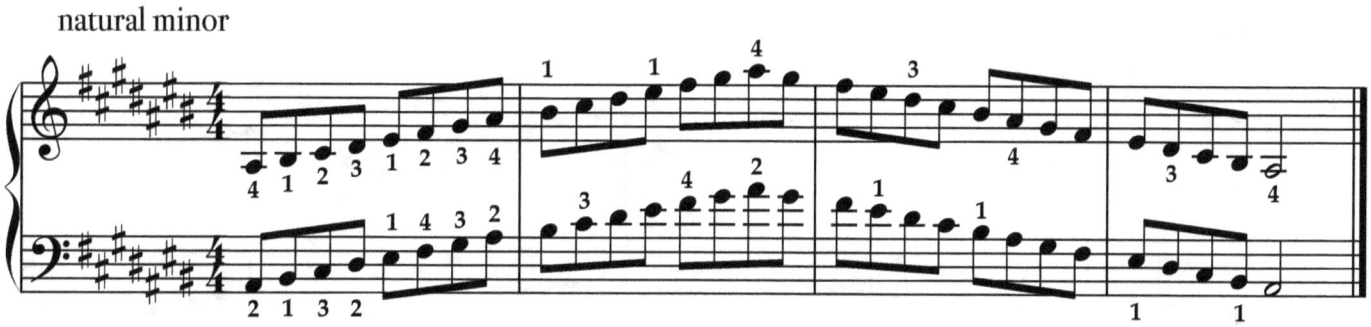

melodic minor

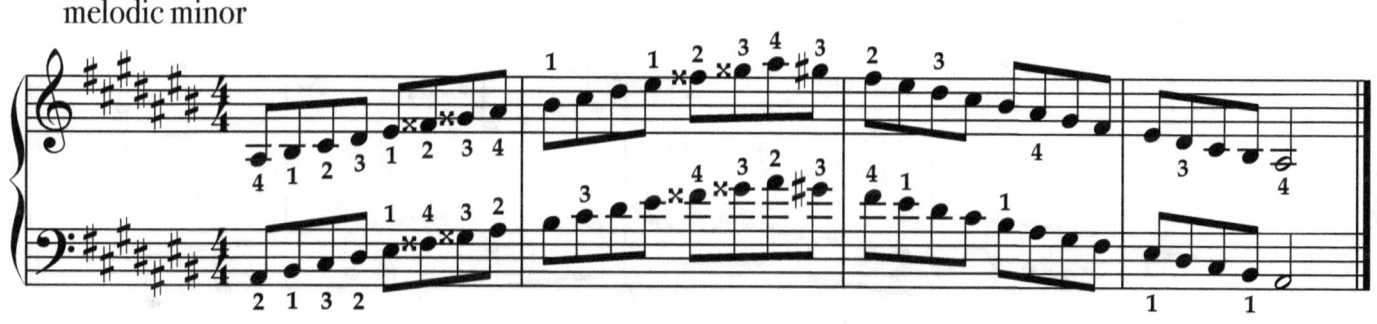

harmonic minor

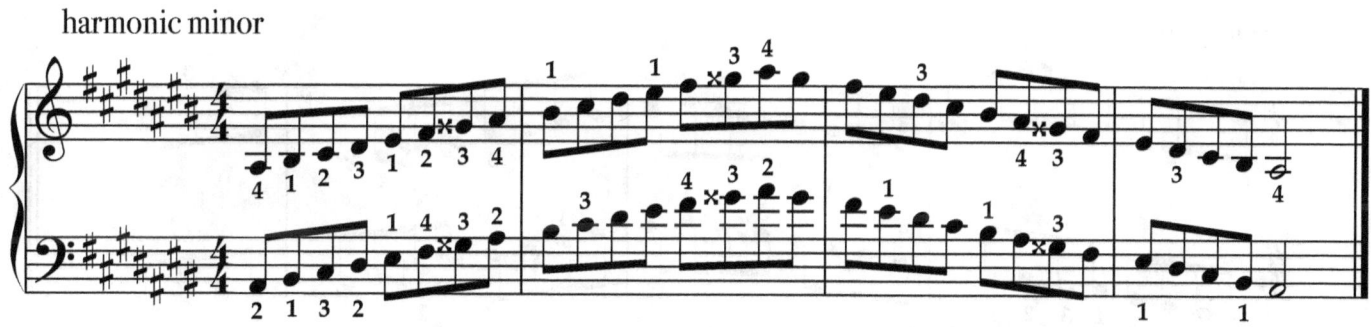

F major
(Relative major of D minor)

D minor
(Relative minor of F major)

natural minor

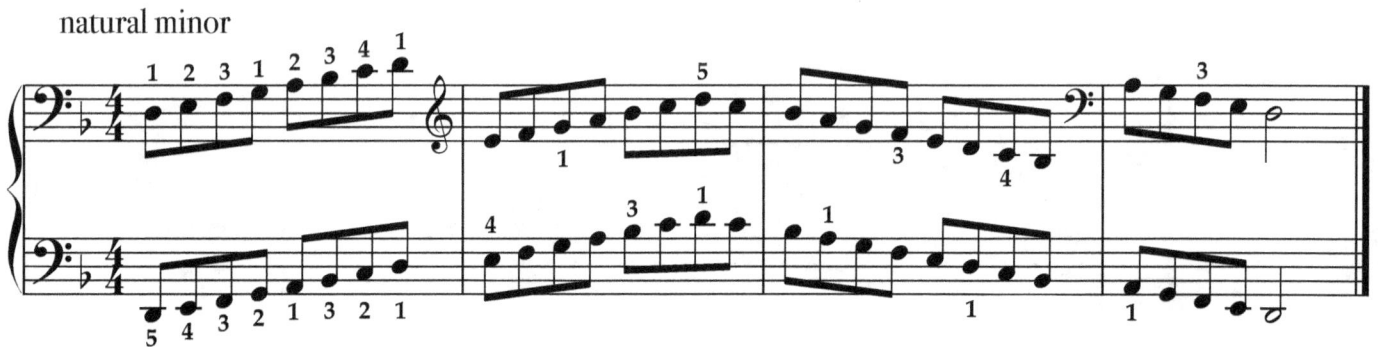

melodic minor

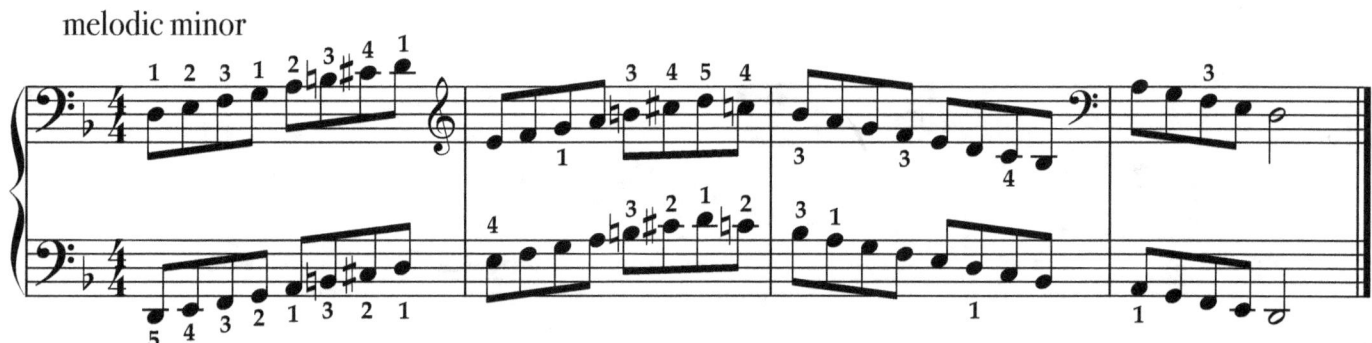

harmonic minor

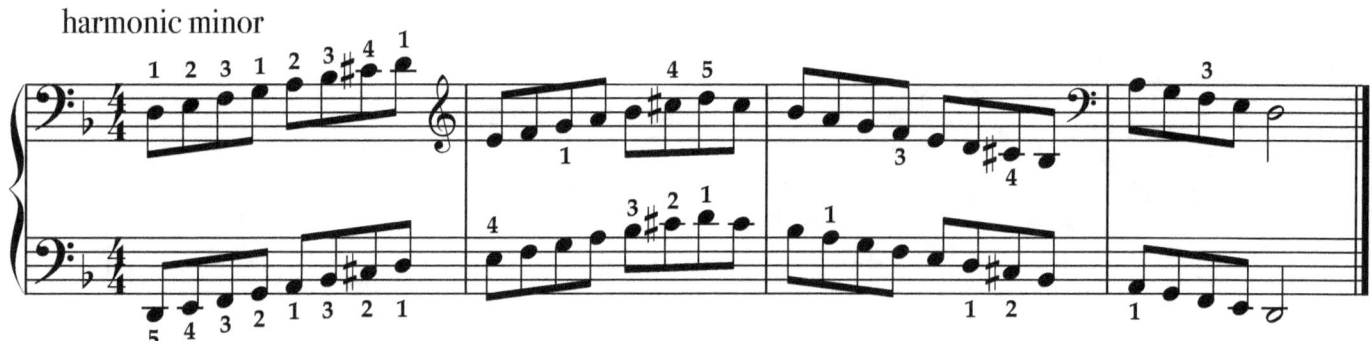

B-flat major
(Relative major of G minor)

G minor
(Relative minor of B-flat major)

natural minor

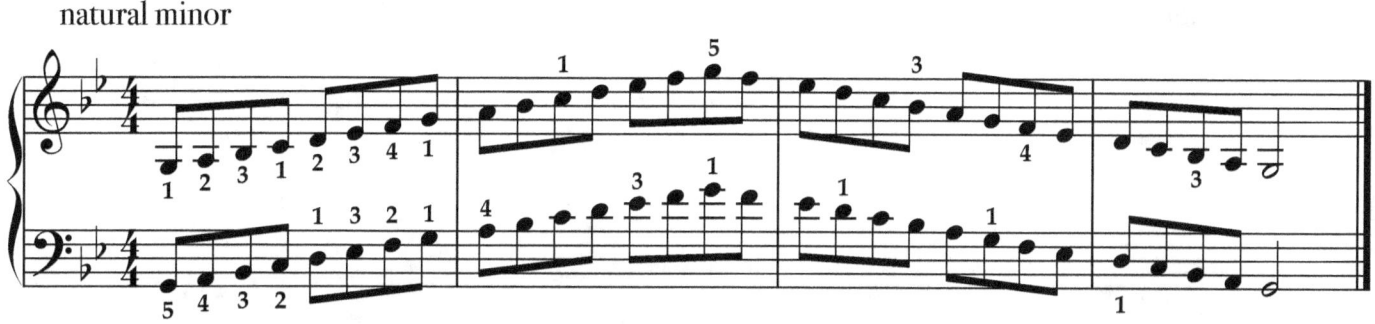

melodic minor

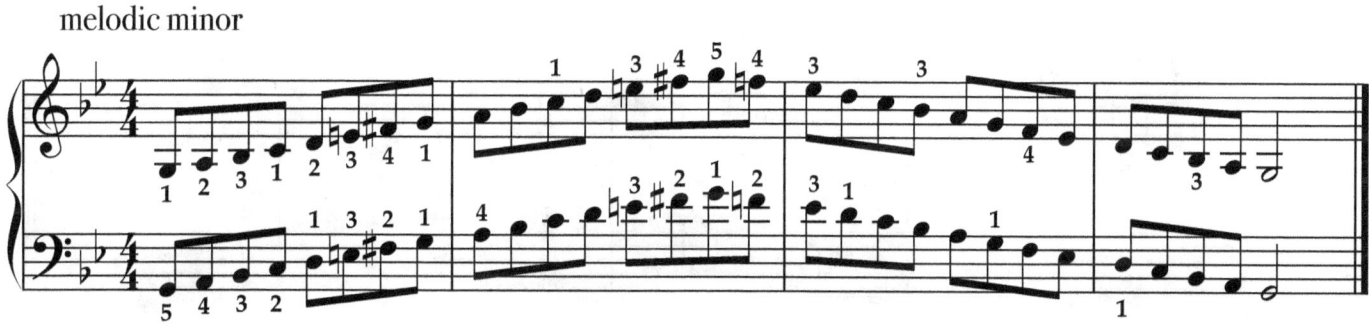

harmonic minor

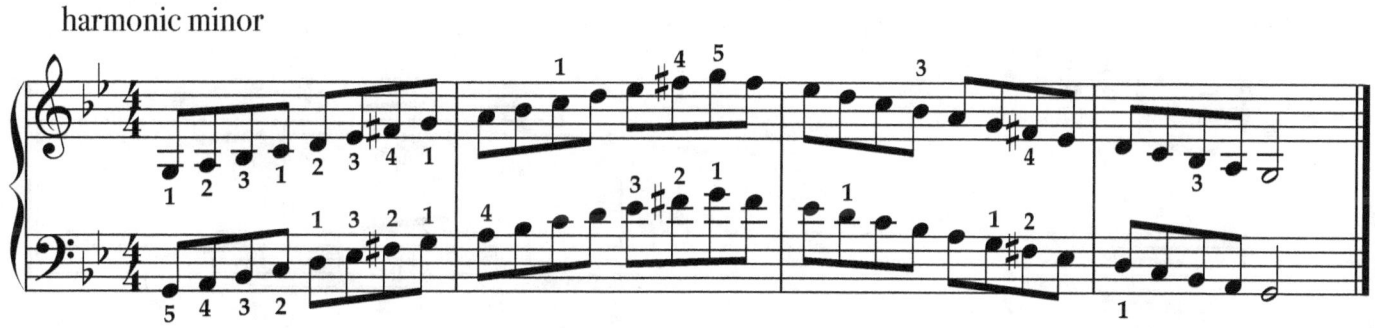

E-flat major
(Relative major of C minor)

C minor
(Relative minor of E-flat major)

natural minor

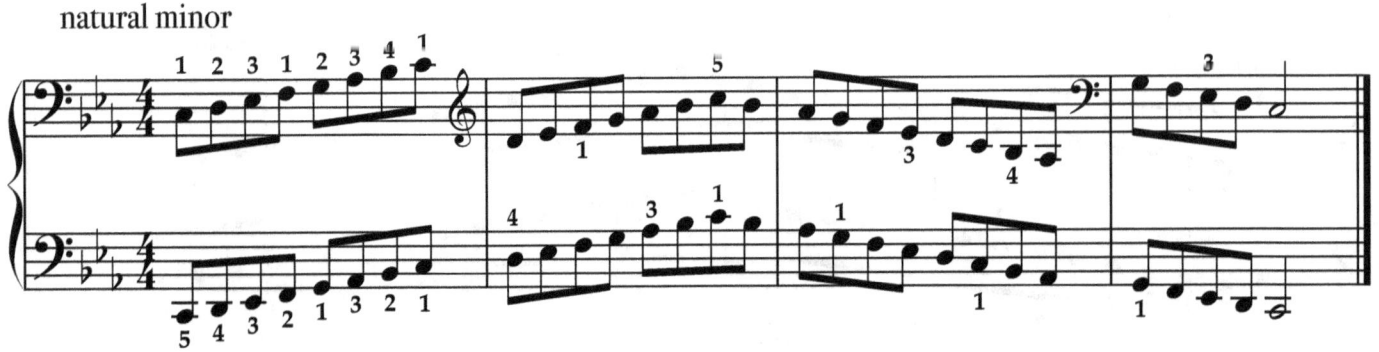

melodic minor

harmonic minor

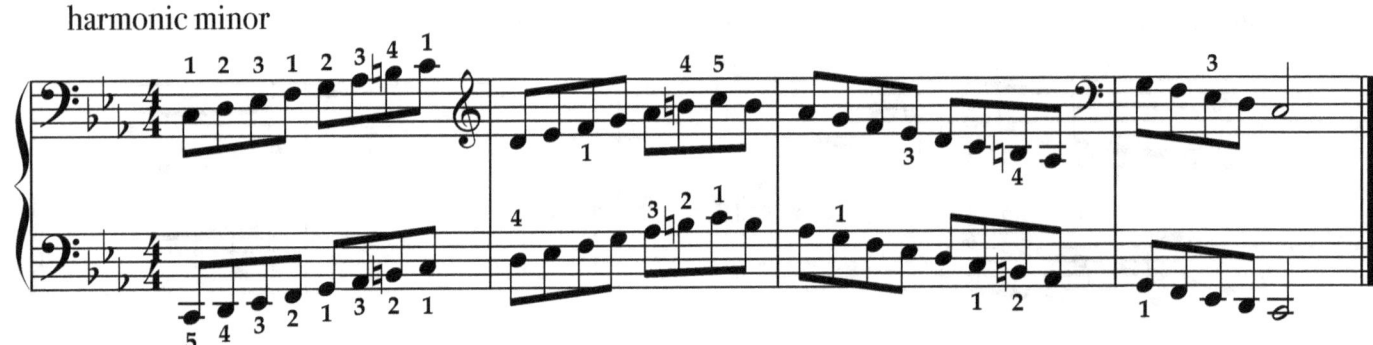

A-flat major
(Relative major of F minor)

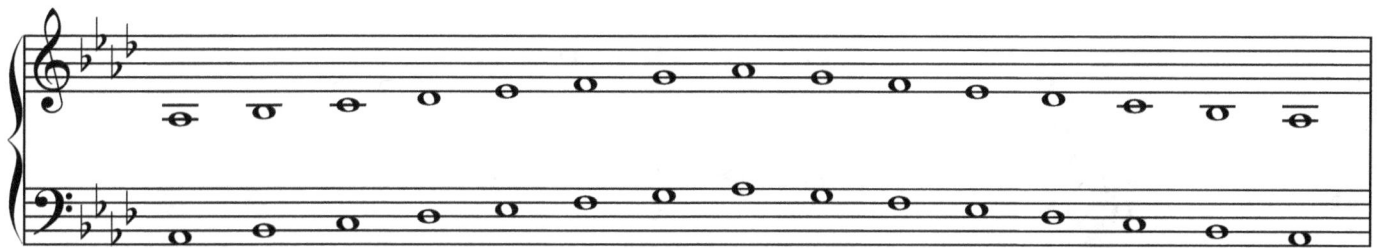

F minor
(Relative minor of A-flat major)

natural minor

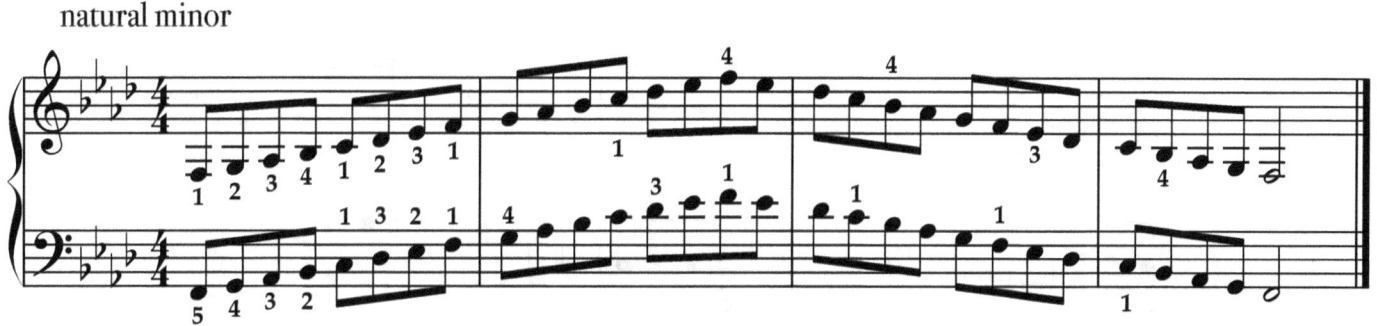

melodic minor

harmonic minor

D-flat major
(Relative major of B-flat minor)

B-flat minor
(Relative minor of D-flat major)

natural minor

melodic minor

harmonic minor

G-flat major
(Relative major of E-flat minor)

E-flat minor
(Relative minor of G-flat major)

natural minor

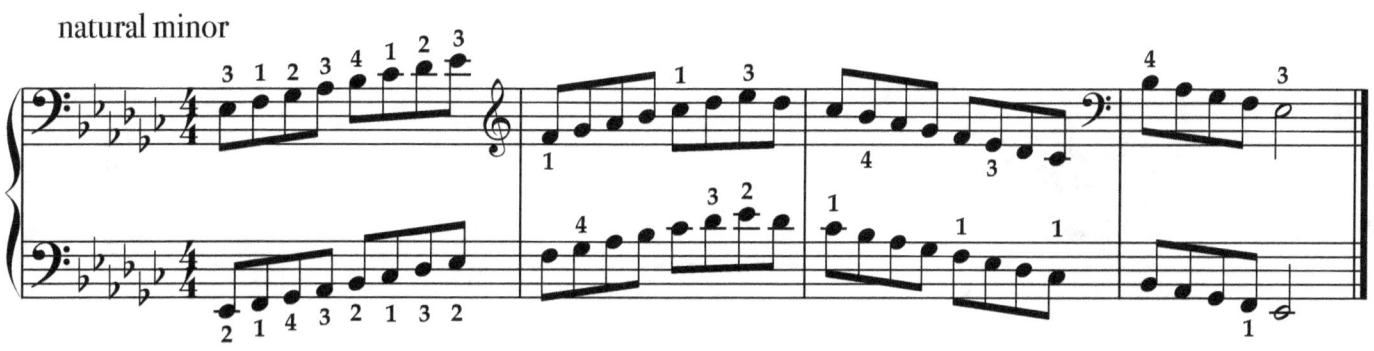

melodic minor

harmonic minor

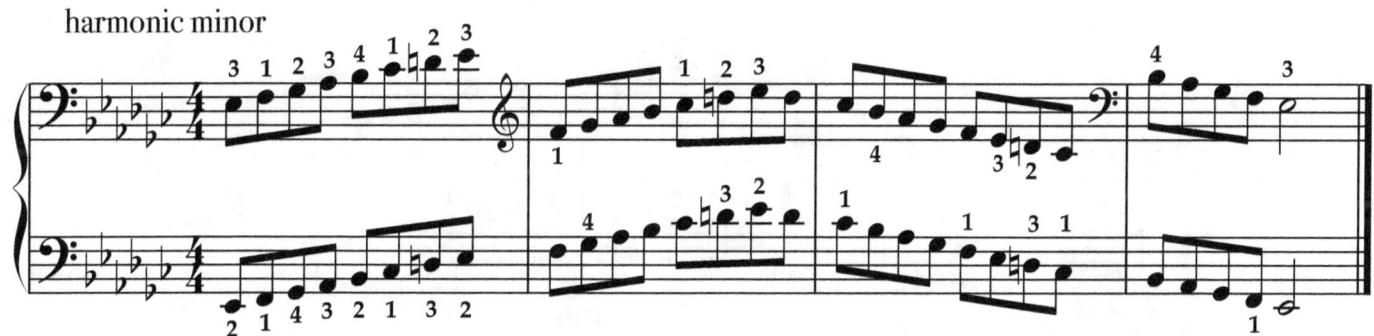

C-flat major
(Relative major of A-flat minor)

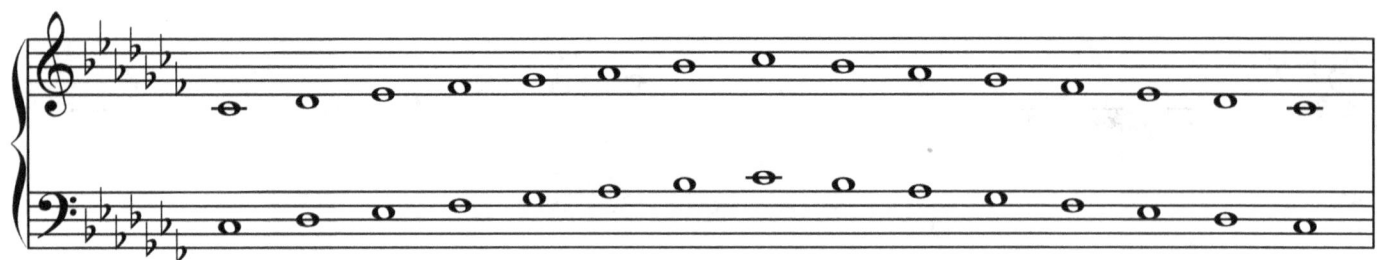

A-flat minor
(Relative minor of C-flat major)

natural minor

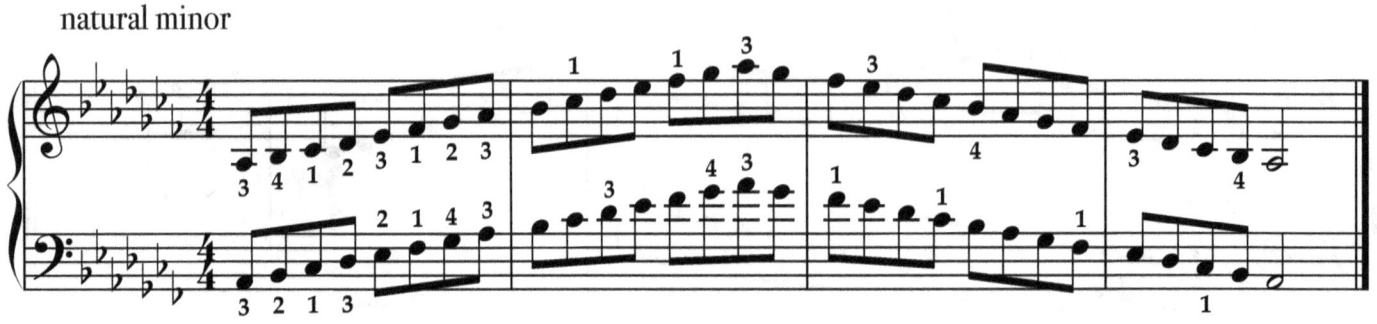

melodic minor

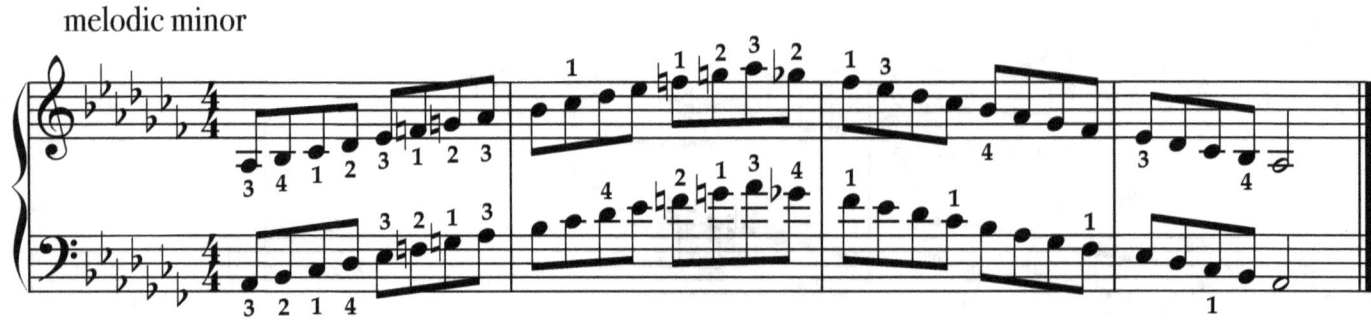

harmonic minor

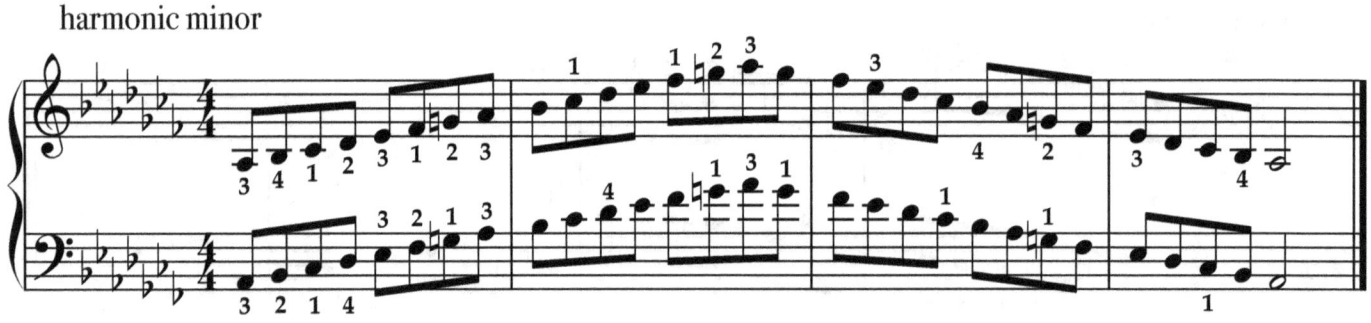

Major & Harmonic Minor Scales in 3rds

C major

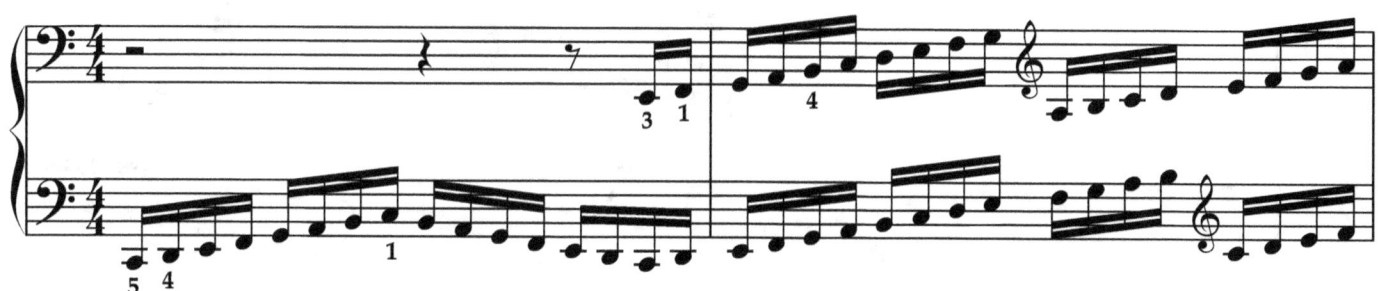

A minor (harmonic)

G major

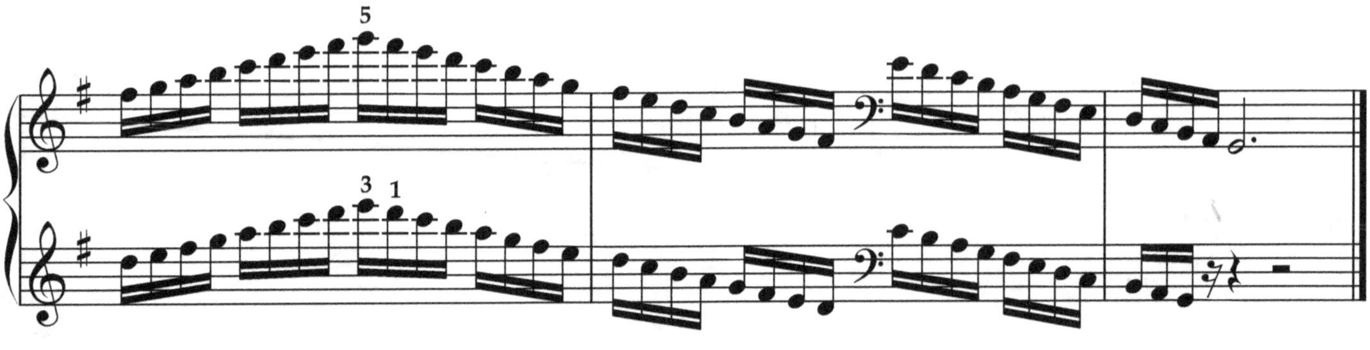

E minor (harmonic)

D major

B minor (harmonic)

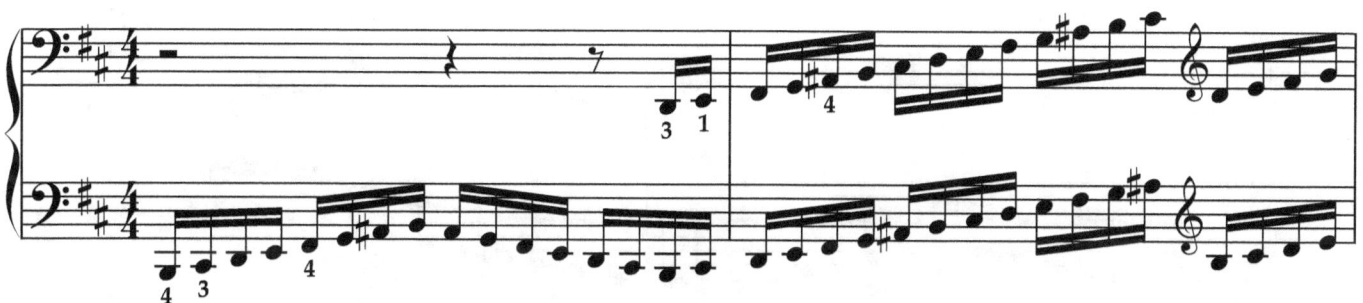

A major

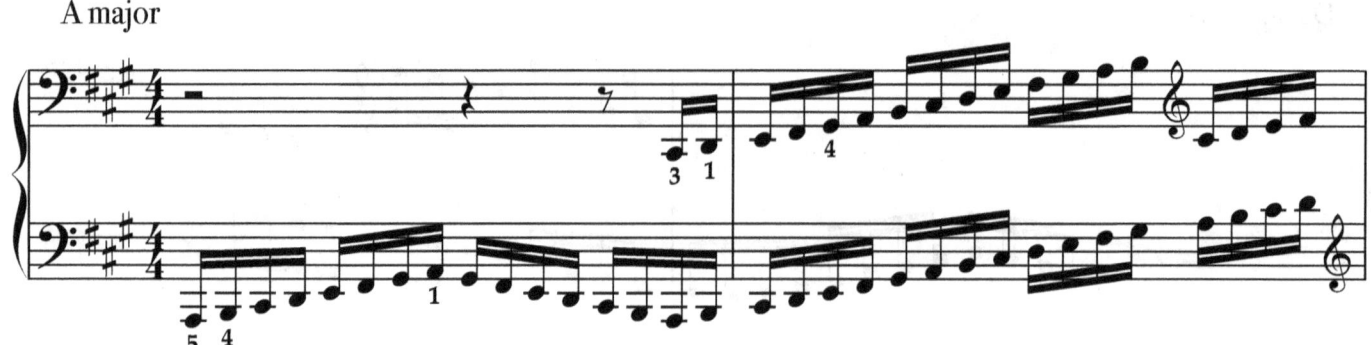

F-sharp minor (harmonic)

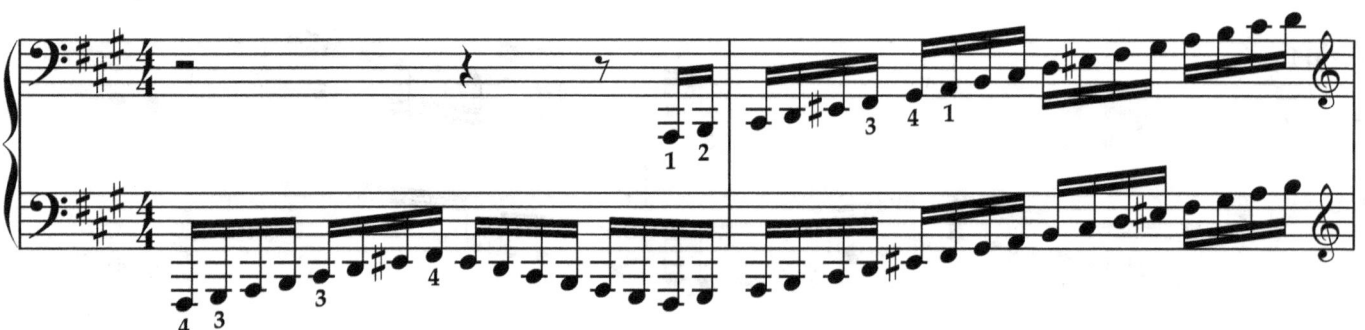

E major

C-sharp minor (harmonic)

B major

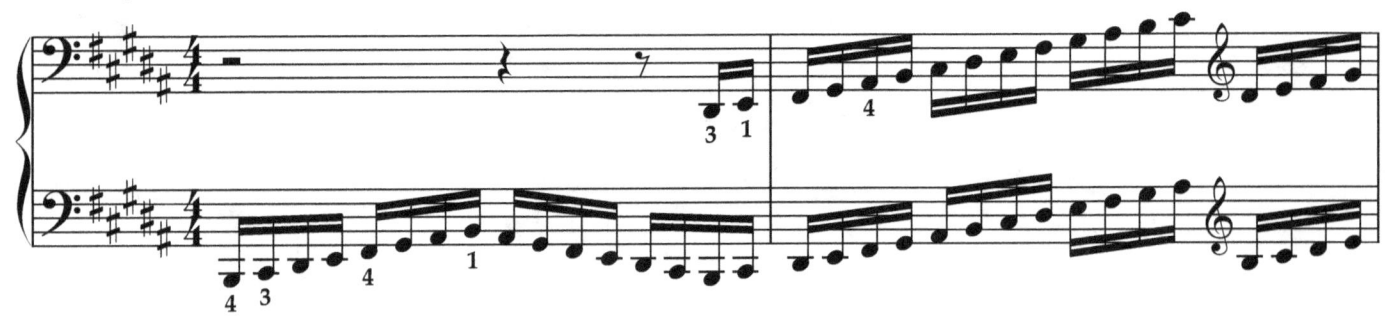

G-sharp minor (harmonic)

F-sharp major

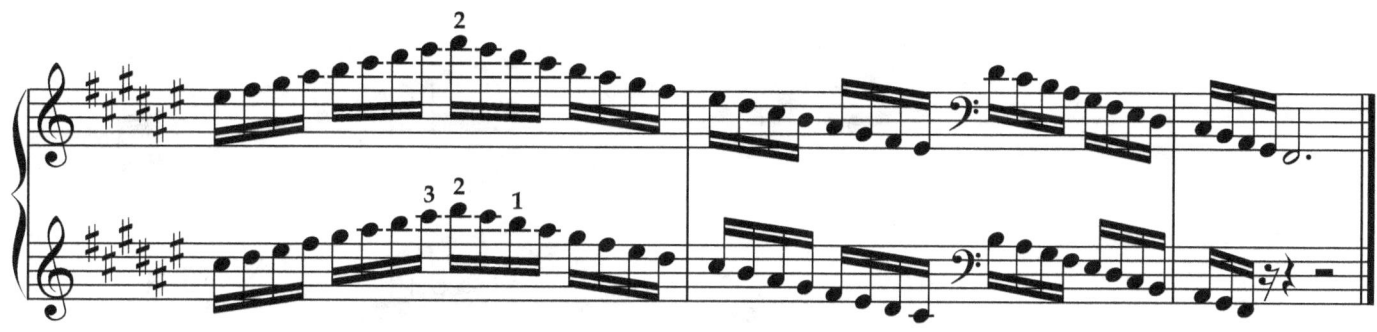

D-sharp minor (harmonic)

66

C-sharp major

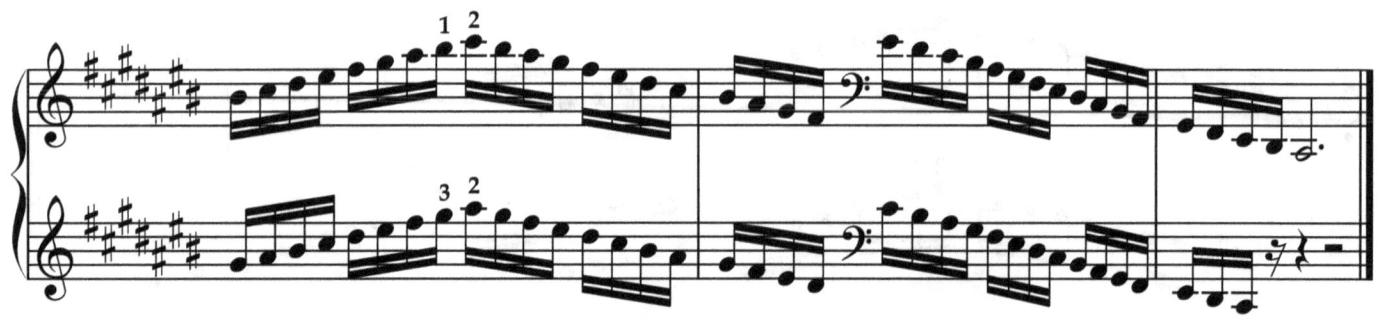

A-sharp minor (harmonic)

F major

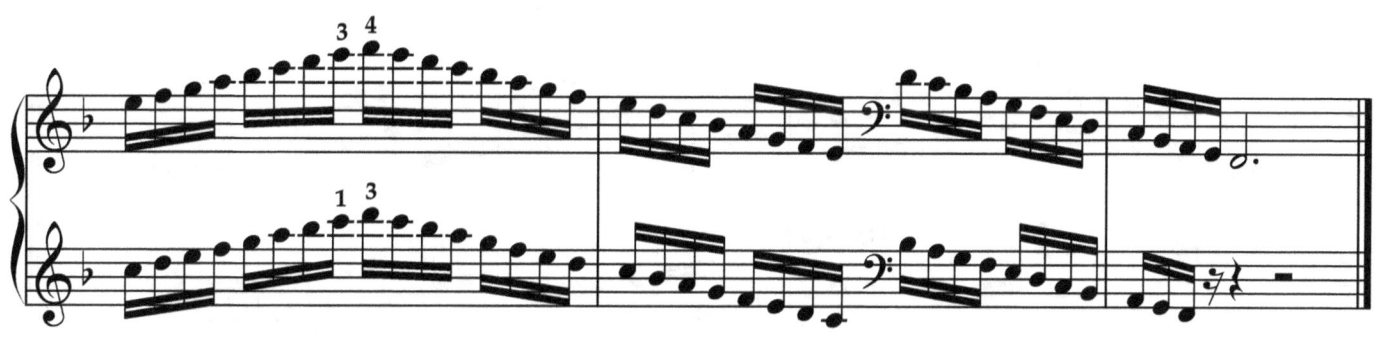

D minor (harmonic)

B-flat major

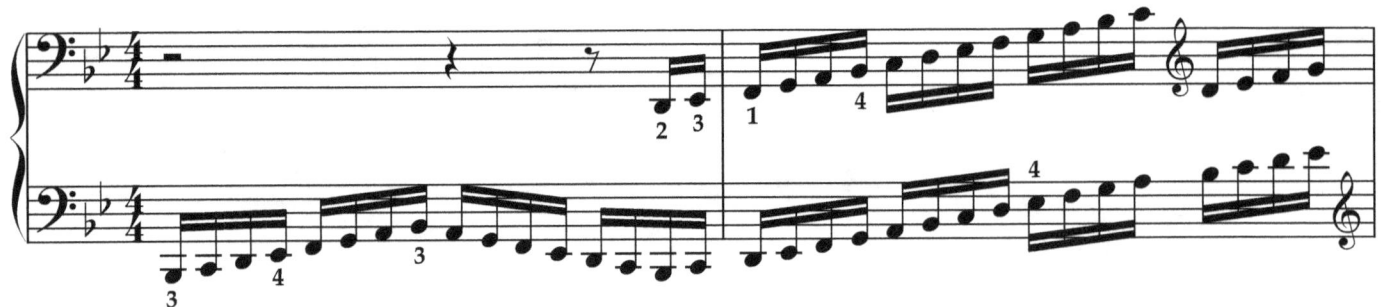

G minor (harmonic)

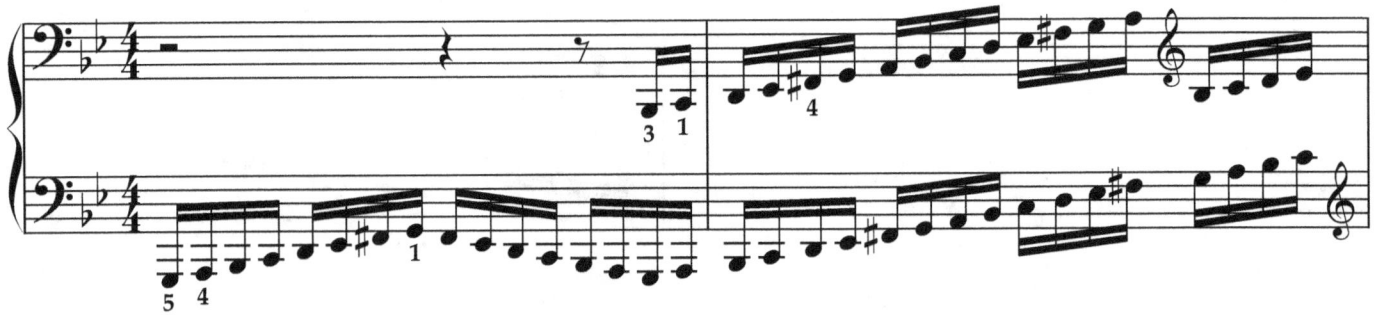

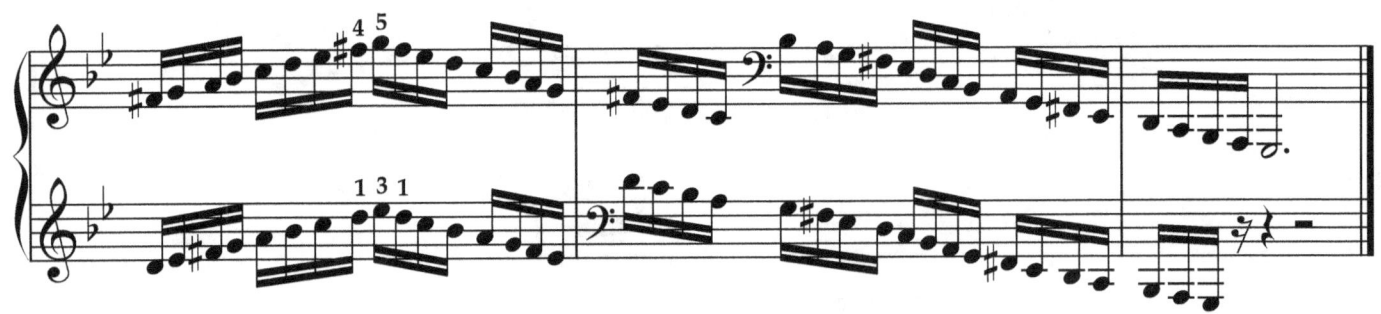

E-flat major

C minor (harmonic)

A-flat major

F minor (harmonic)

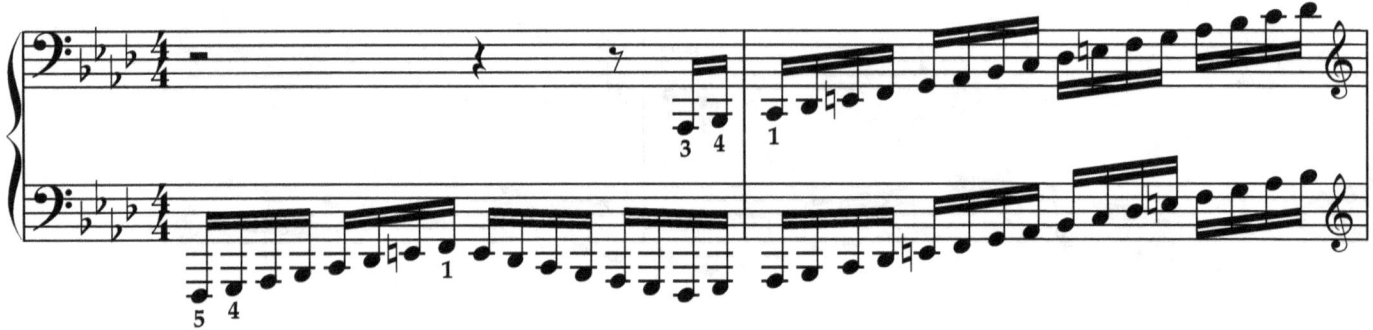

D-flat major

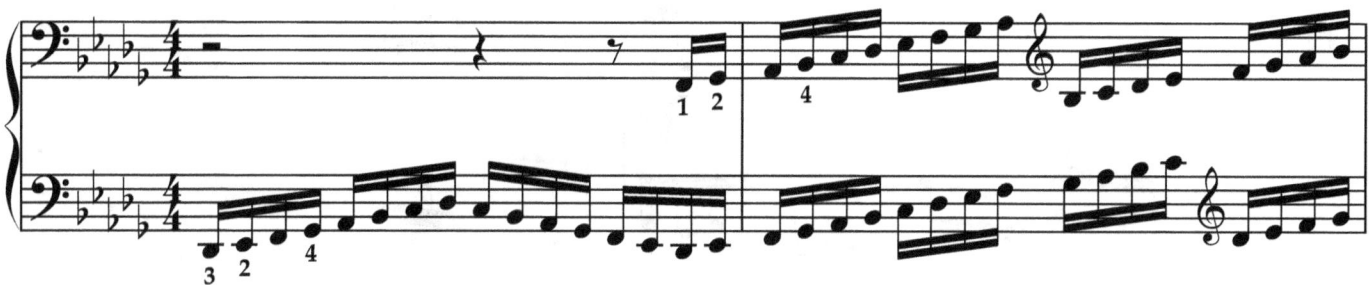

B-flat minor (harmonic)

G-flat major

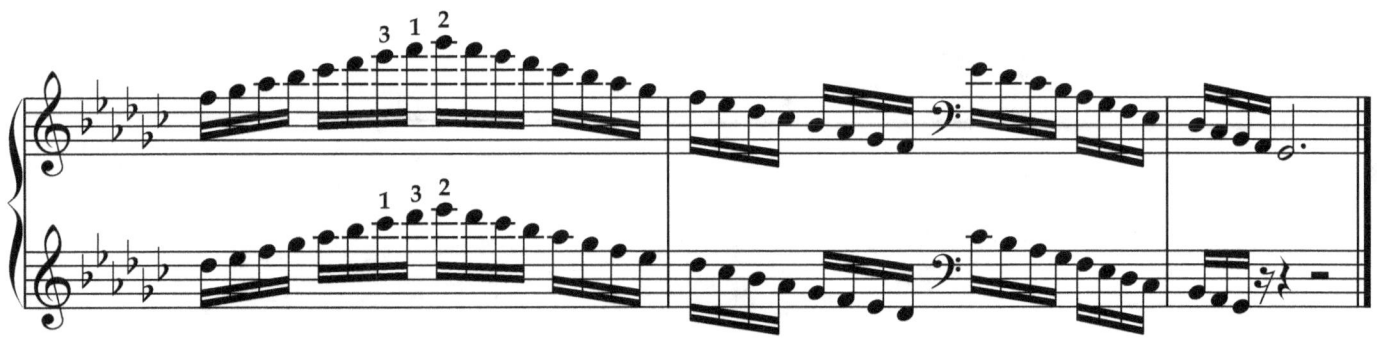

E-flat minor (harmonic)

C-flat major

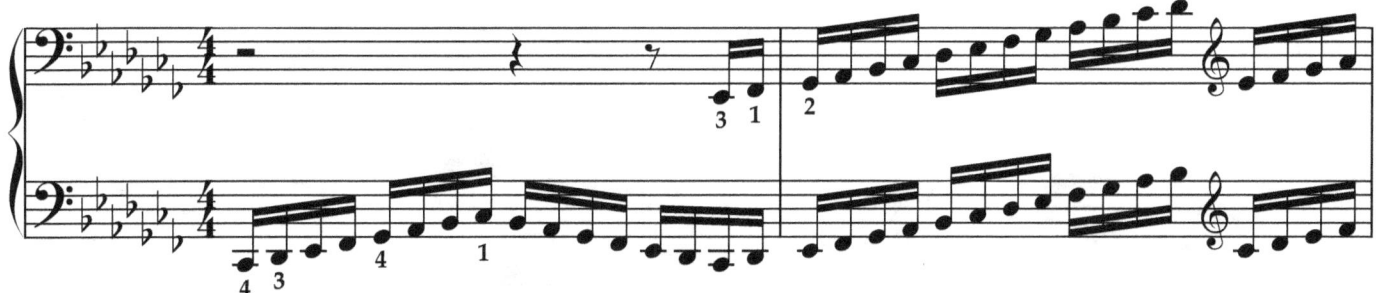

A-flat minor (harmonic)

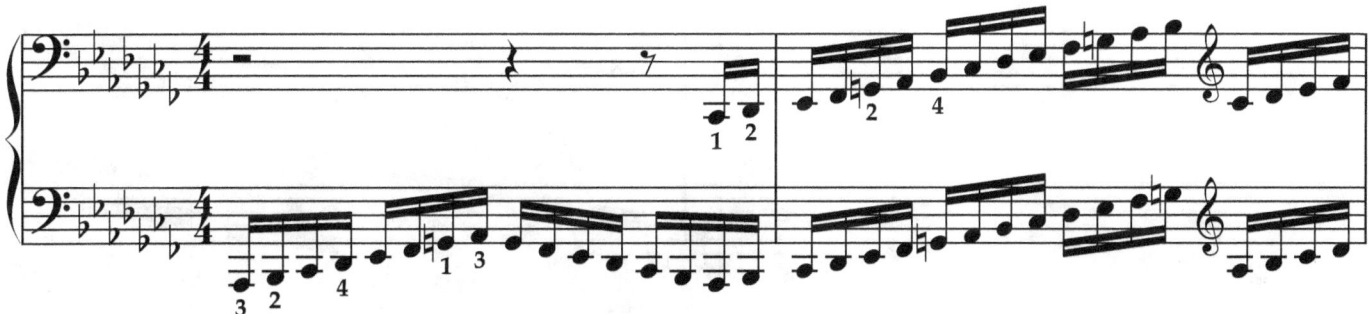

Major & Harmonic Minor Scales in 6ths

C major

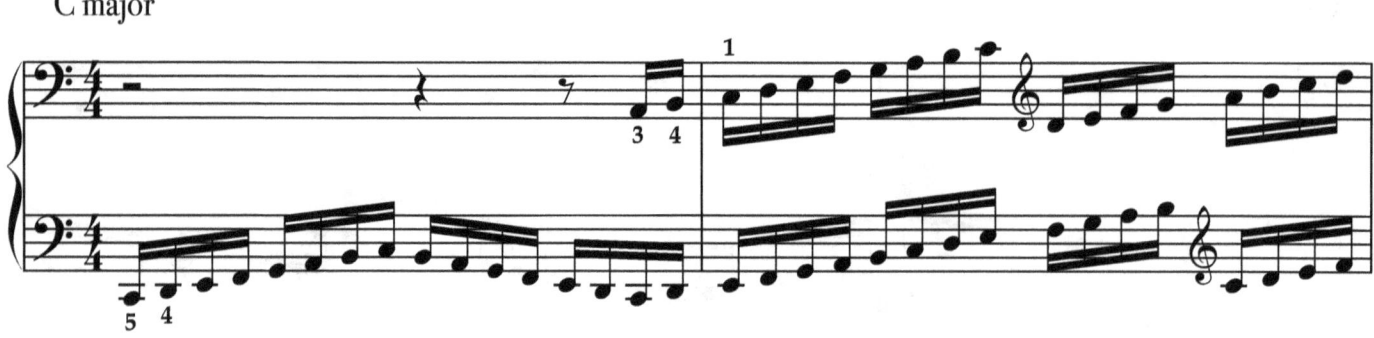

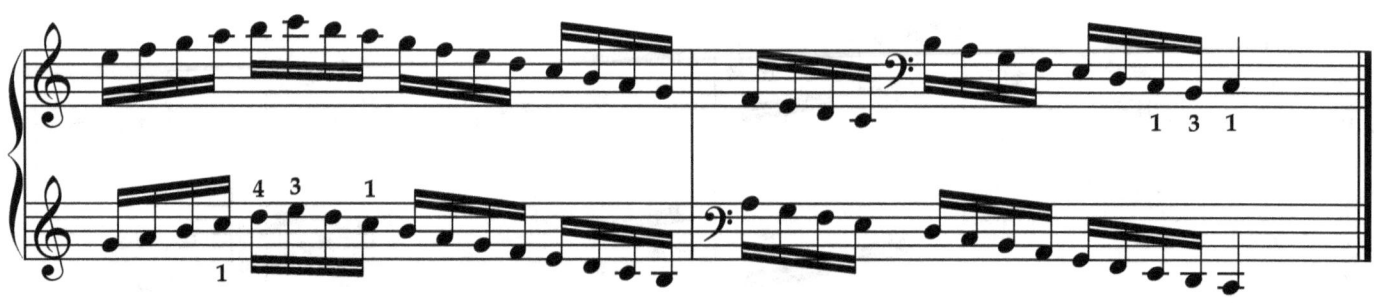

A minor (harmonic)

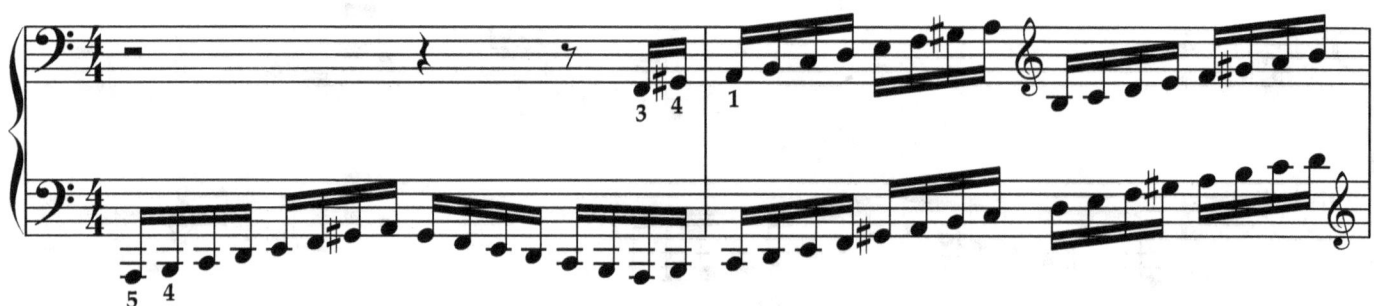

G major

E minor (harmonic)

D major

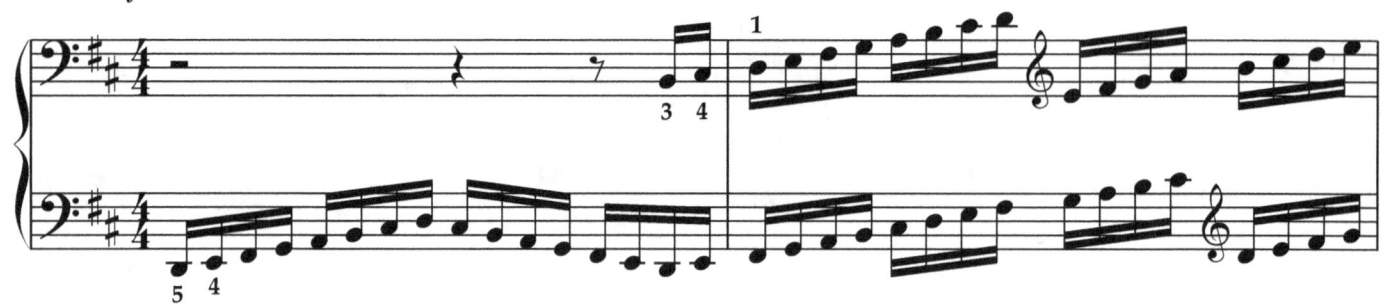

B minor (harmonic)

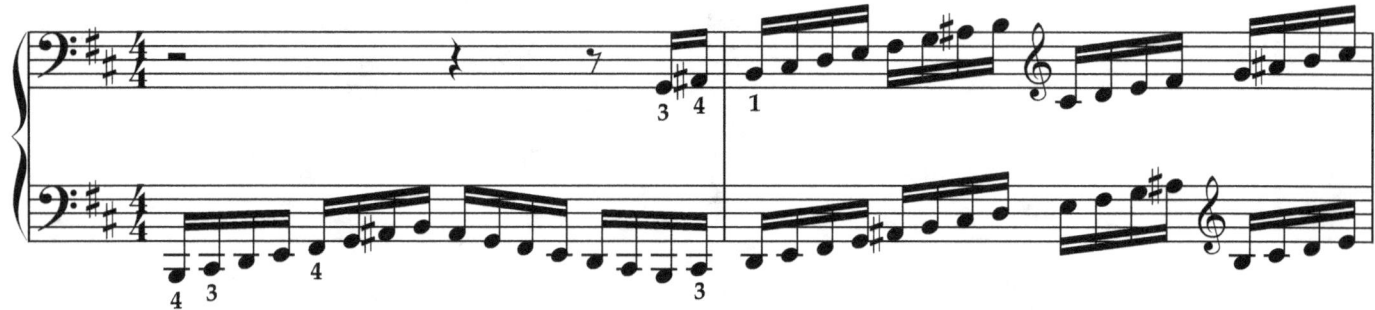

A major

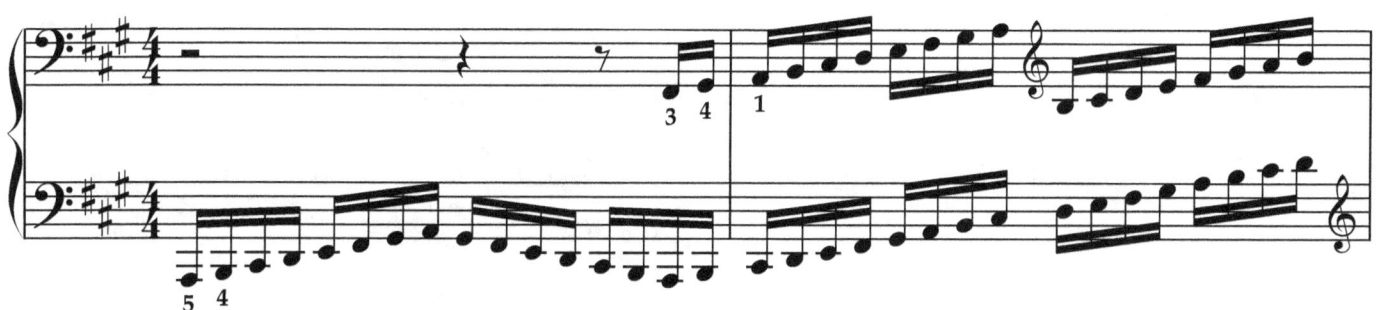

F-sharp minor (harmonic)

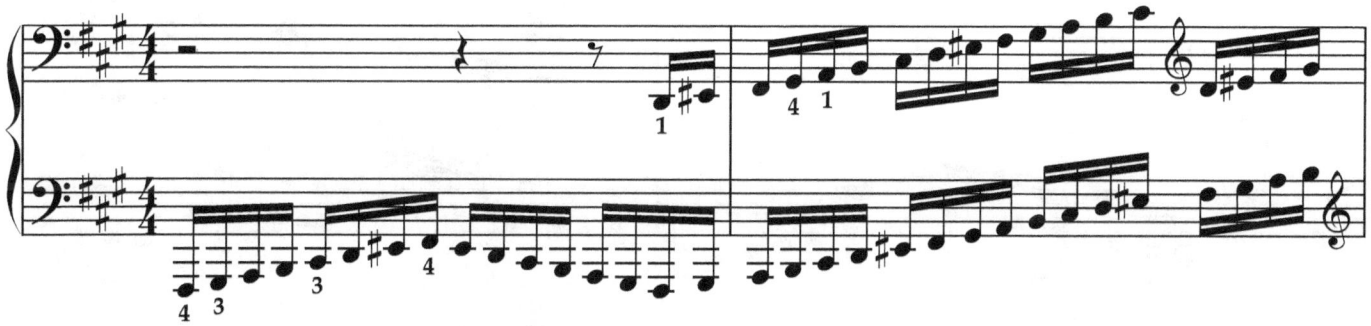

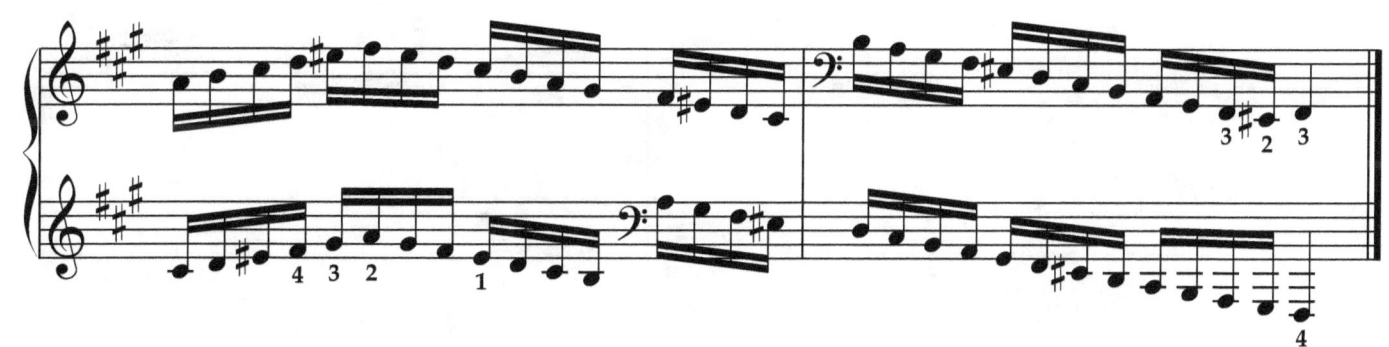

E major

C-sharp minor (harmonic)

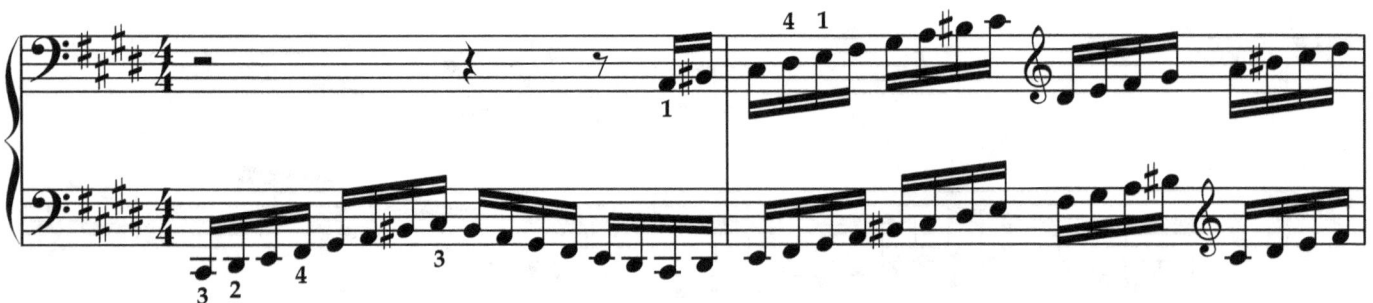

79

B major

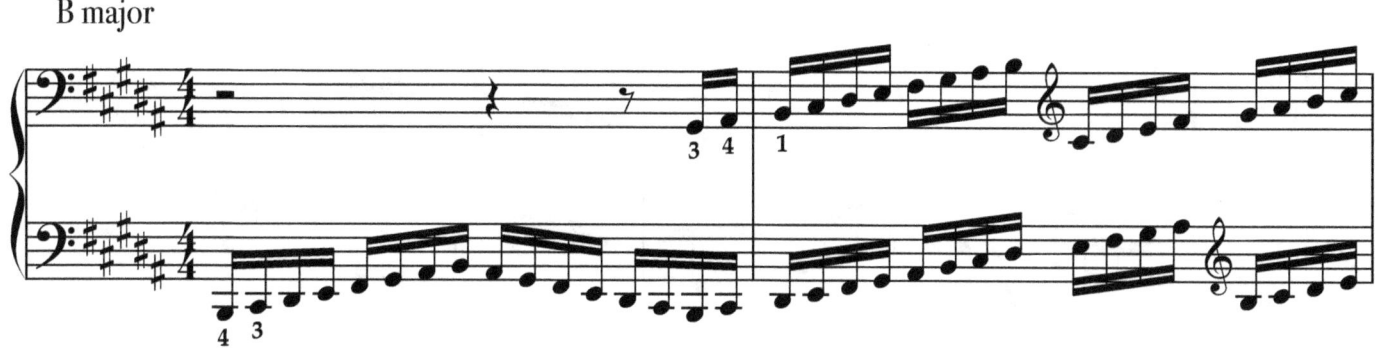

G-sharp minor (harmonic)

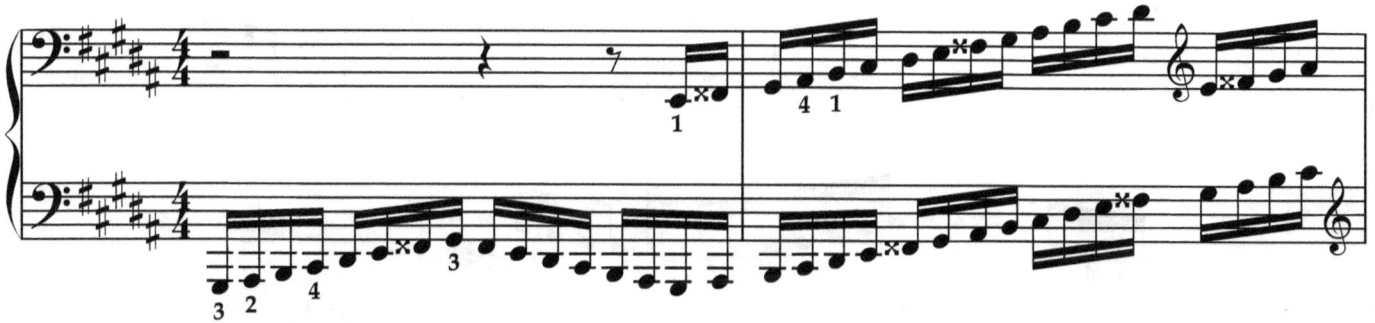

F-sharp major

D-sharp minor (harmonic)

C-sharp major

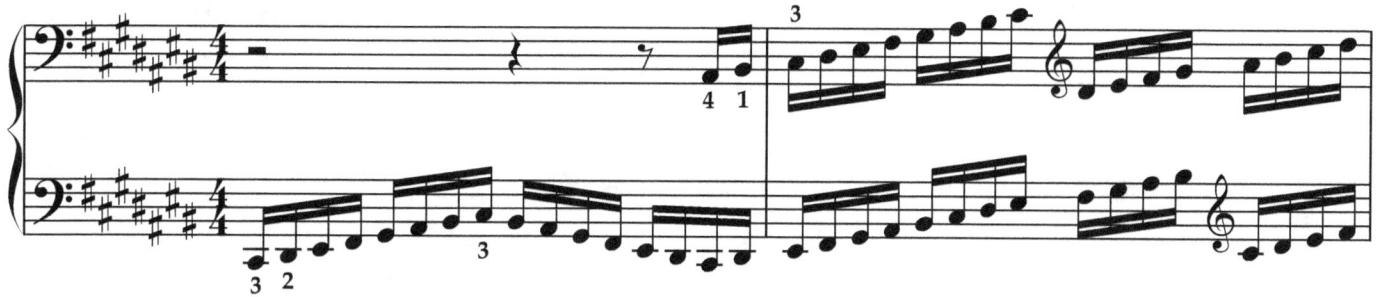

A-sharp minor (harmonic)

F major

D minor (harmonic)

B-flat major

G minor (harmonic)

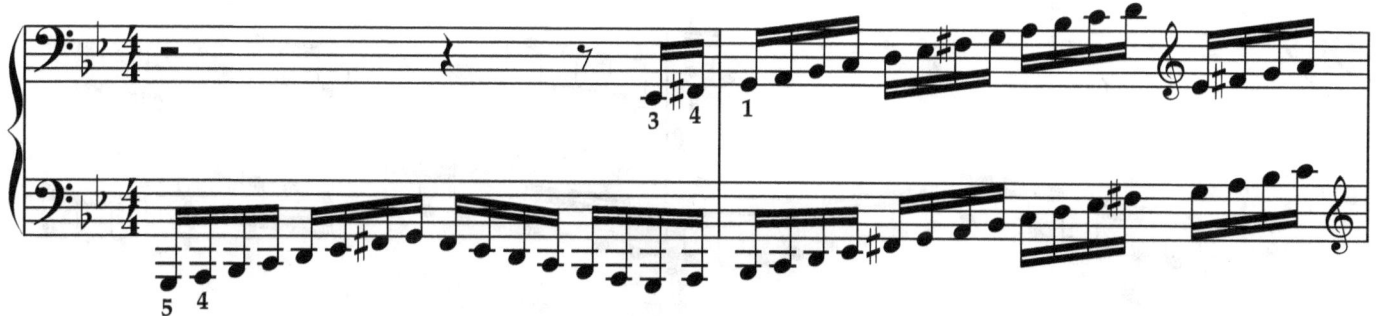

E-flat major

C minor (harmonic)

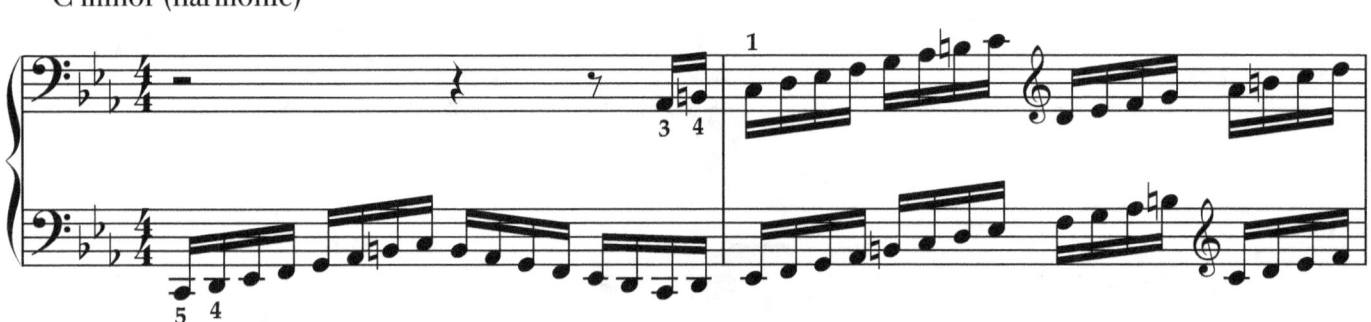

A-flat major

F minor (harmonic)

D-flat major

B-flat minor (harmonic)

87

G-flat major

E-flat minor (harmonic)

C-flat major

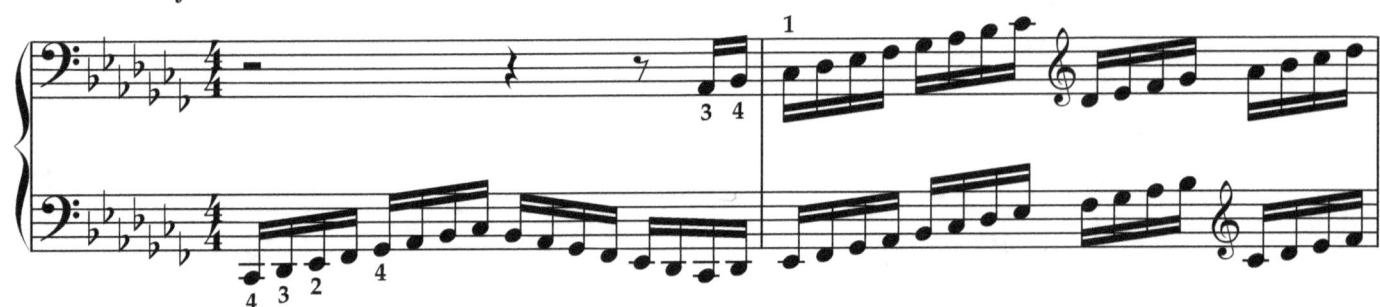

A-flat minor (harmonic)

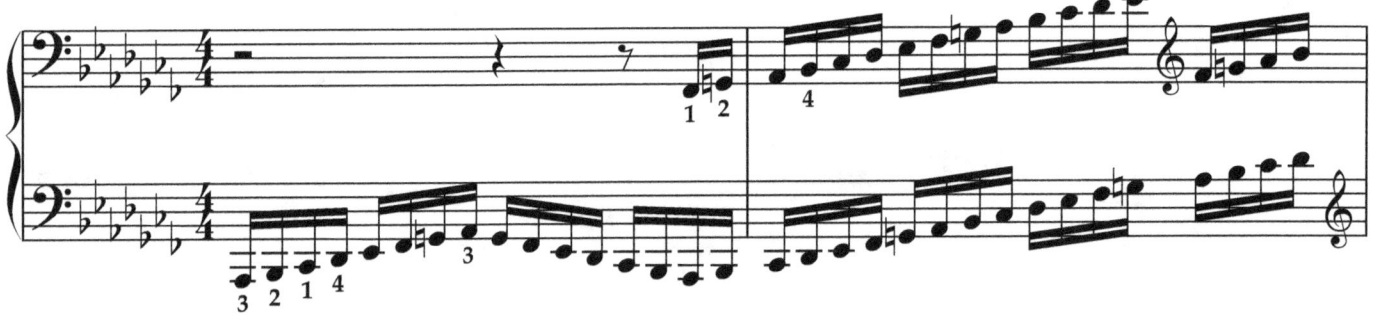

Major & Harmonic Minor Scales in 10ths

C major

A minor (harmonic)

G major

E minor (harmonic)

D major

B minor (harmonic)

A major

F-sharp minor (harmonic)

E major

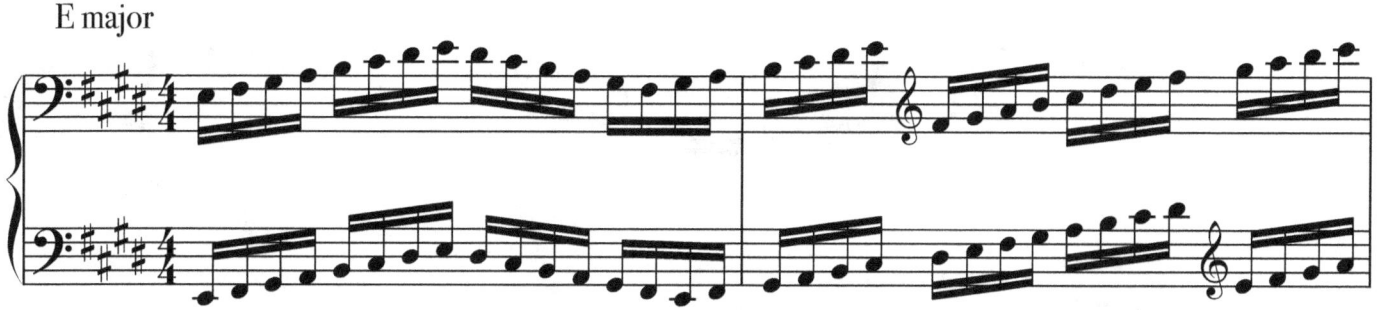

C-sharp minor (harmonic)

94

B major

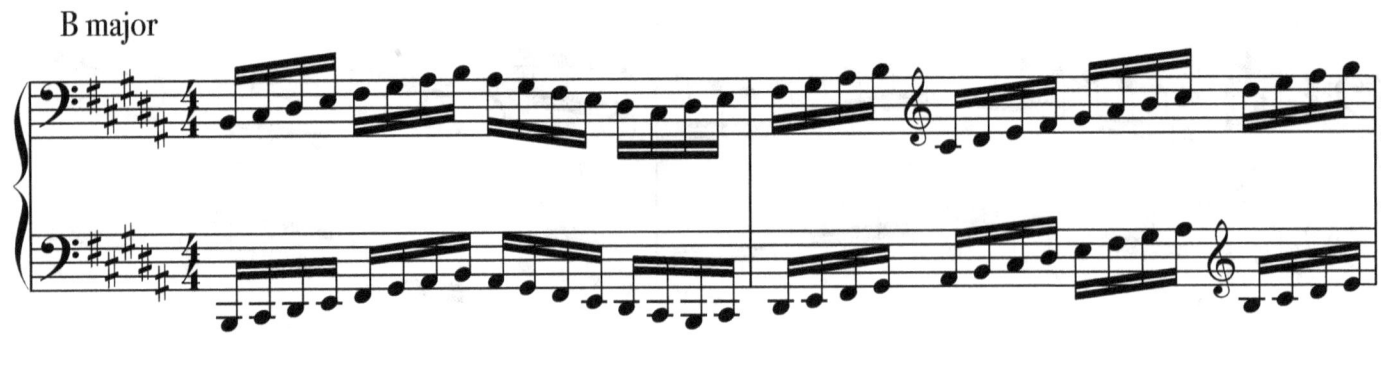

G-sharp minor (harmonic)

F-sharp major

D-sharp minor (harmonic)

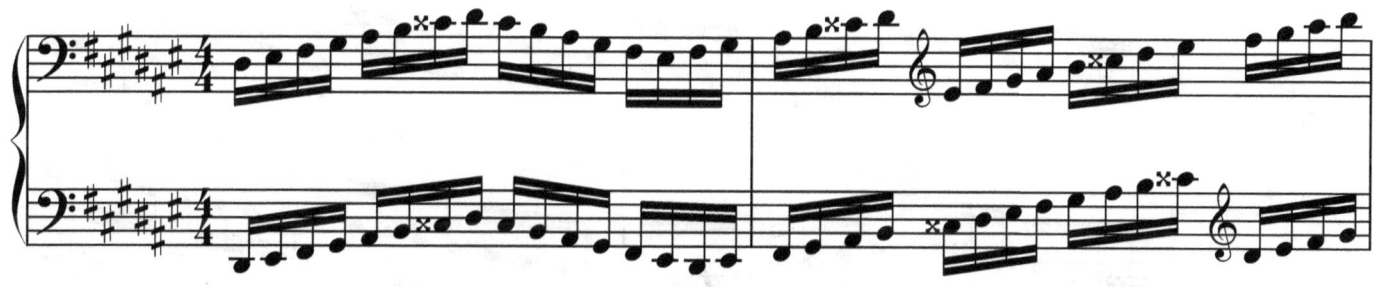

C-sharp major

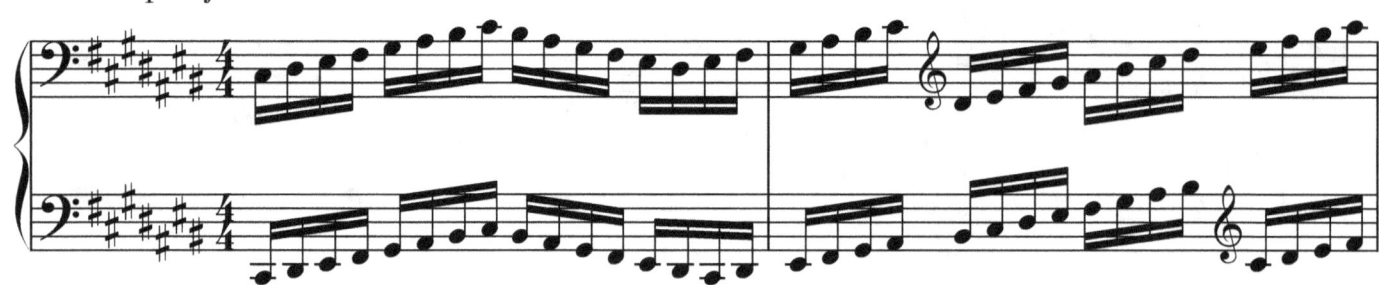

A-sharp minor (harmonic)

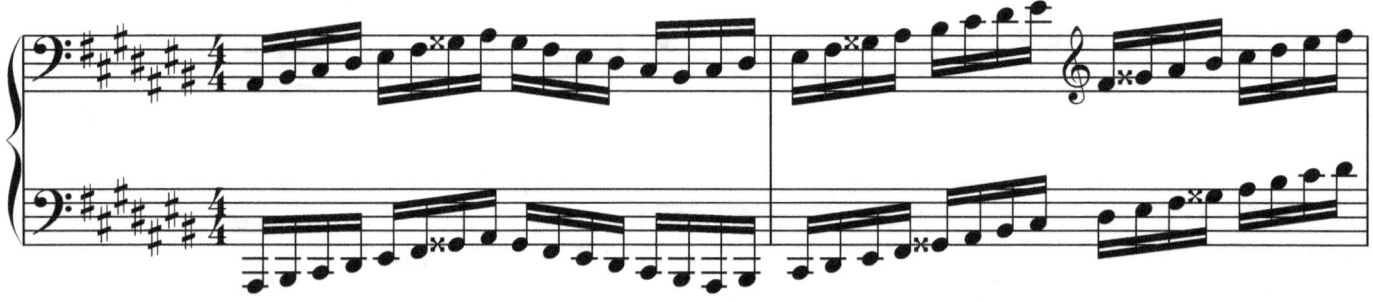

97

F major

D minor (harmonic)

B-flat major

G minor (harmonic)

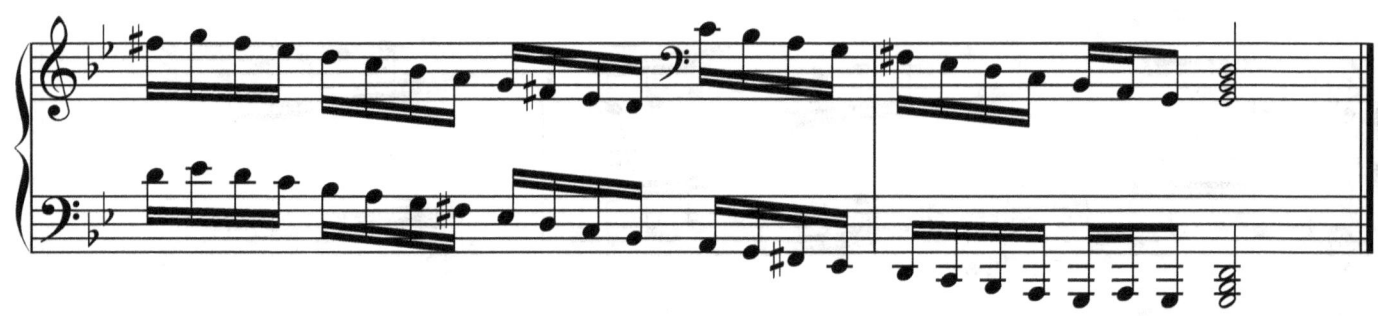

E-flat major

C minor (harmonic)

100

A-flat major

F minor (harmonic)

D-flat major

B-flat minor (harmonic)

G-flat major

E-flat minor (harmonic)

C-flat major

A-flat minor (harmonic)

A minor (harmonic)

Note: The 4th finger of either hand may be used to play the black keys when playing octaves

E minor (harmonic)

B minor (harmonic)

F-sharp minor (harmonic)

E major

Offset Octaves

Broken Octaves

Unison Octaves

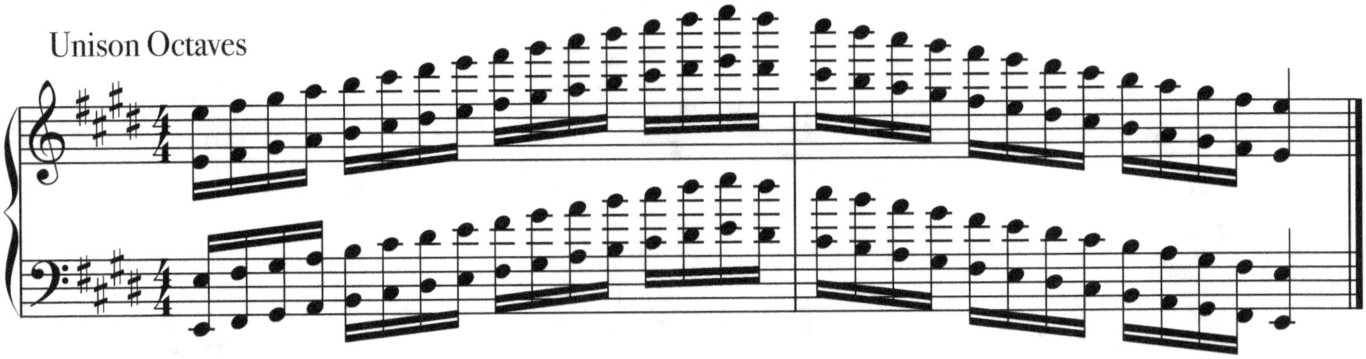

C-sharp minor (harmonic)

B major

G-sharp minor (harmonic)

F-sharp major

D-sharp minor (harmonic)

C-sharp major

A-sharp minor (harmonic)

D minor (harmonic)

B-flat major

G minor (harmonic)

E-flat major

C minor (harmonic)

A-flat major

F minor (harmonic)

D-flat major

B-flat minor (harmonic)

G-flat major

E-flat minor (harmonic)

C-flat major

A-flat minor (harmonic)

Chromatic Scales

Unison

Beginning on the minor 3rd

136

Beginning on the major 3rd

Beginning on the minor 6th

138

Beginning on the major 6th

Arpeggios with a root note of C

139

Major

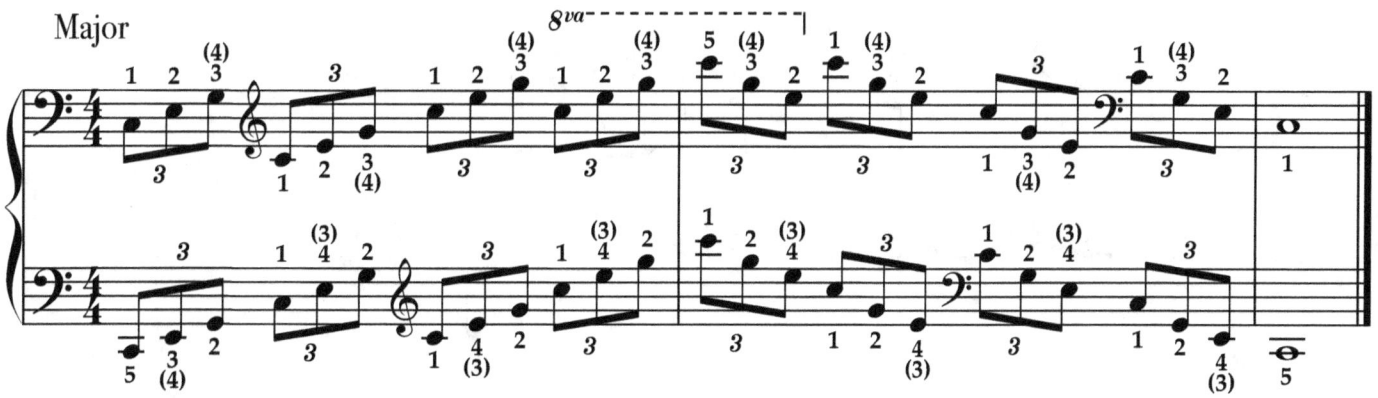

Minor

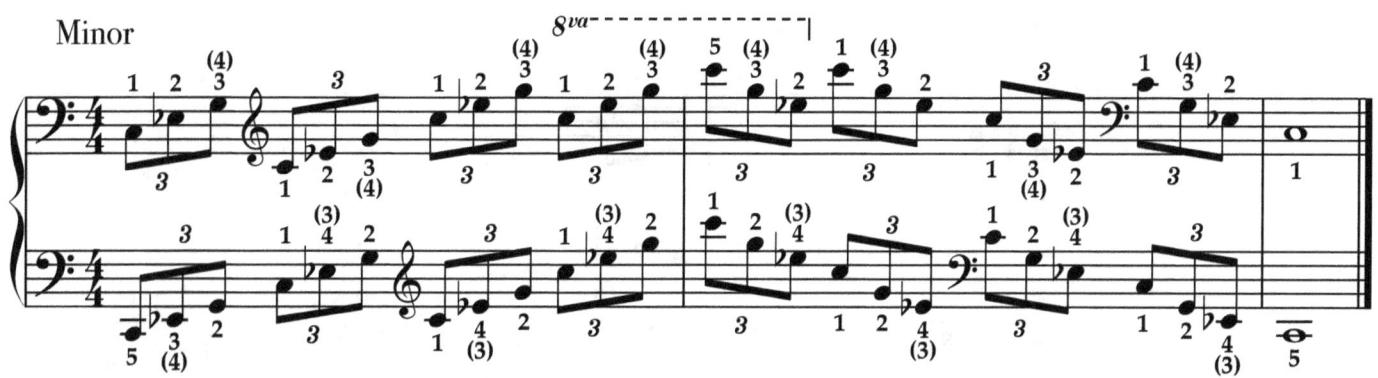

Dominant 7th

Diminished 7th

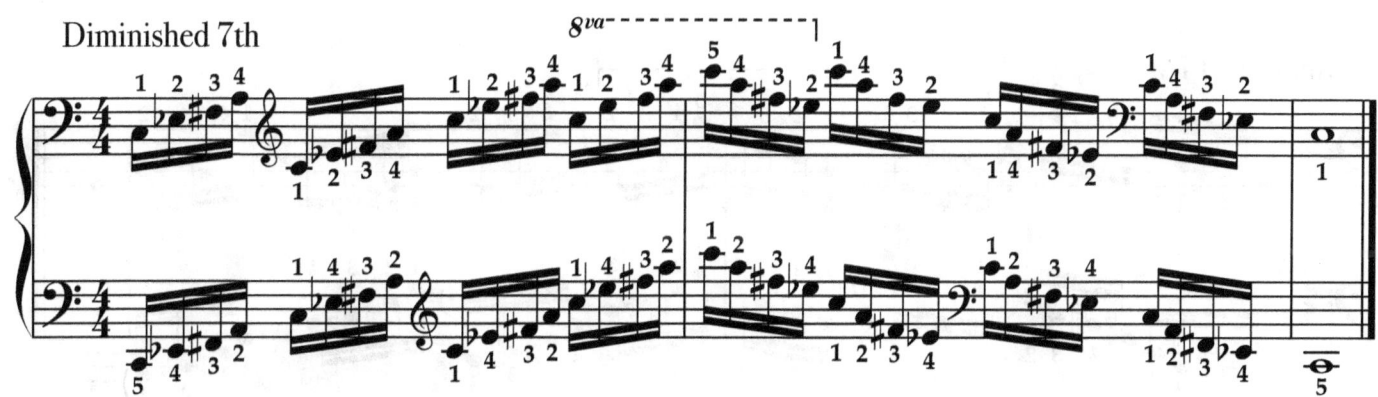

Note: For an explanation of arpeggios, see *Appendix B*, page *ii*

Arpeggios with a root note of G

Major

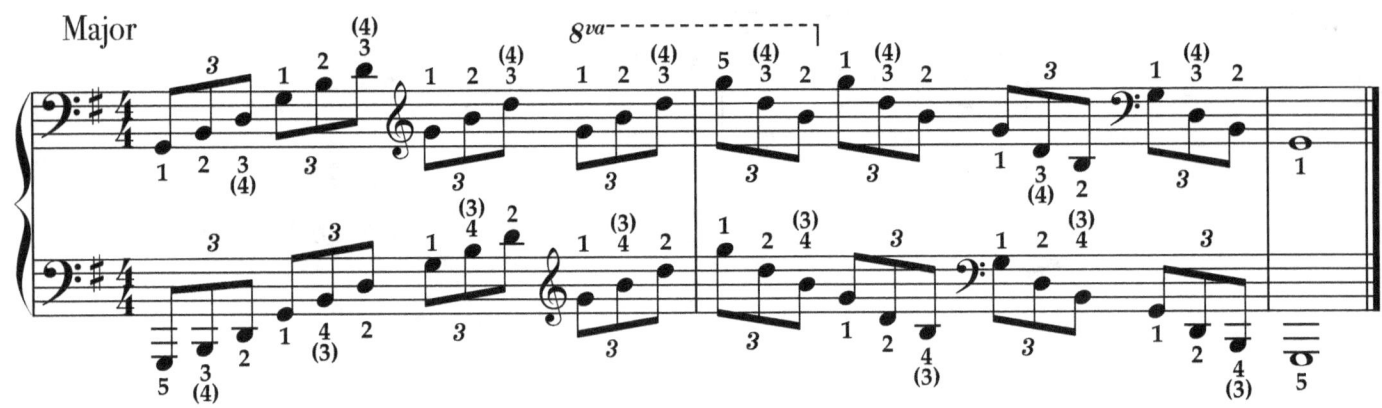

Minor

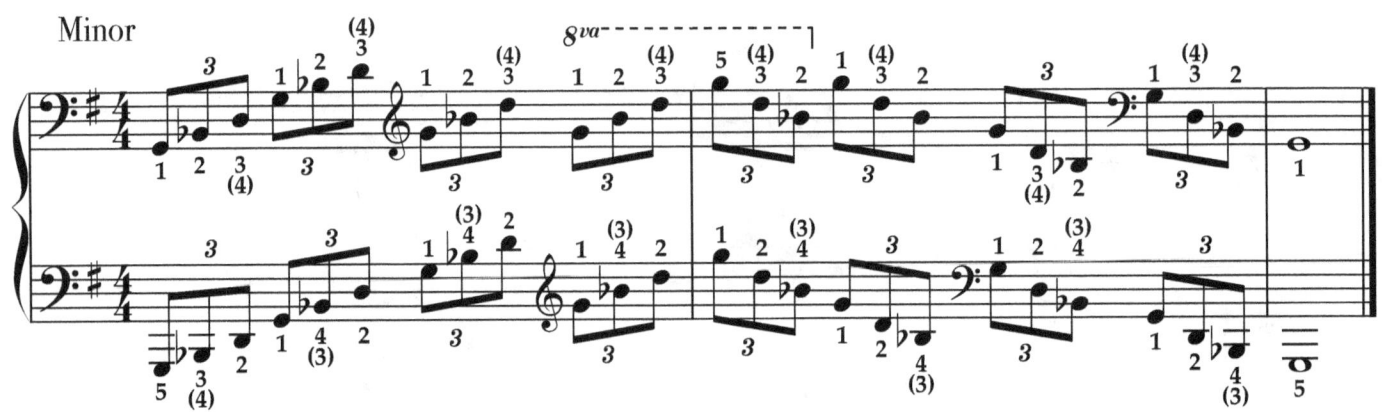

Dominant 7th

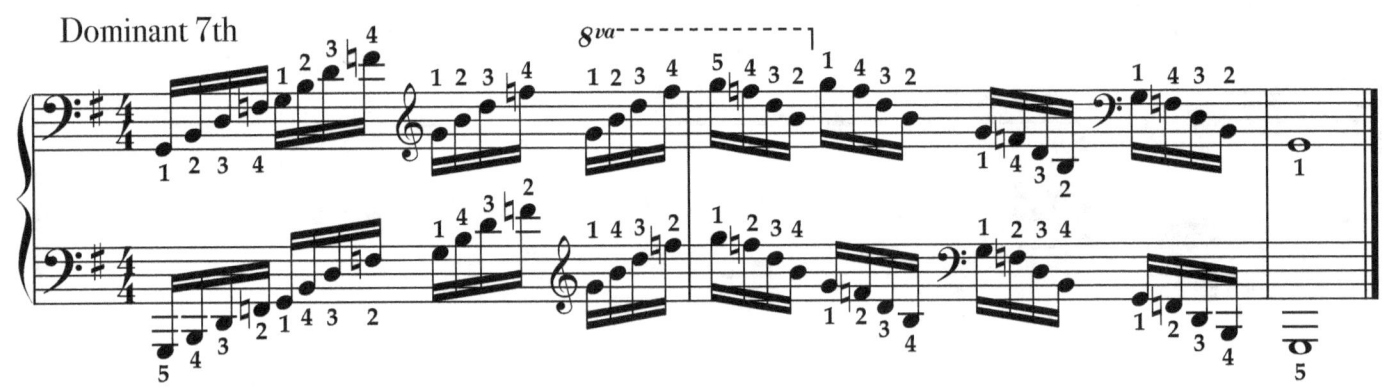

Diminished 7th

Arpeggios with a root note of D

141

Major

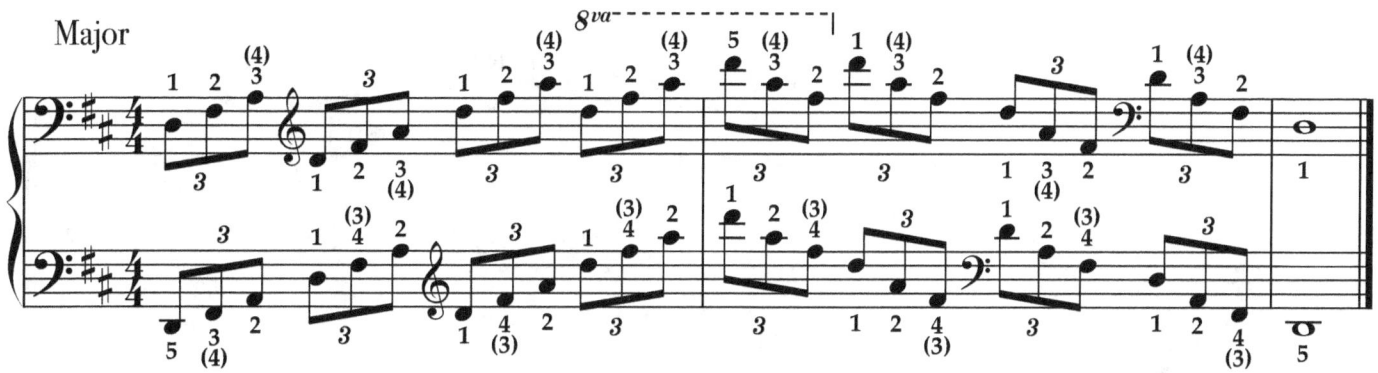

Minor

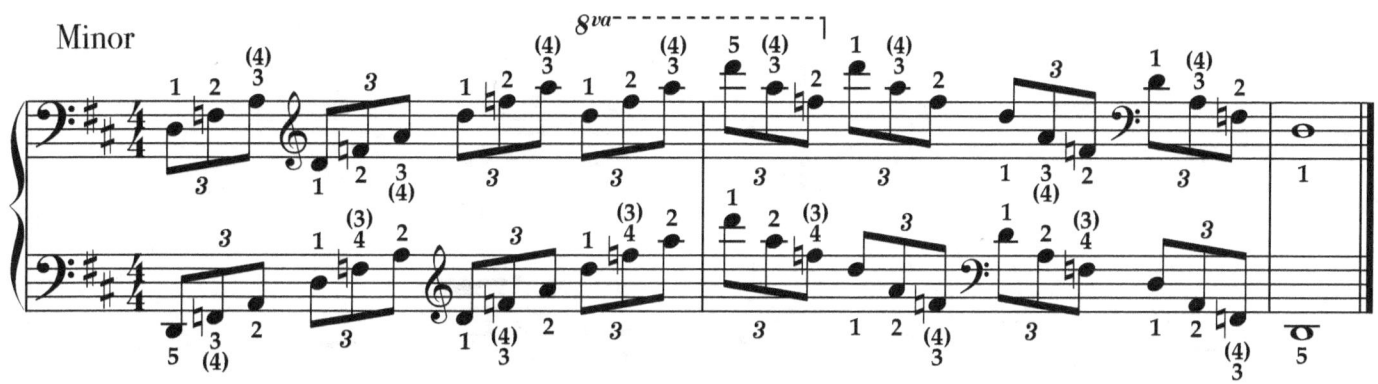

Dominant 7th

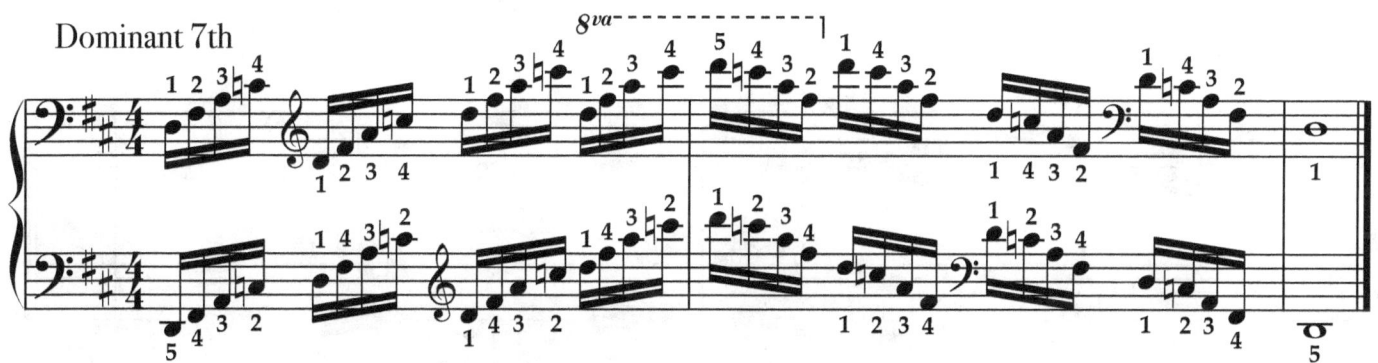

Diminished 7th

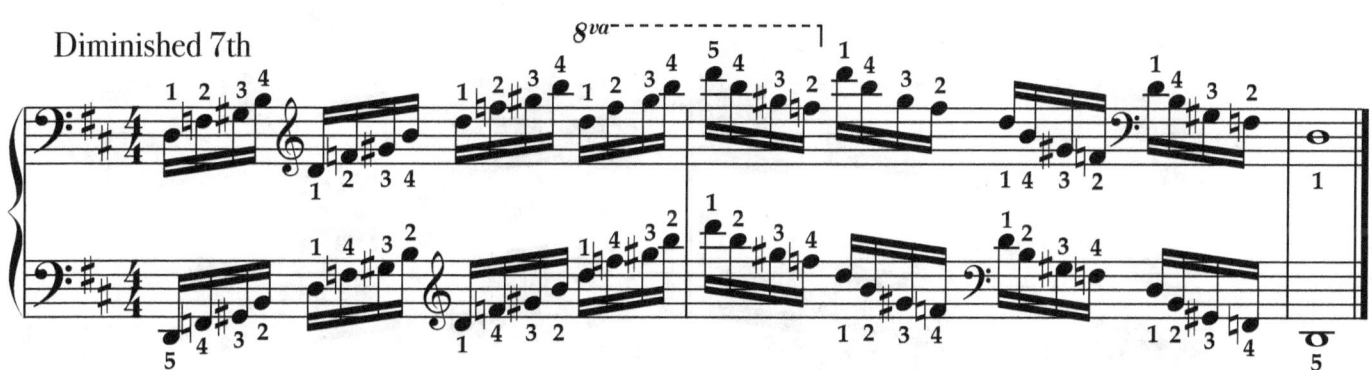

Arpeggios with a root note of A

Major

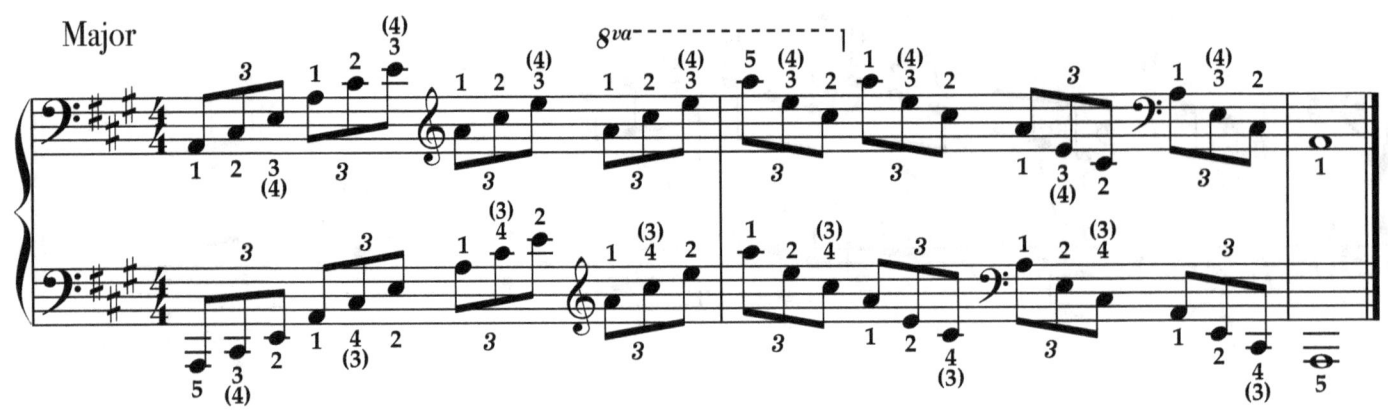

Minor

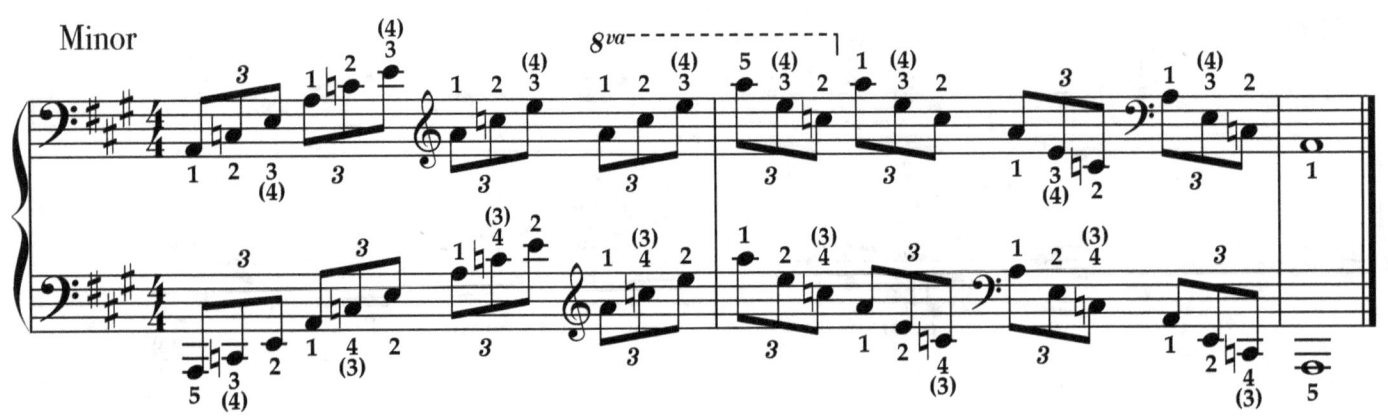

Dominant 7th

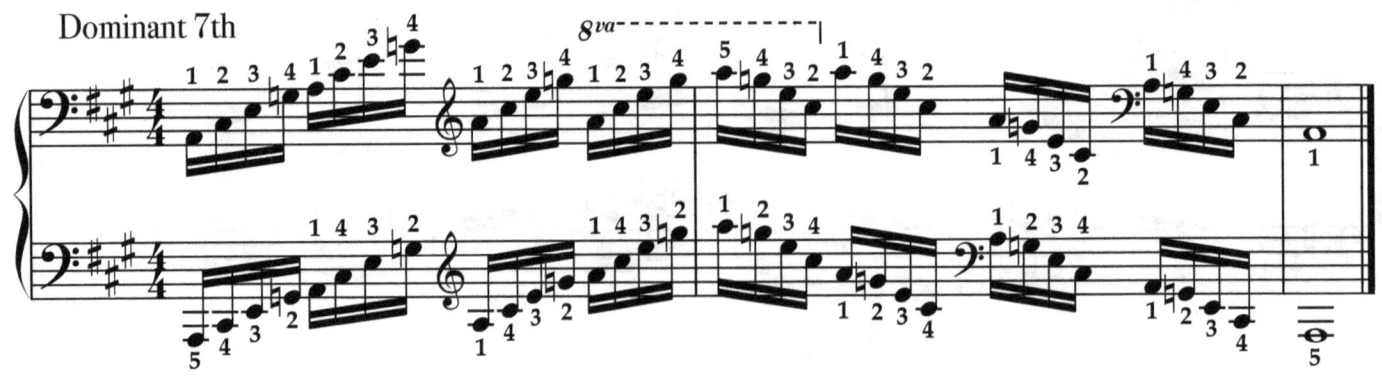

Diminished 7th

Arpeggios with a root note of E

143

Major

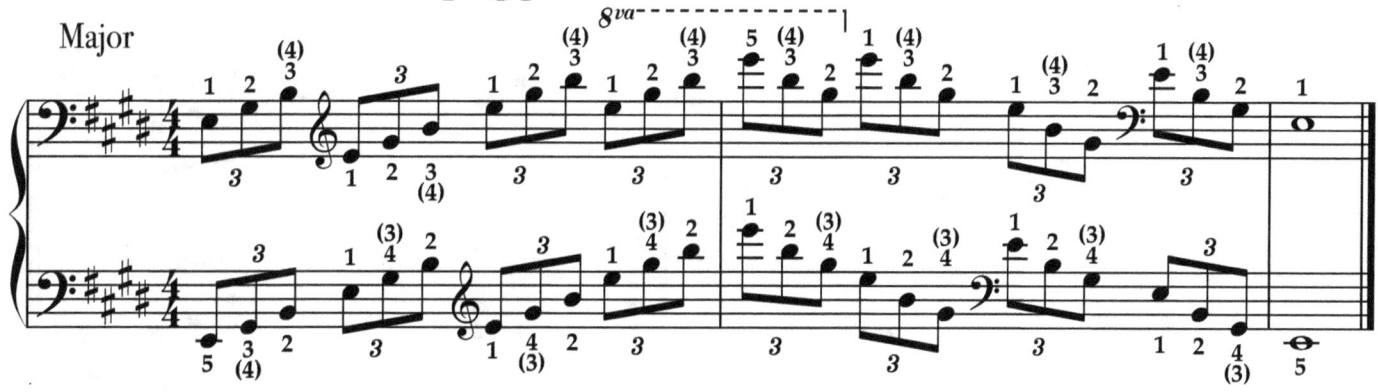

Minor

Dominant 7th

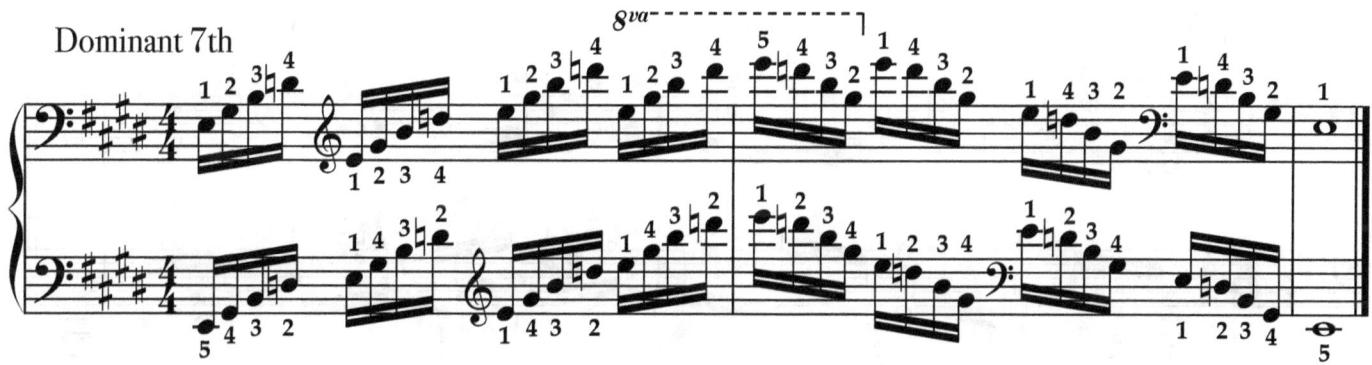

Diminished 7th

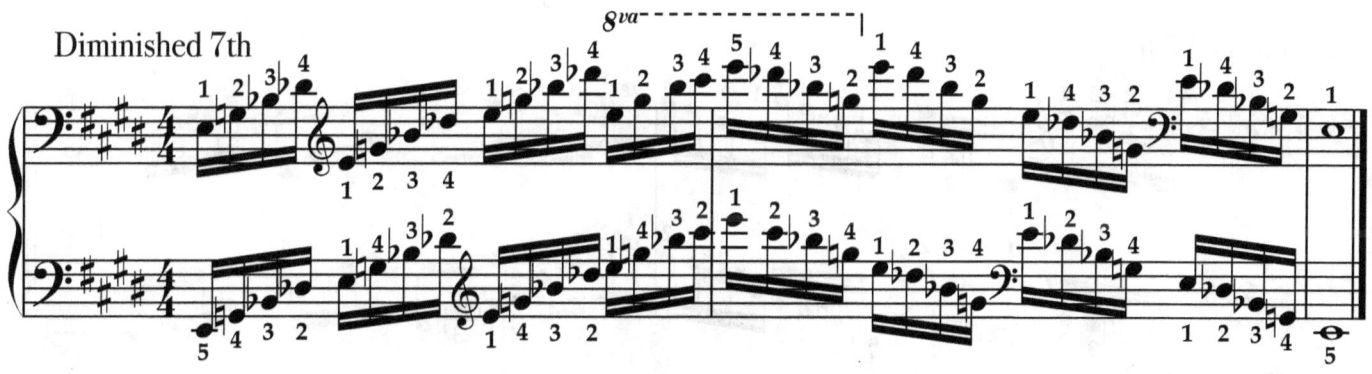

144

Arpeggios with a root note of B

Major

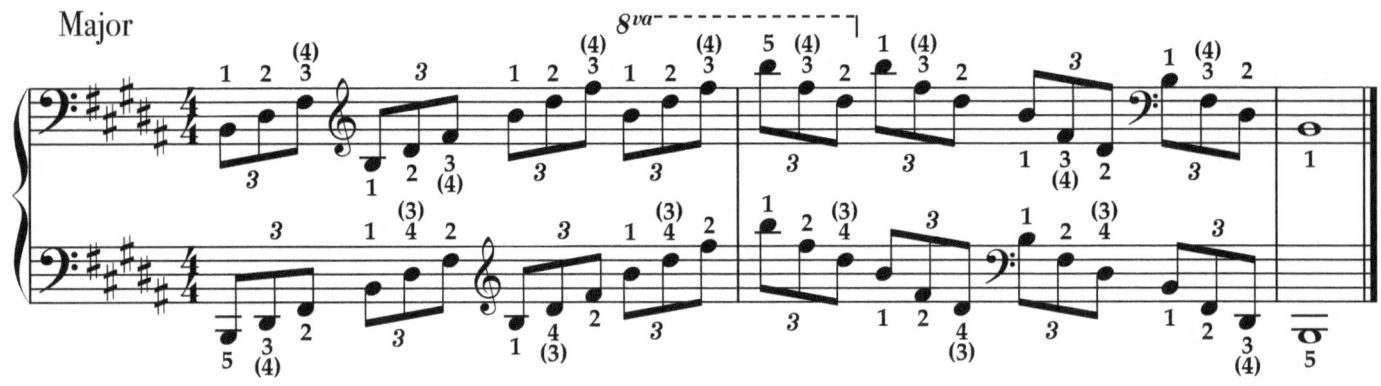

Minor

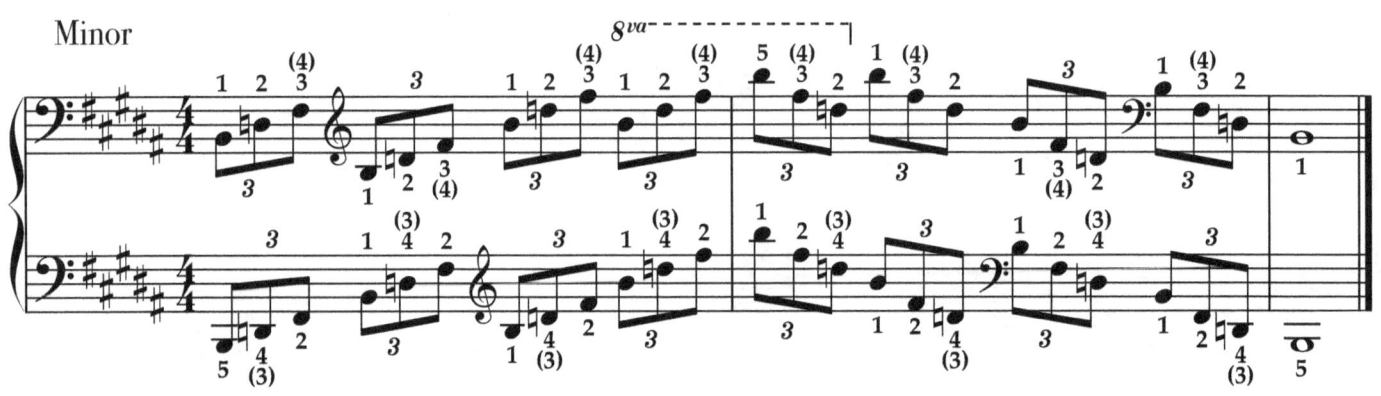

Dominant 7th

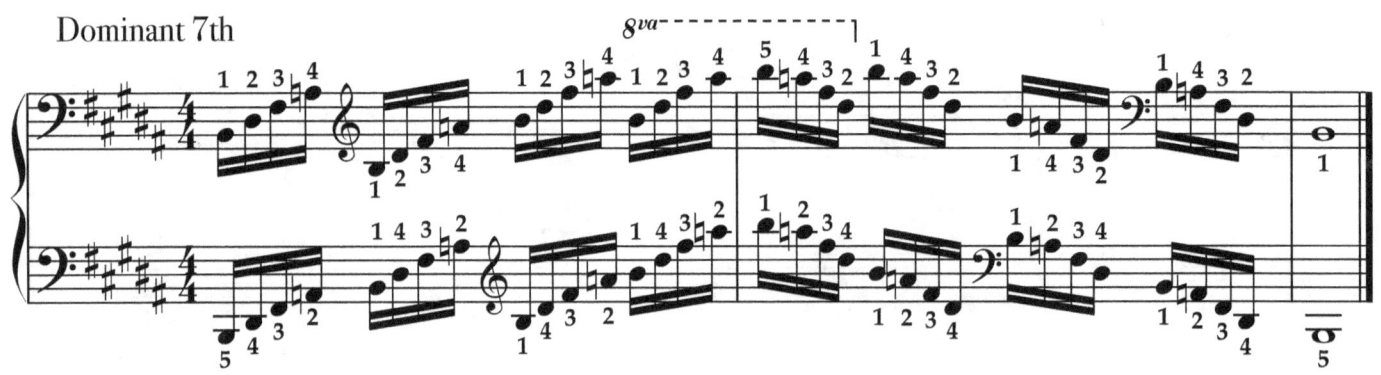

Diminished 7th

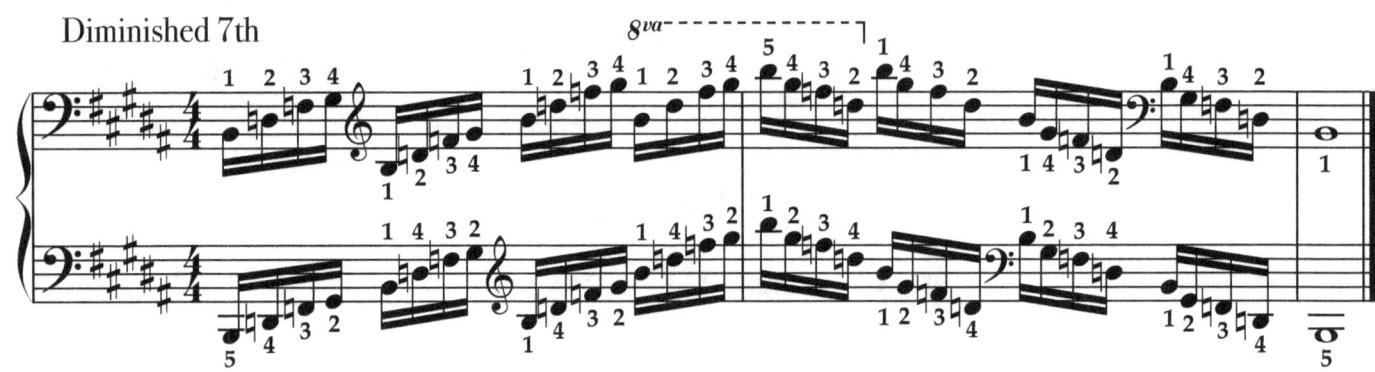

Arpeggios with a root note of F-sharp

Major

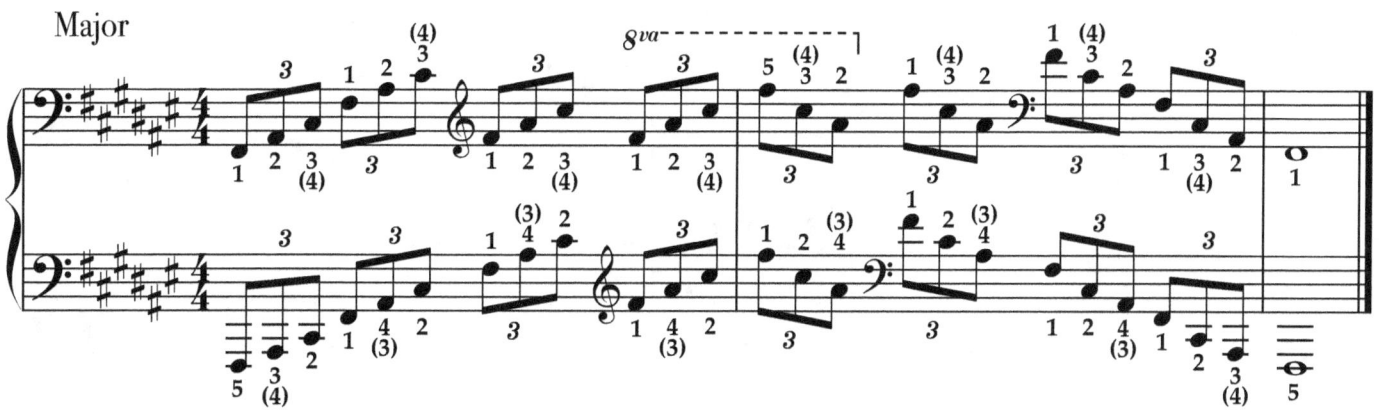

Minor

Dominant 7th

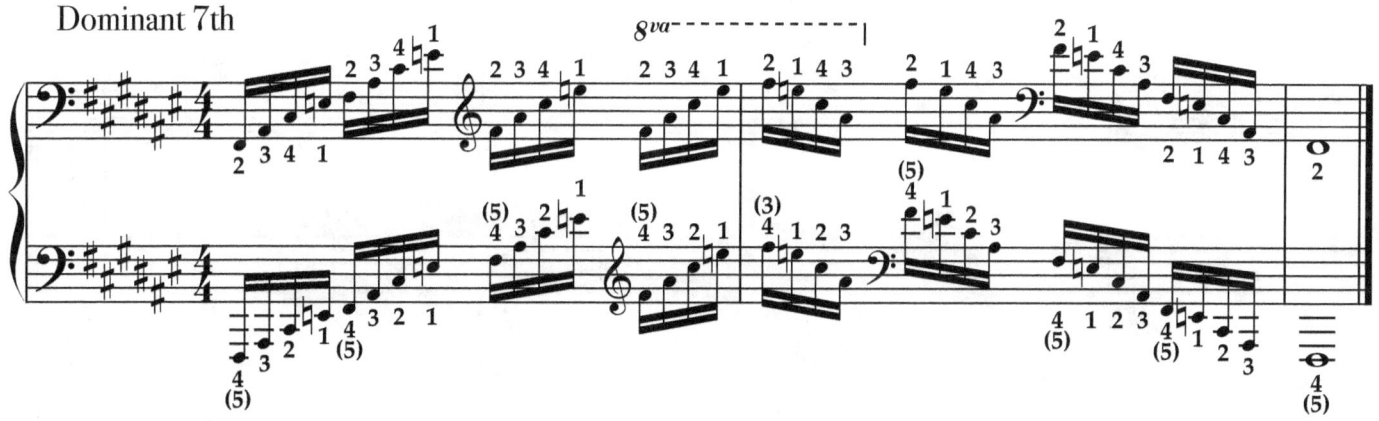

Diminished 7th

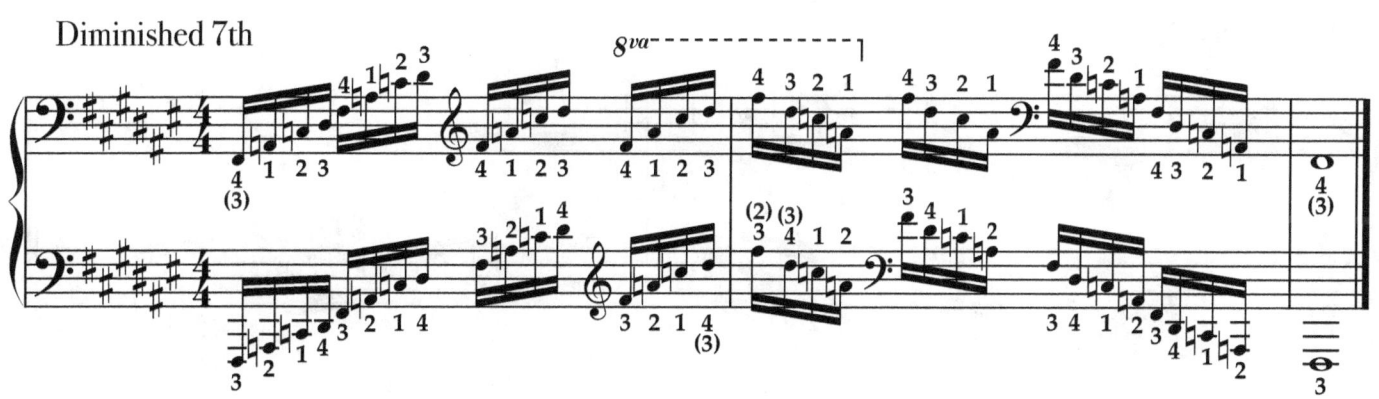

Arpeggios with a root note of C-sharp

Major

Minor

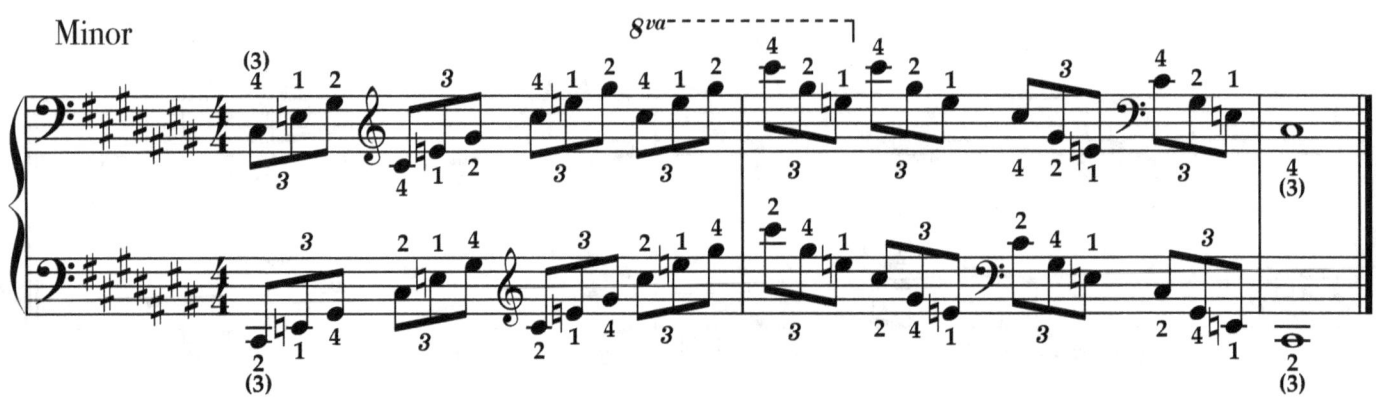

Dominant 7th

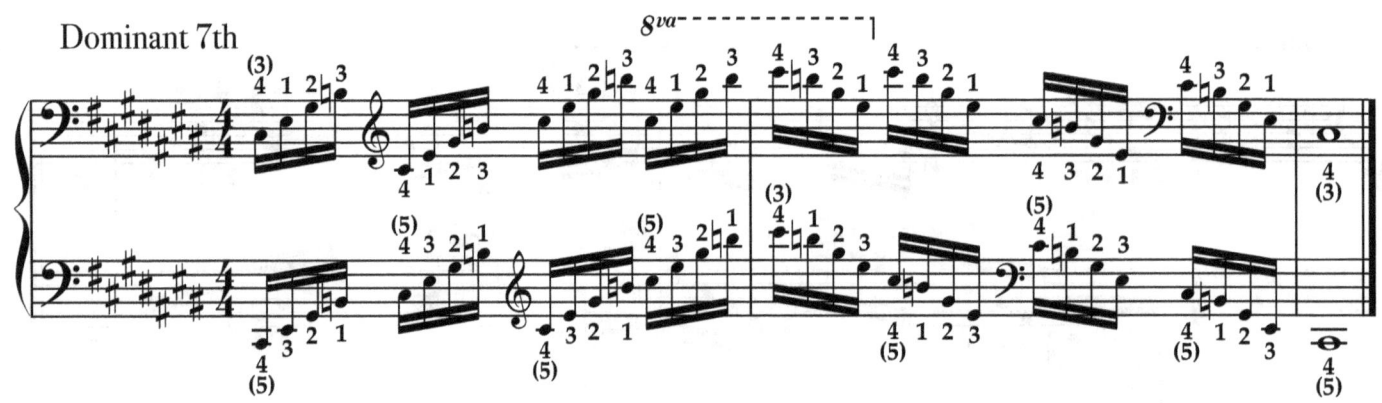

Diminished 7th

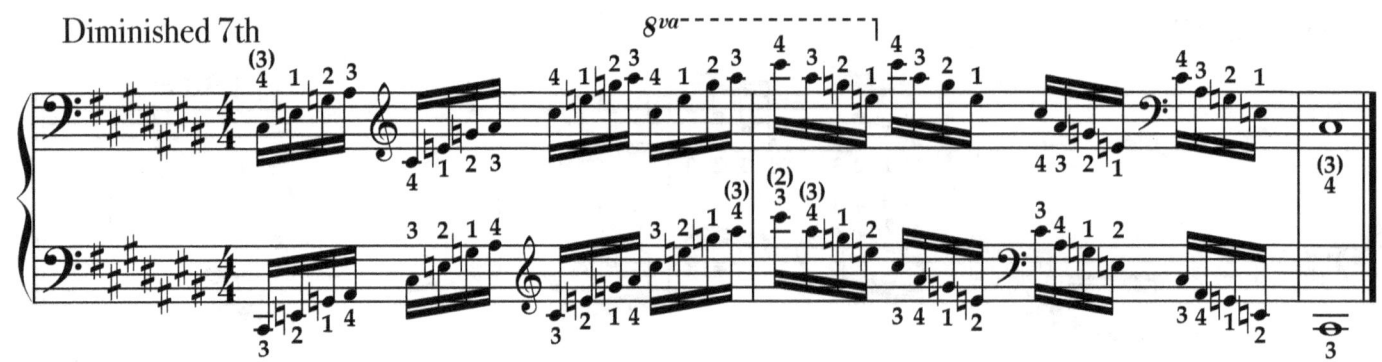

Arpeggios with a root note of F

147

Major

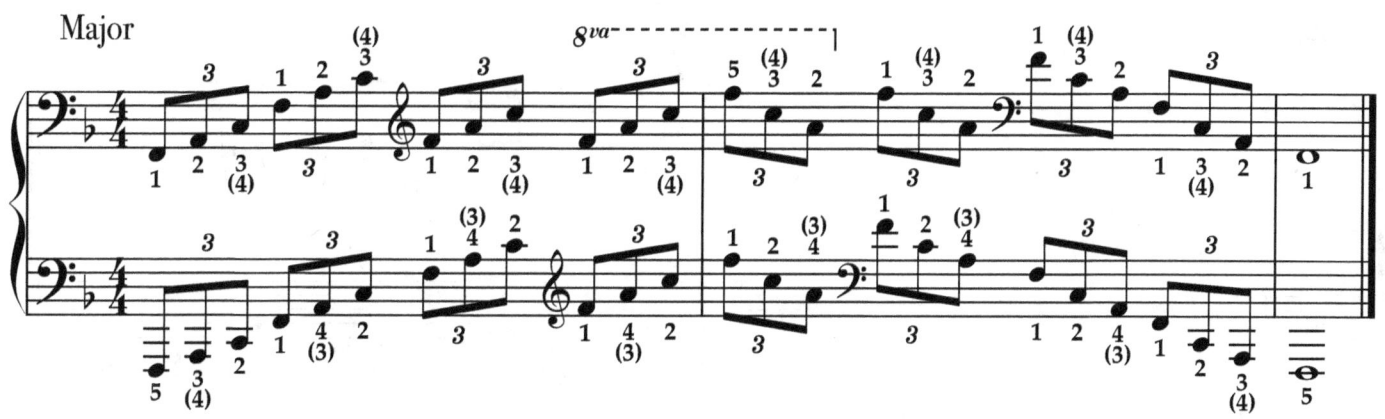

Minor

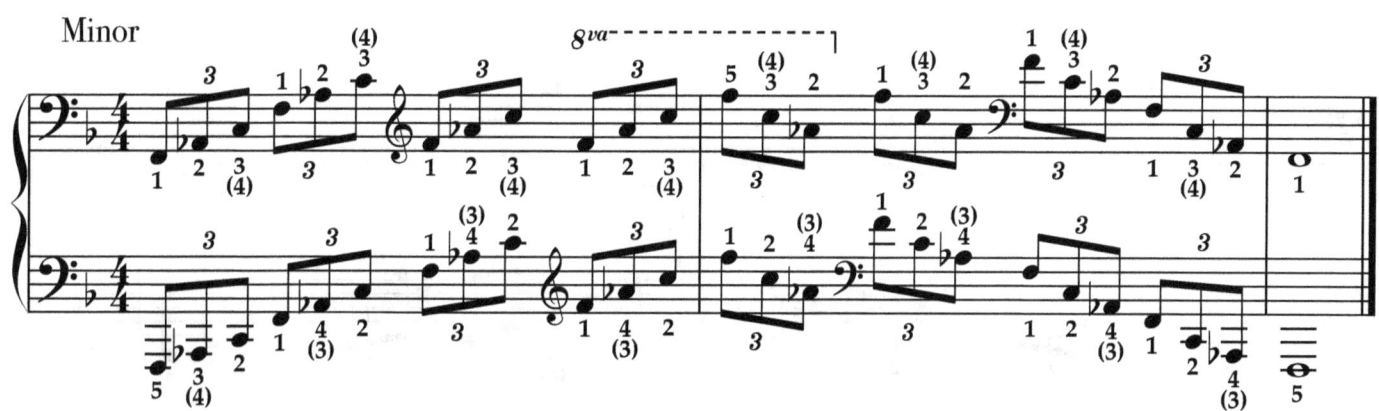

Dominant 7th

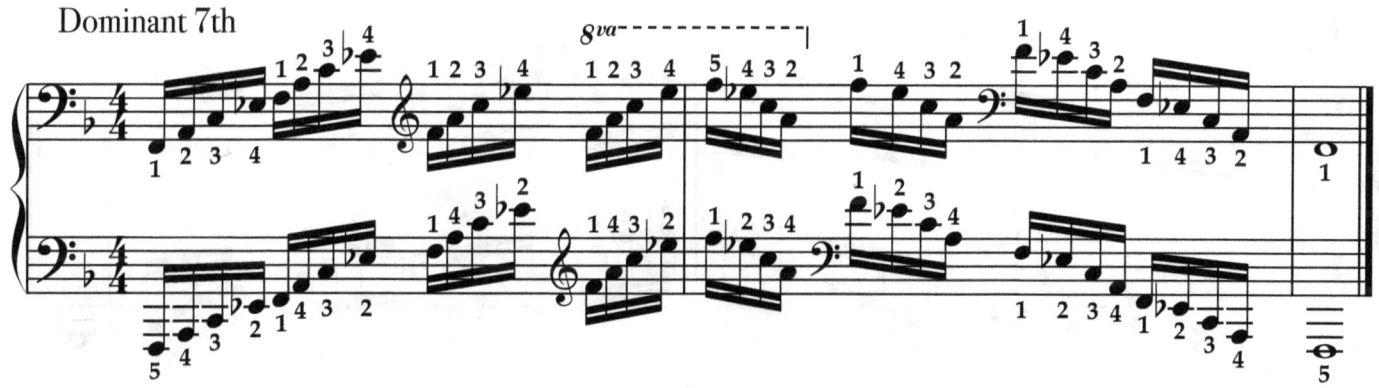

Diminished 7th

148

Arpeggios with a root note of B-flat

Major

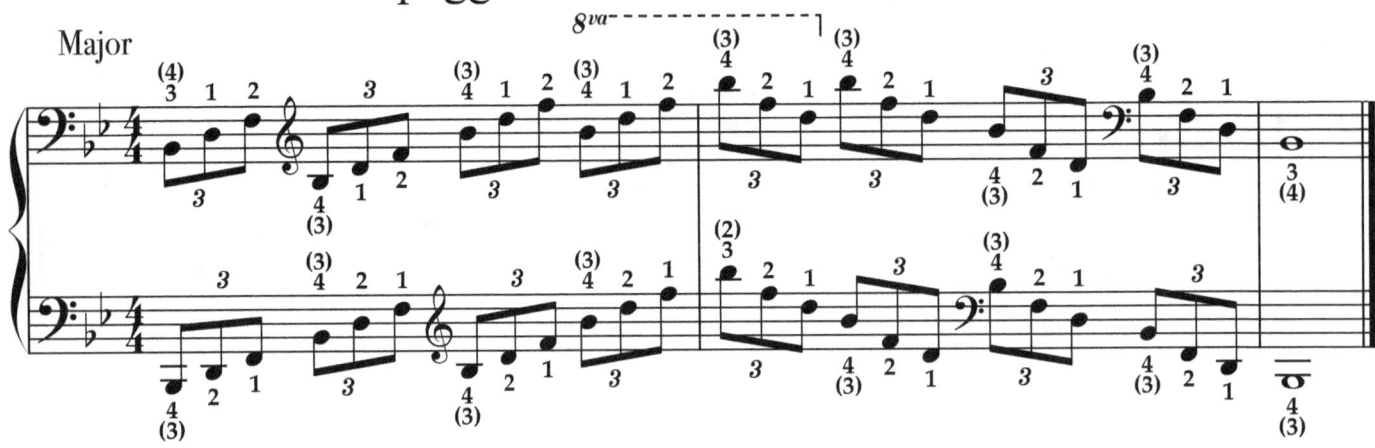

Minor

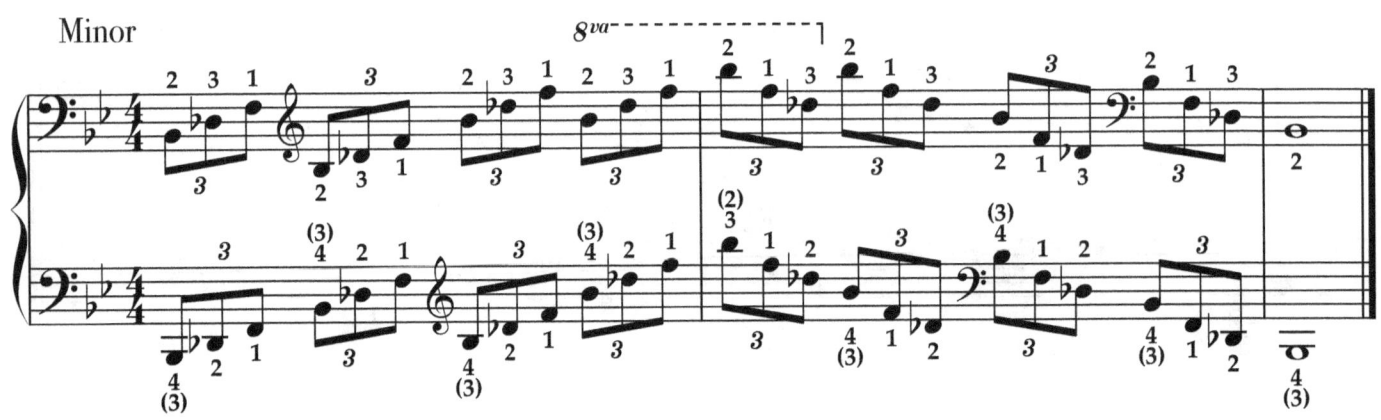

Dominant 7th

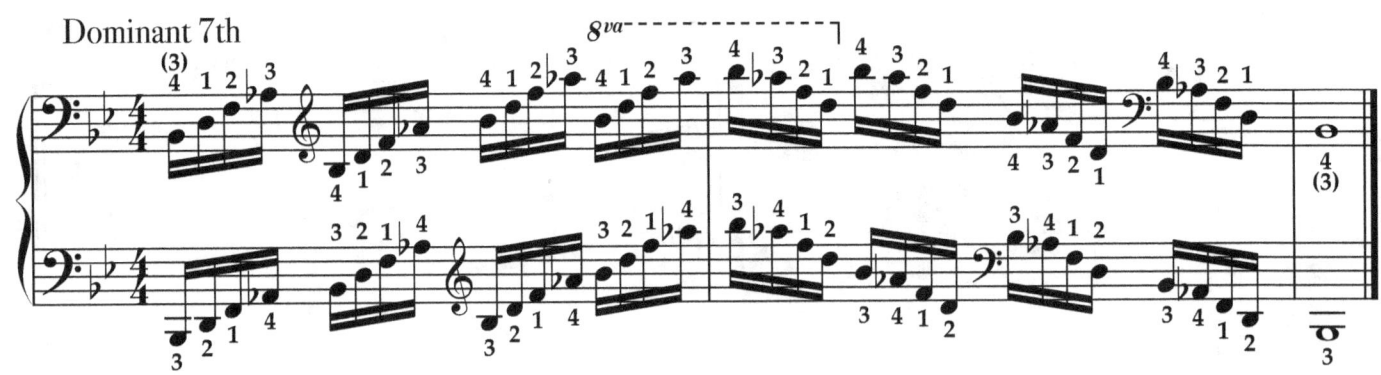

Diminished 7th

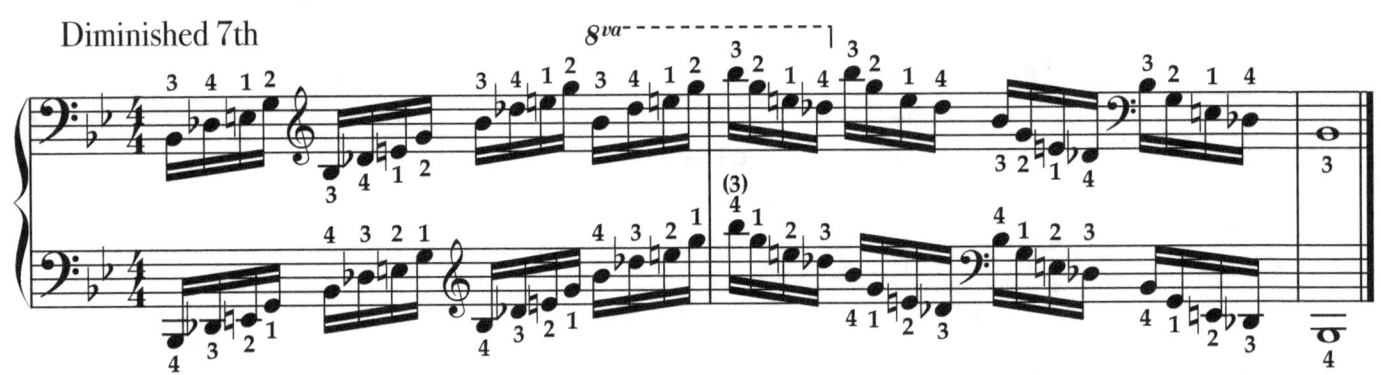

Arpeggios with a root note of E-flat

Major

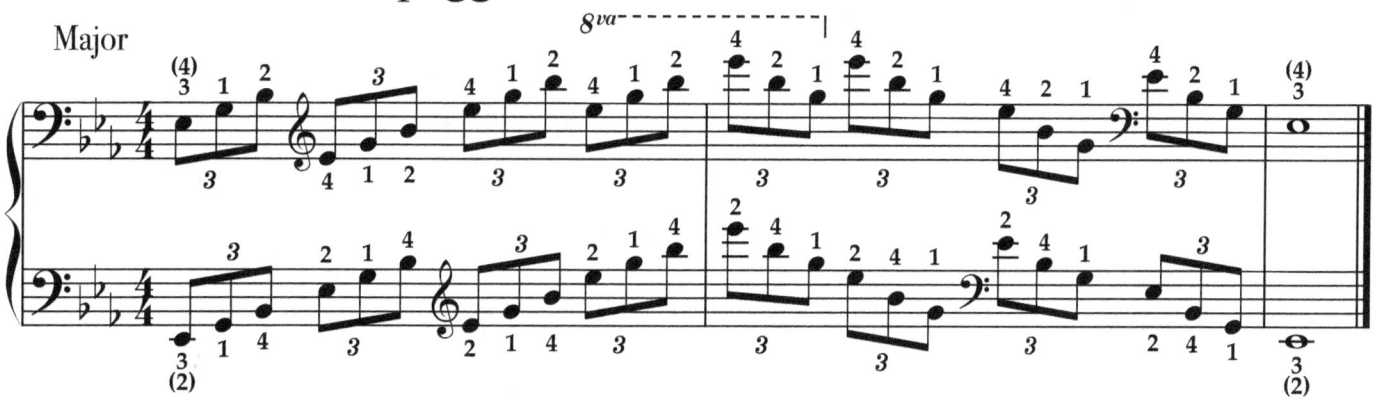

Minor

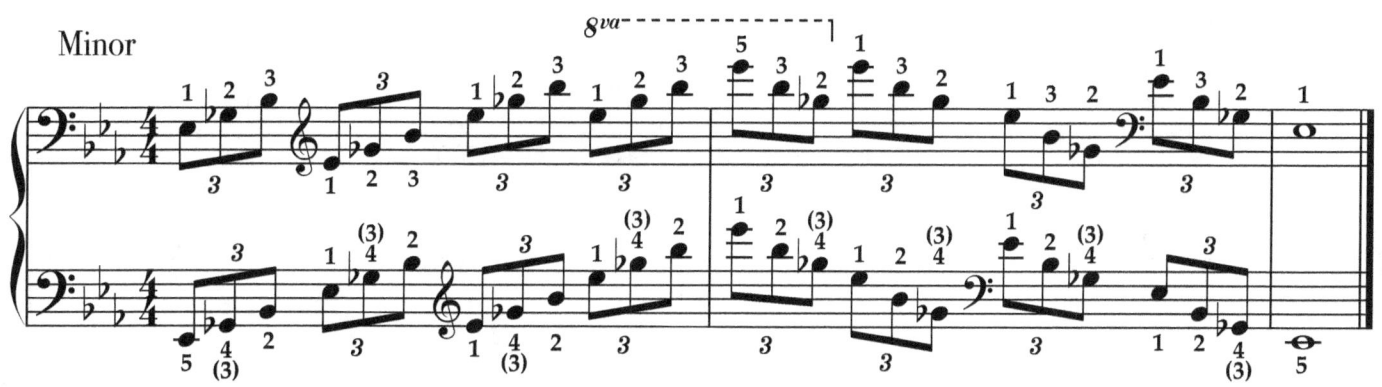

Dominant 7th

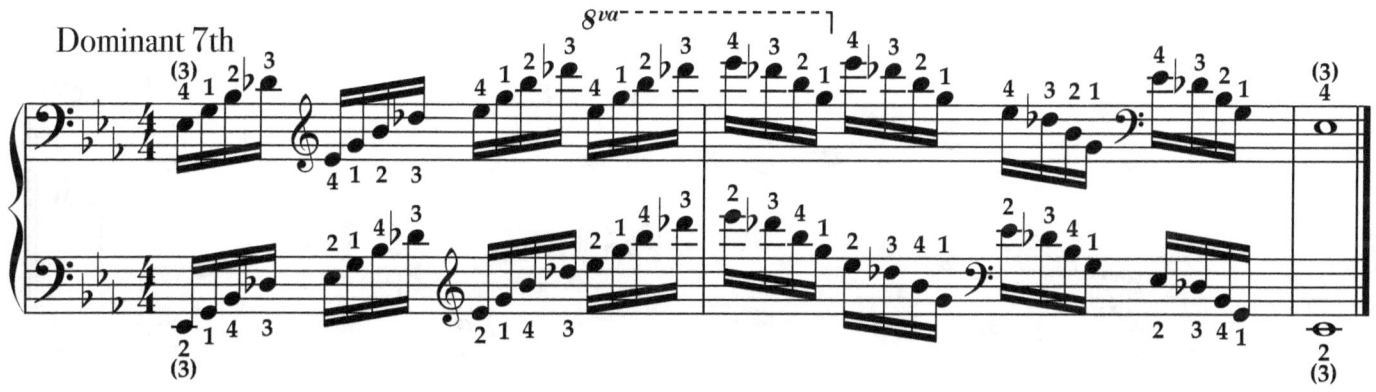

Diminished 7th

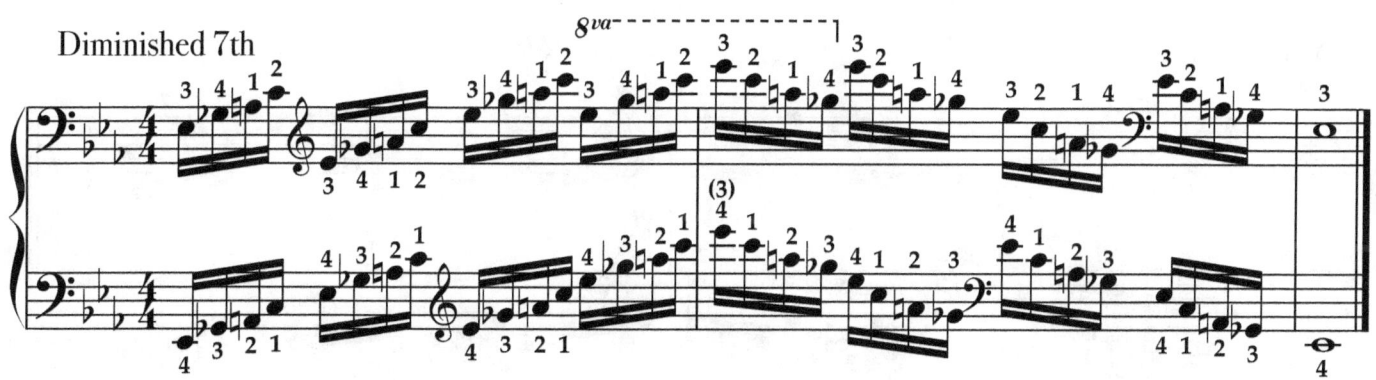

Arpeggios with a root note of A-flat

150

Major

Minor

Dominant 7th

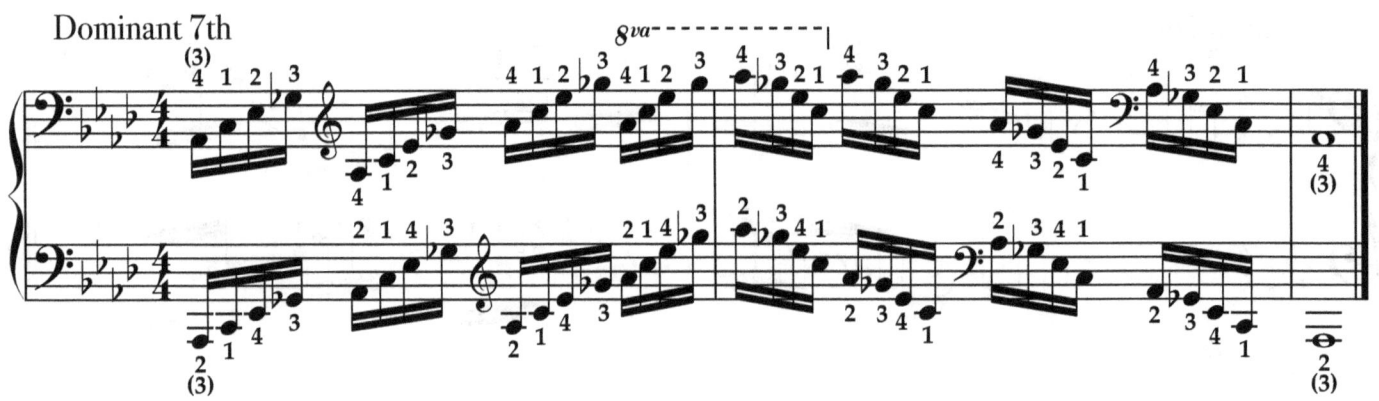

Diminished 7th

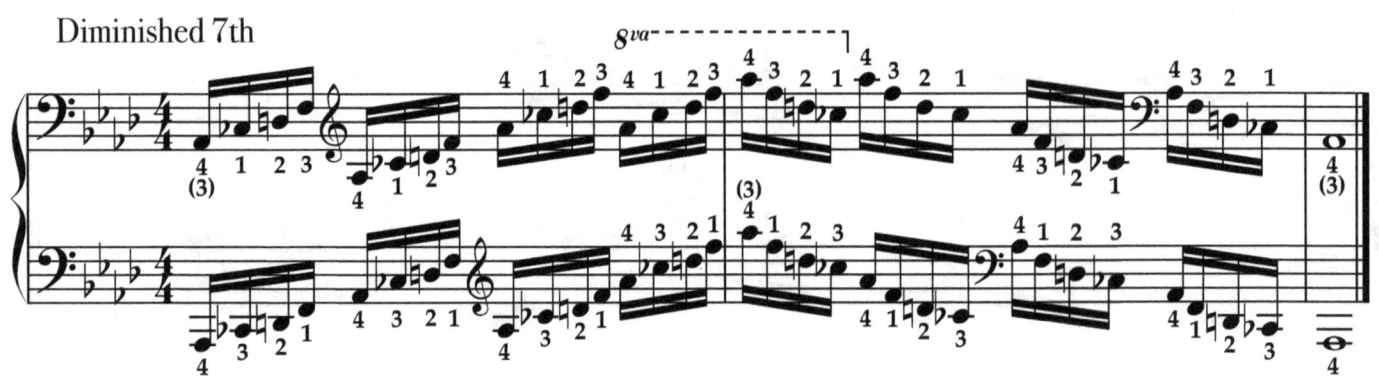

Arpeggios with a root note of D-flat

Major

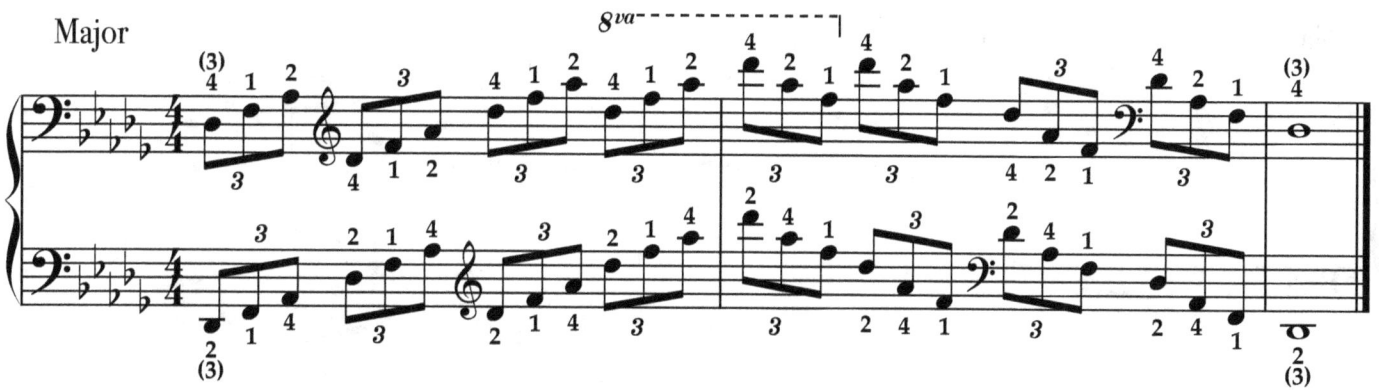

Minor

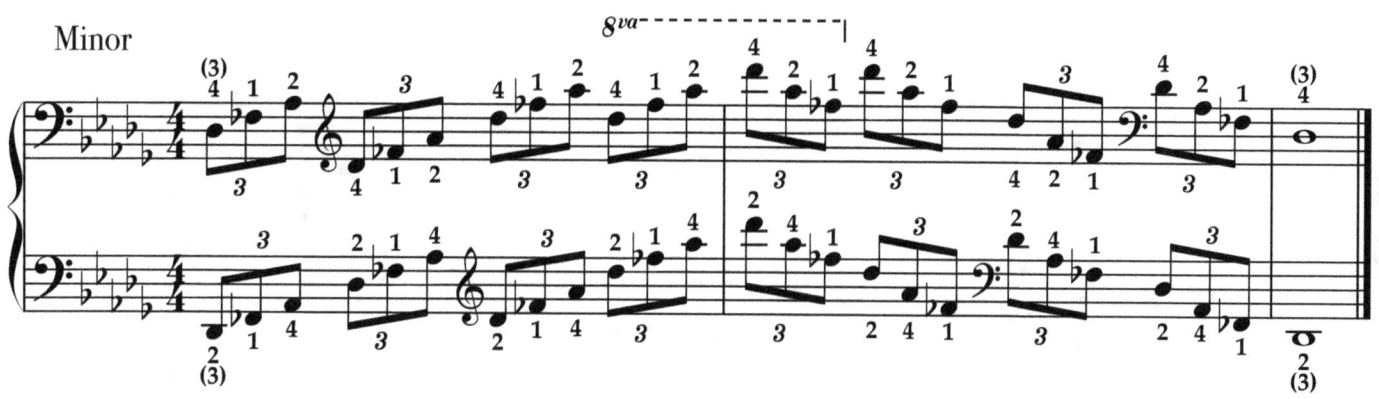

Dominant 7th

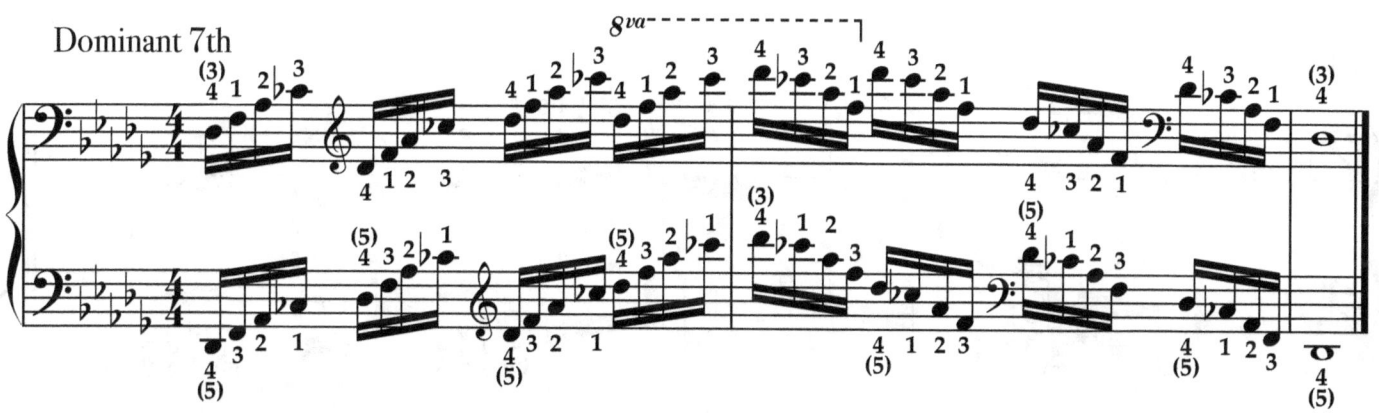

Diminished 7th

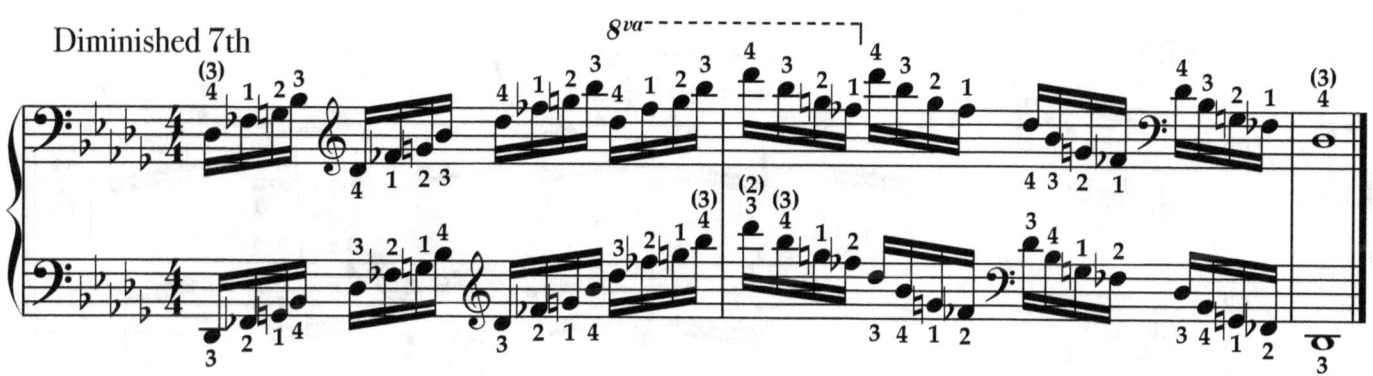

Arpeggios with a root note of G-flat

Major

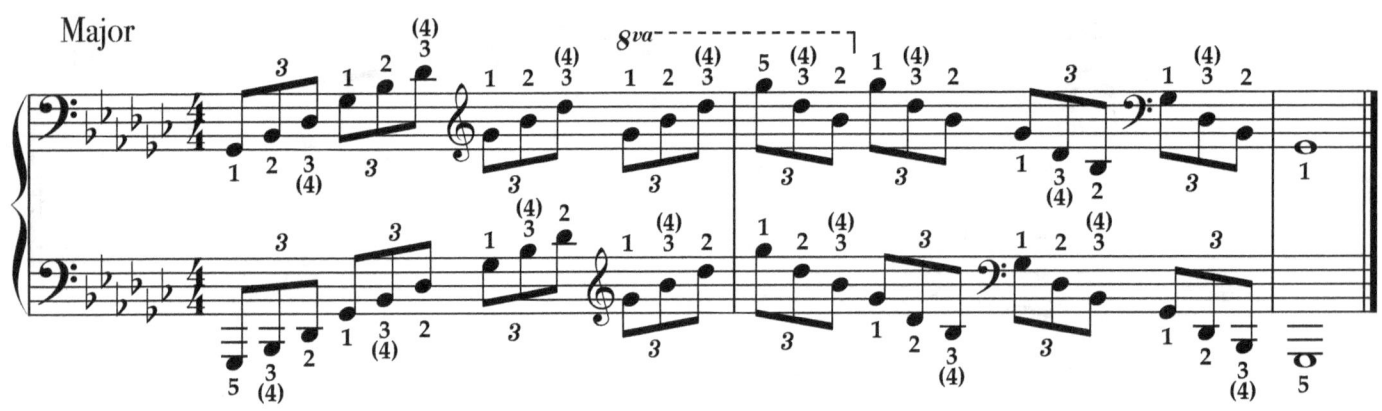

Minor

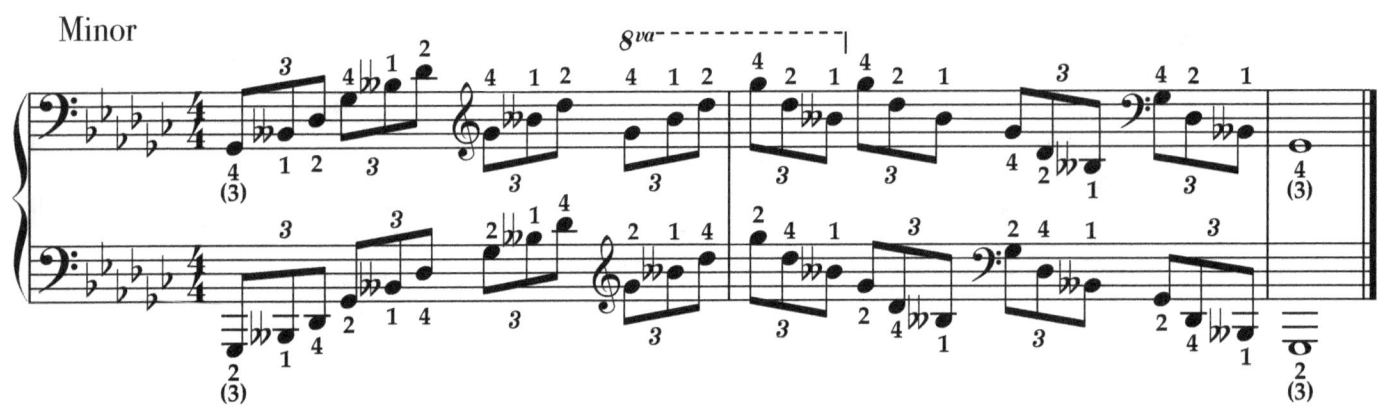

Dominant 7th

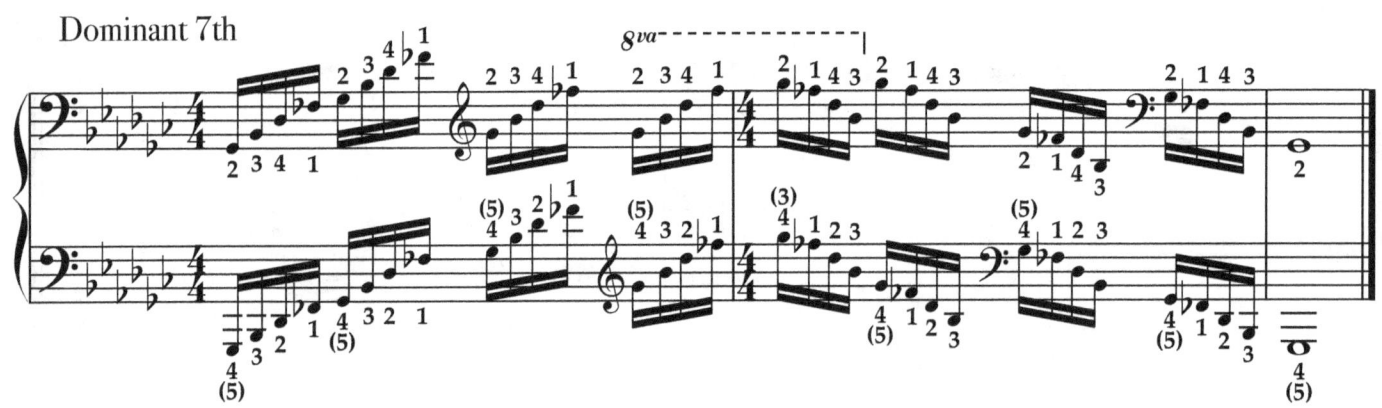

Diminished 7th

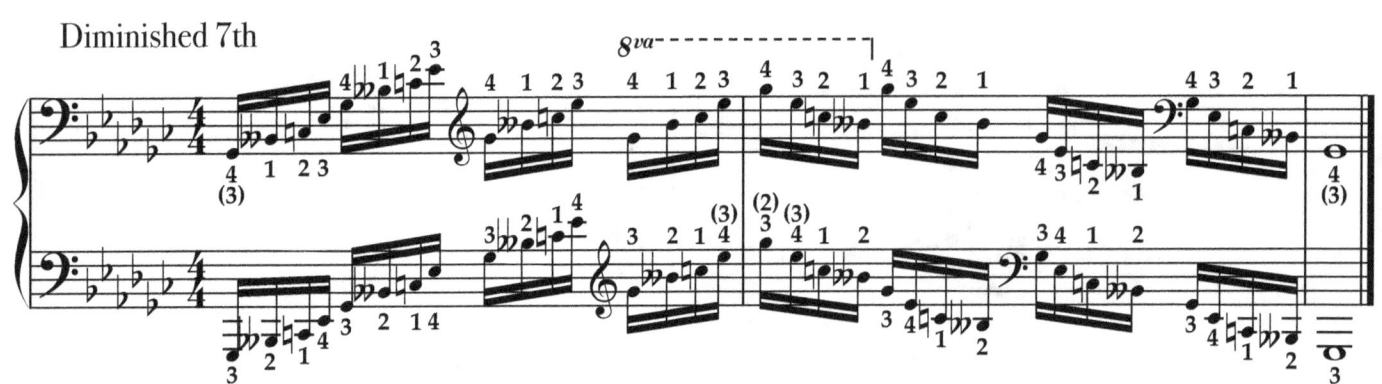

Arpeggios with a root note of C-flat

Major

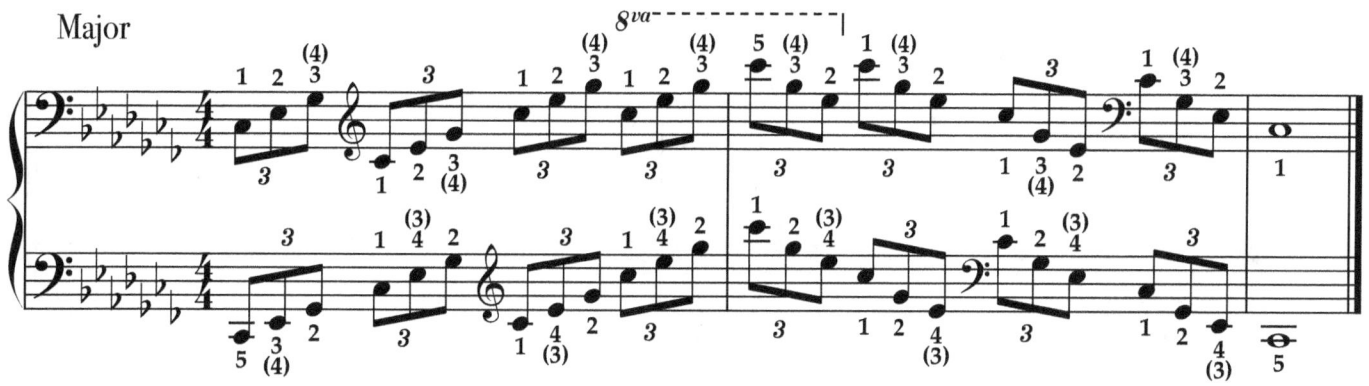

Minor

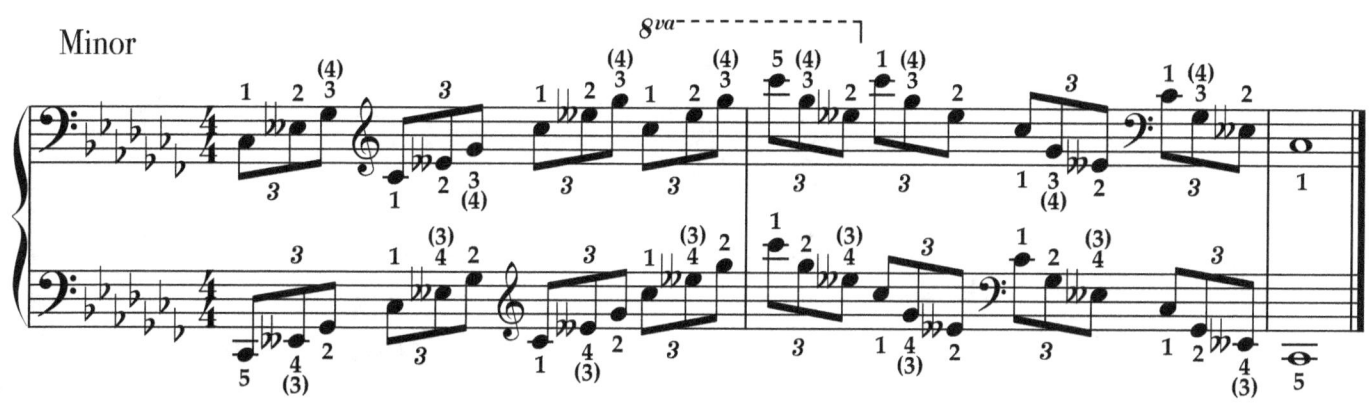

Dominant 7th

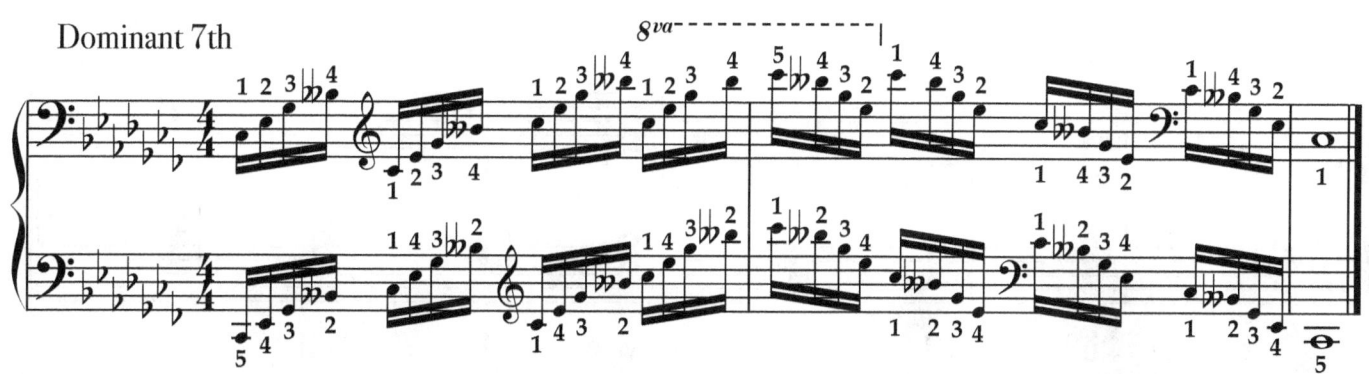

Diminished 7th

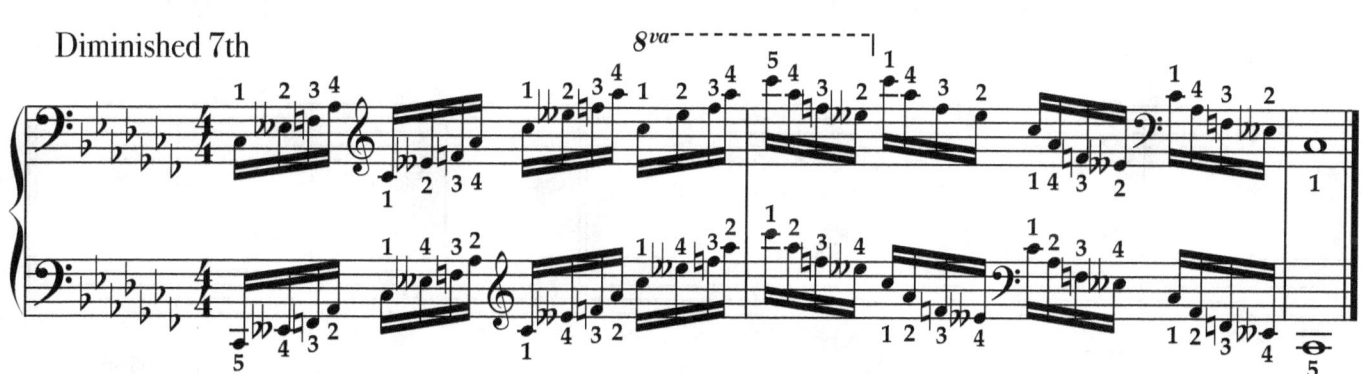

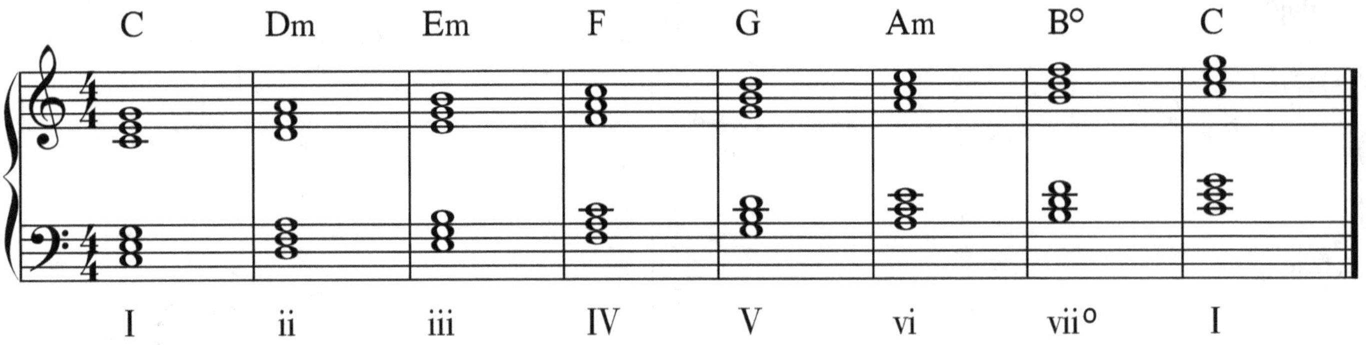

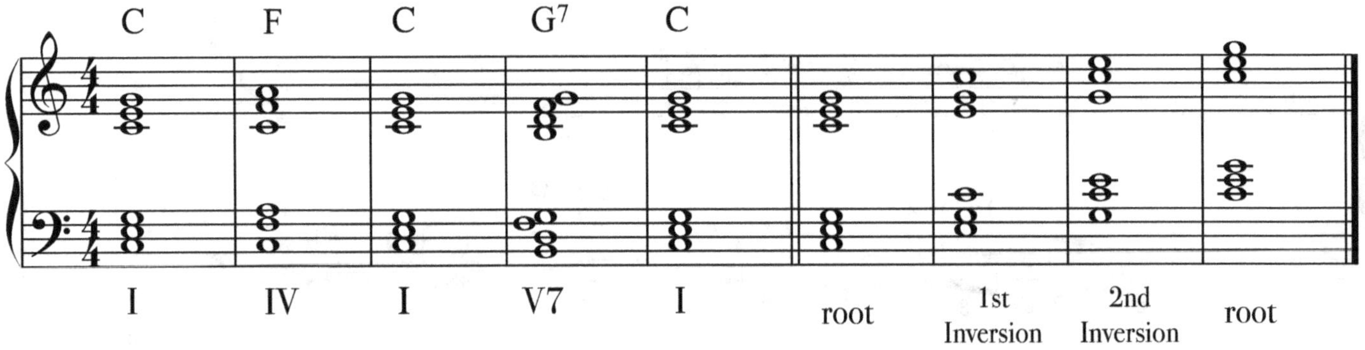

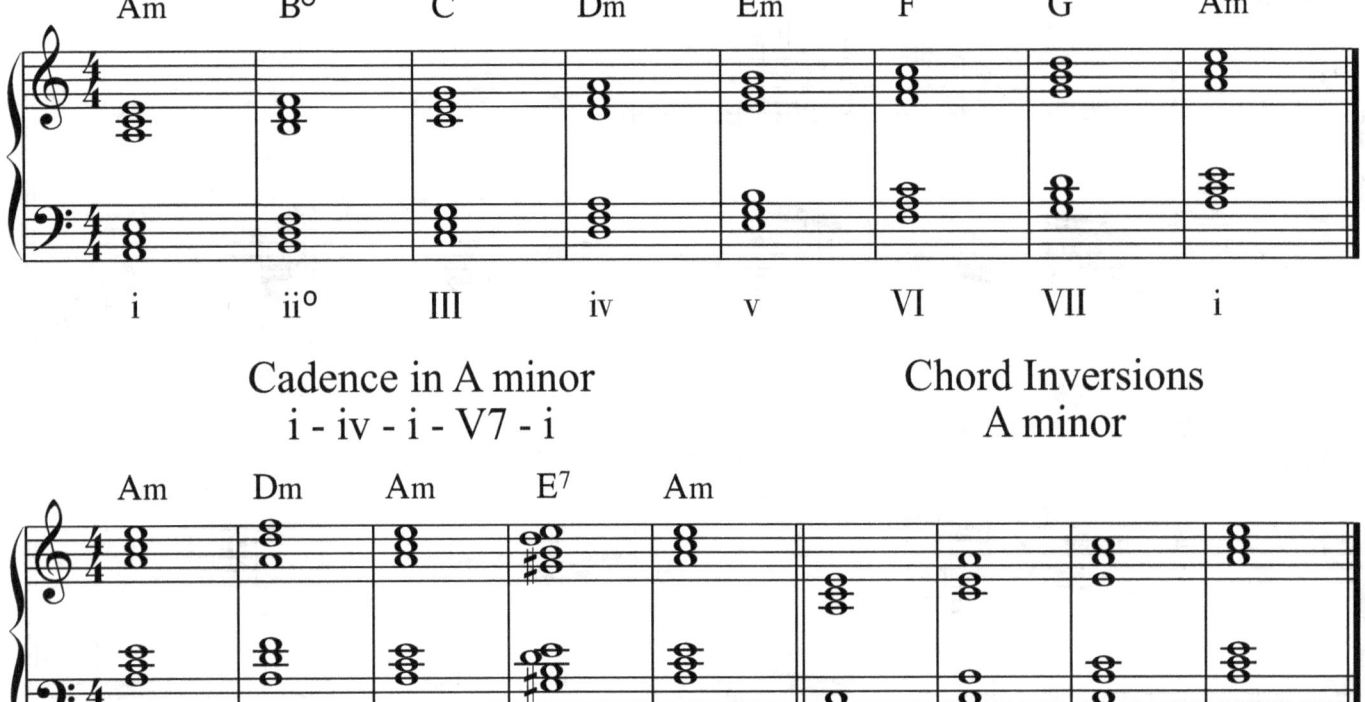

Scale-tone triads in the key of G major

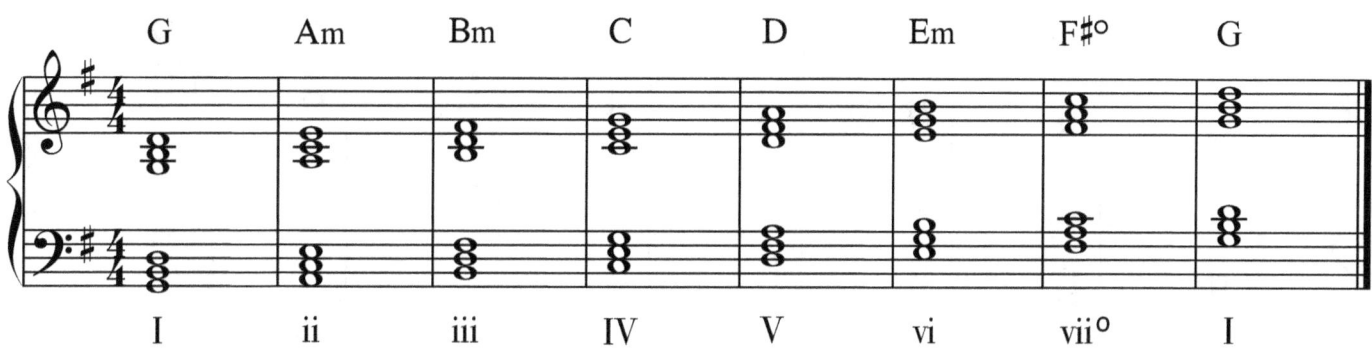

Cadence in G major
I - IV - I - V7 - I

Chord Inversions
G major

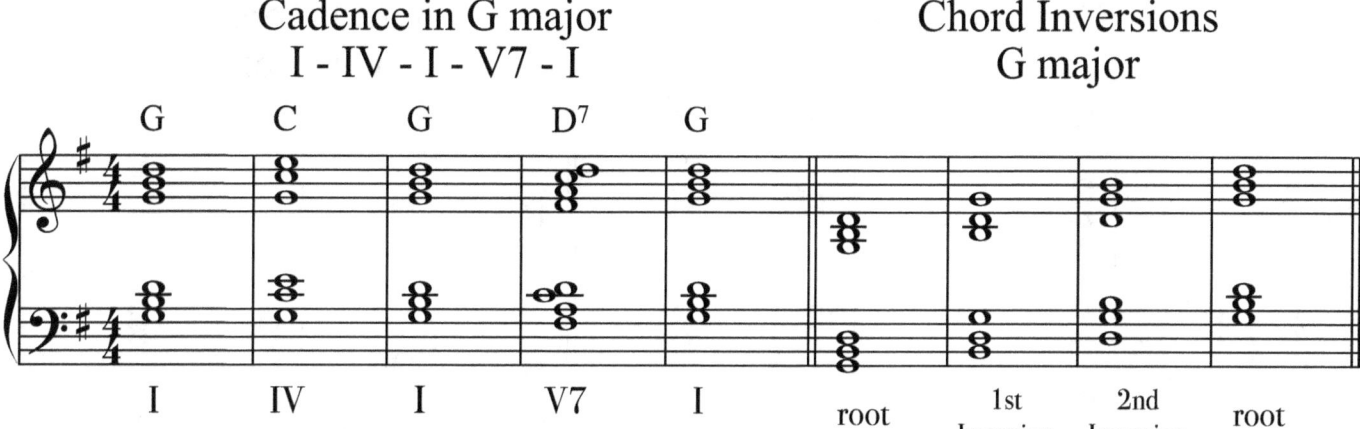

Scale-tone triads in the key of E minor

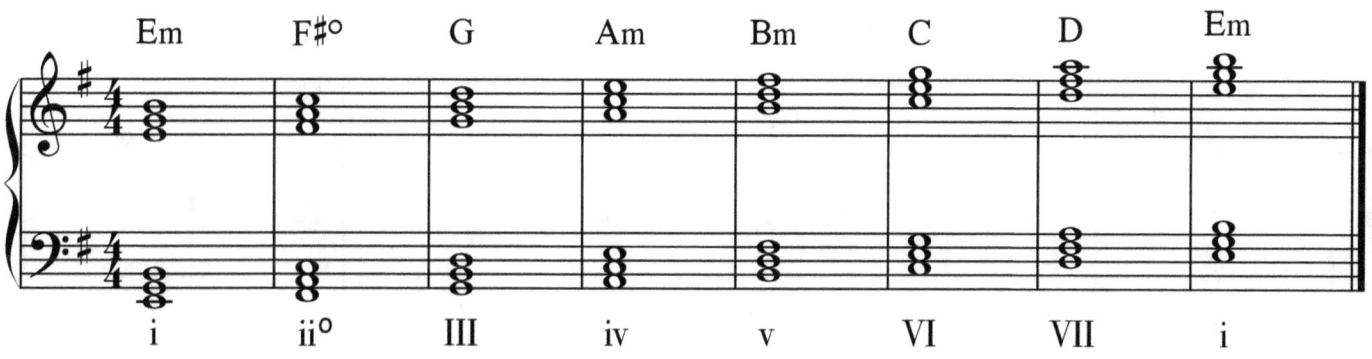

Cadence in E minor
i - iv - i - V7 - i

Chord Inversions
E minor

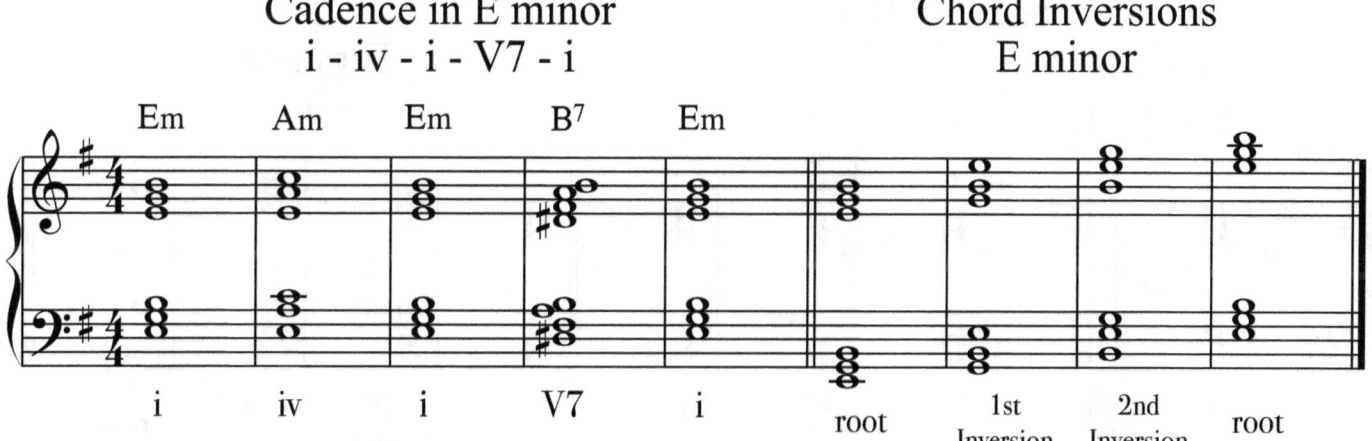

Scale-tone triads in the key of D major

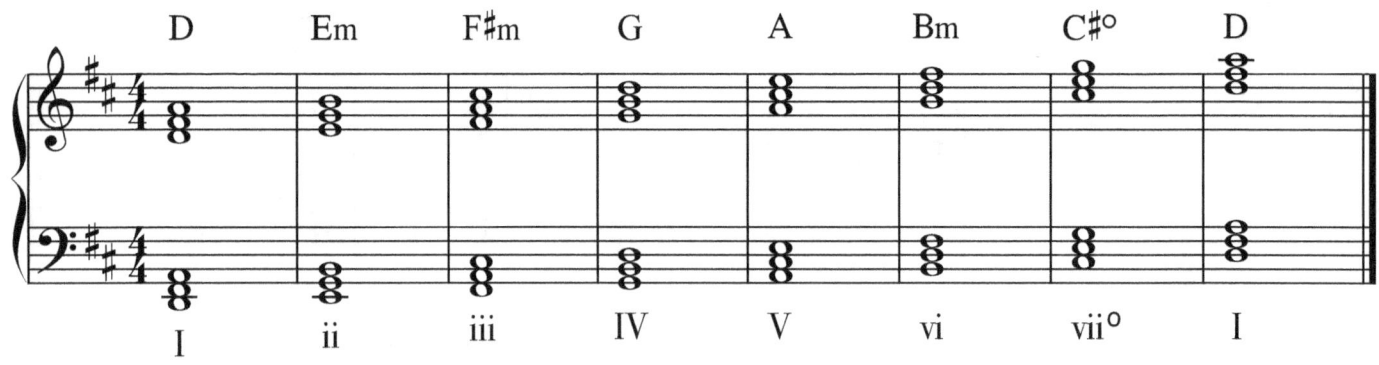

Cadence in D major
I - IV - I - V7 - I

Chord Inversions
D major

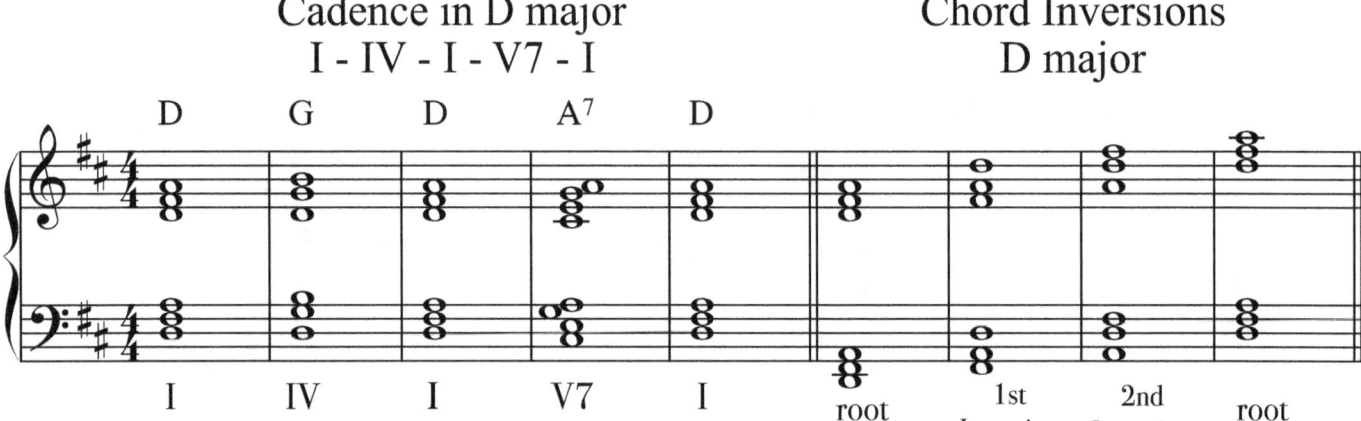

Scale-tone triads in the key of B minor

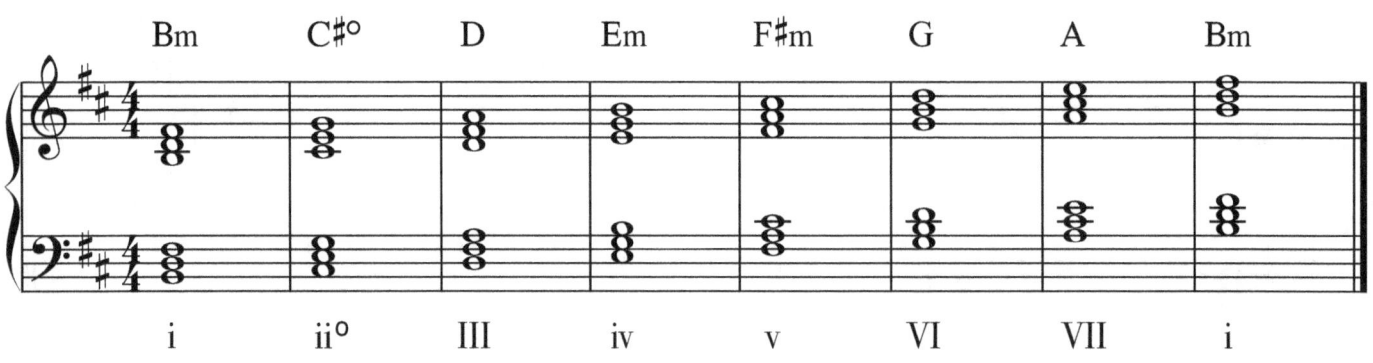

Cadence in B minor
i - iv - i - V7 - i

Chord Inversions
B minor

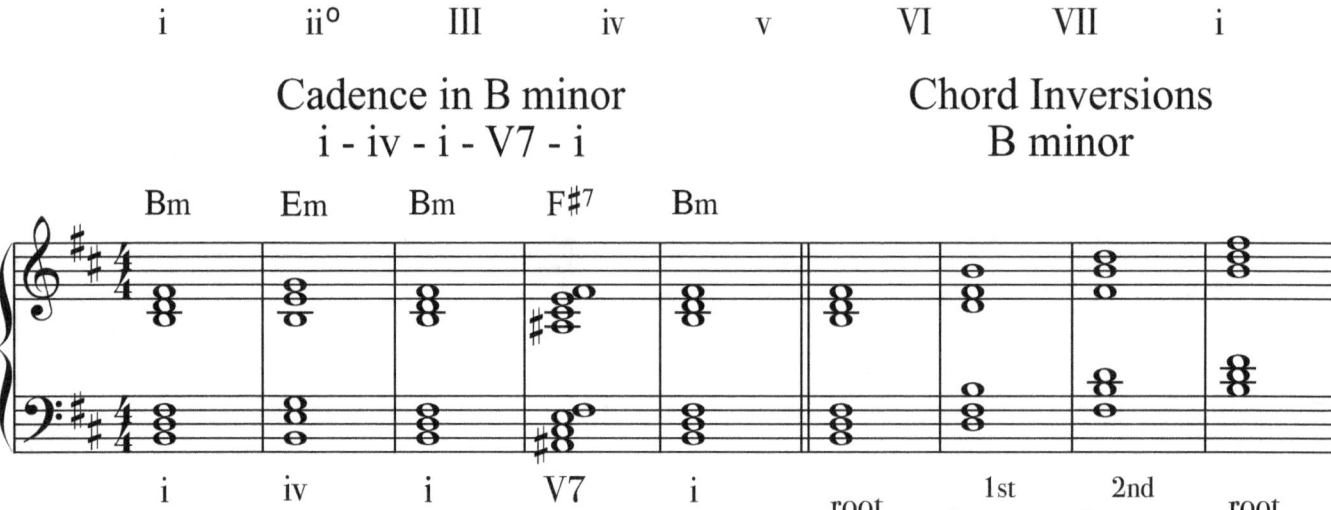

Scale-tone triads in the key of A major

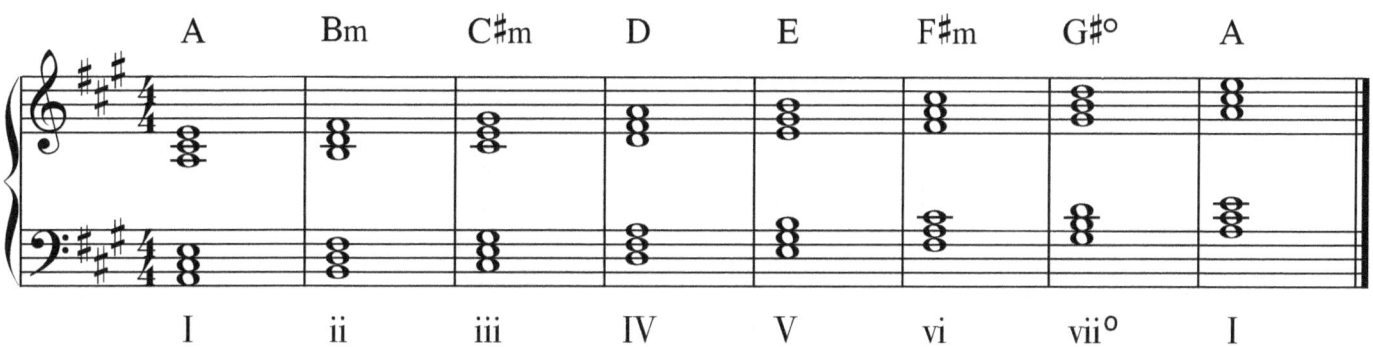

Cadence in A major
I - IV - I - V7 - I

Chord Inversions
A major

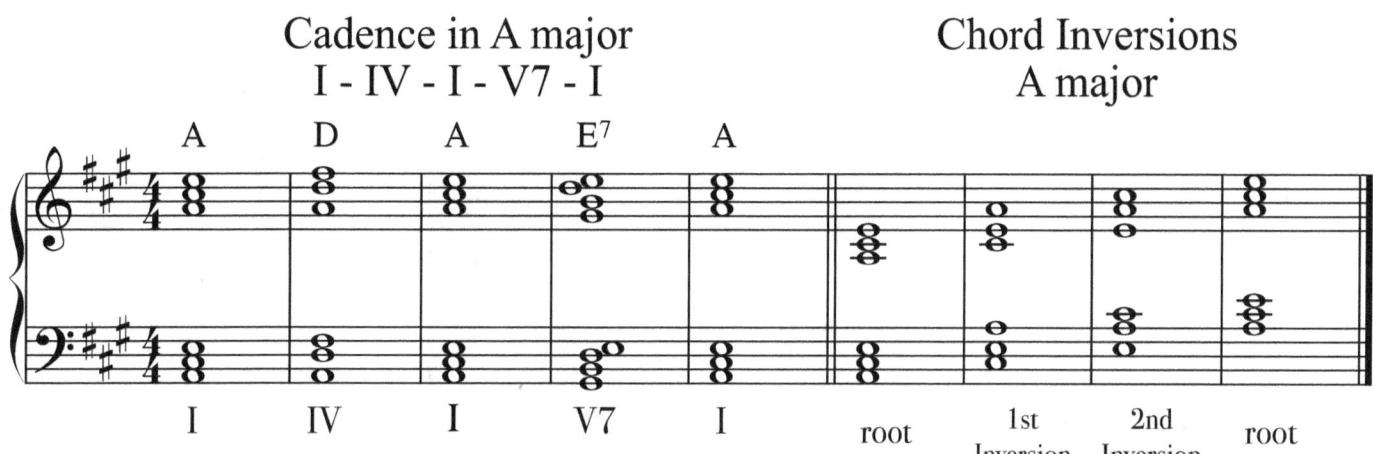

Scale-tone triads in the key of F-sharp minor

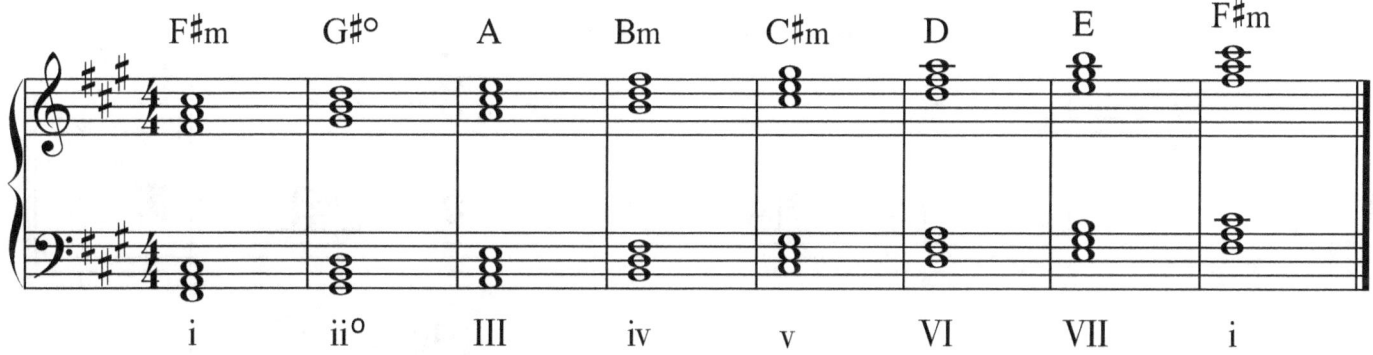

Cadence in F-sharp minor
i - iv - i - V7 - i

Chord Inversions
F-sharp minor

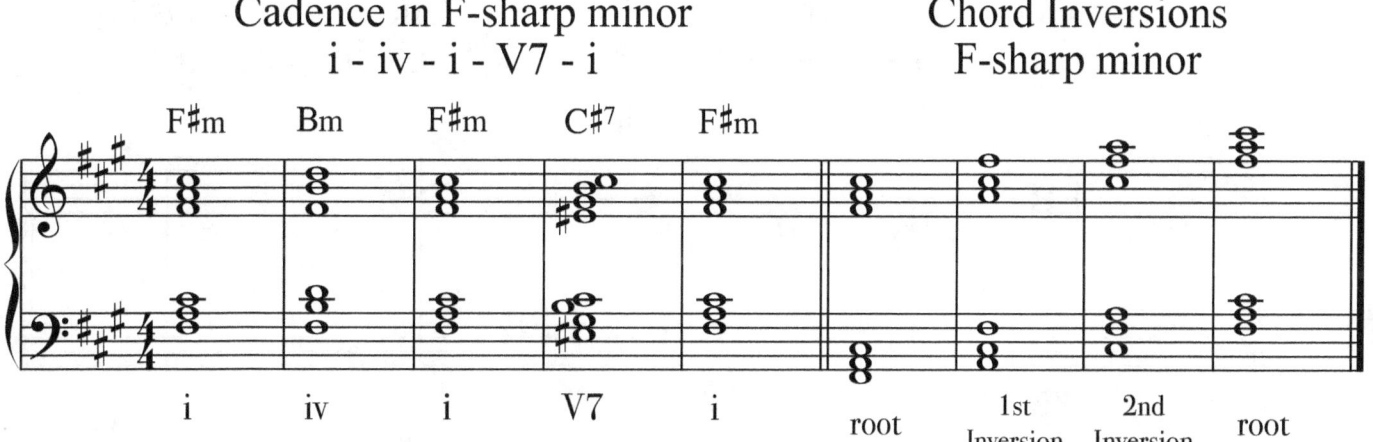

Scale-tone triads in the key of E major

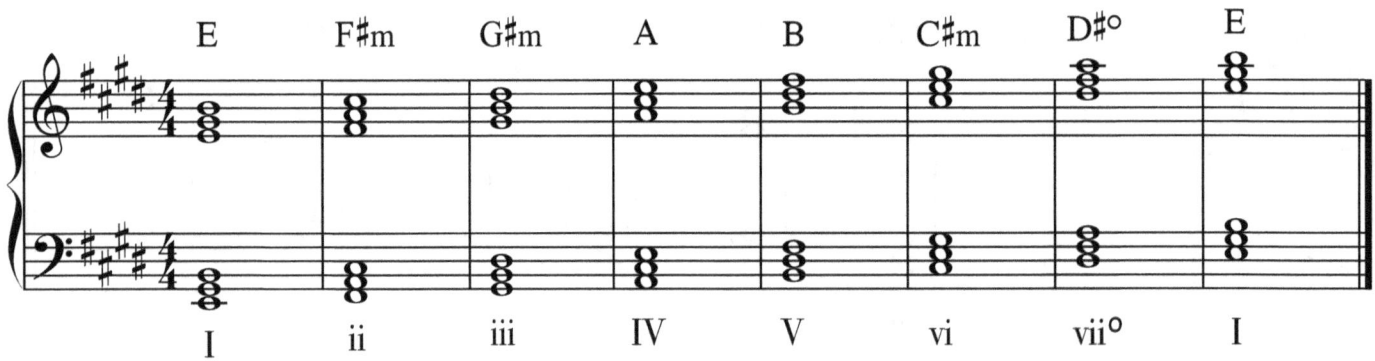

Cadence in E major
I - IV - I - V7 - I

Chord Inversions
E major

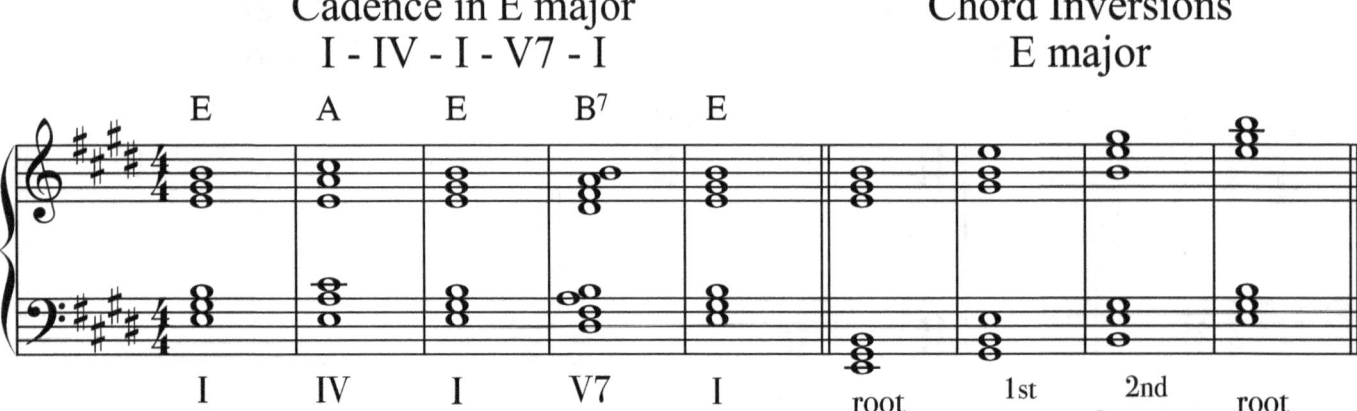

Scale-tone triads in the key of C-sharp minor

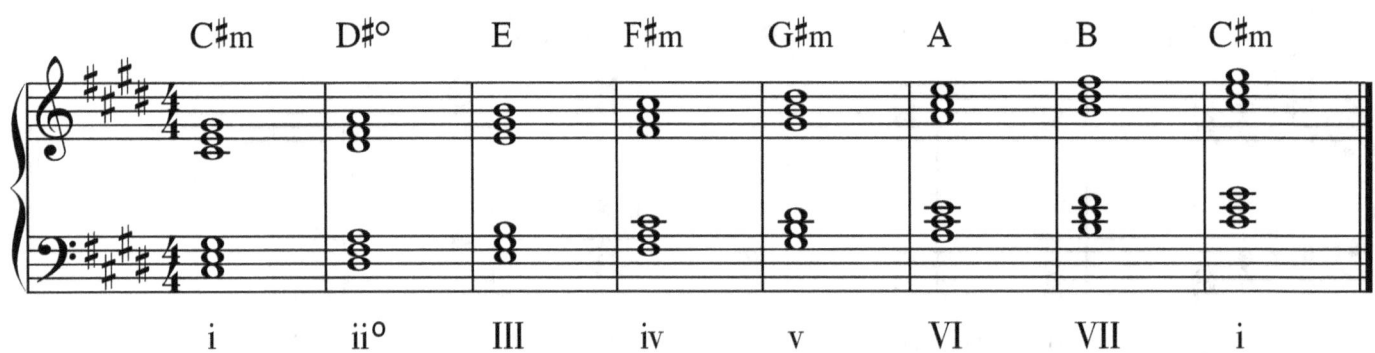

Cadence in C-sharp minor
i - iv - i - V7 - i

Chord Inversions
C-sharp minor

The scale-tone triads in the key of B major

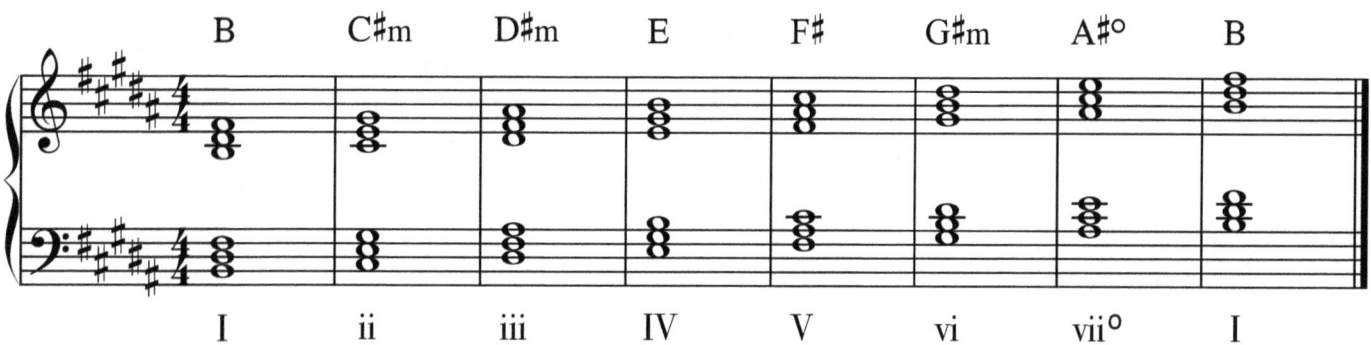

Cadence in B major
I - IV - I - V7 - I

Chord Inversions
B major

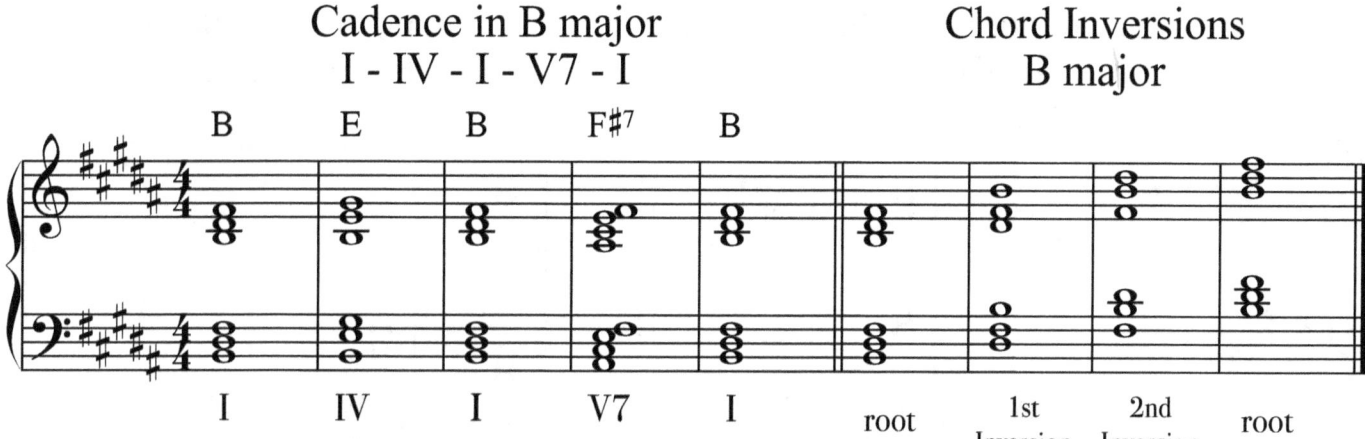

Scale-tone triads in the key of G-sharp minor

Cadence in G-sharp minor
i - iv - i - V7 - i

Chord Inversions
G-sharp minor

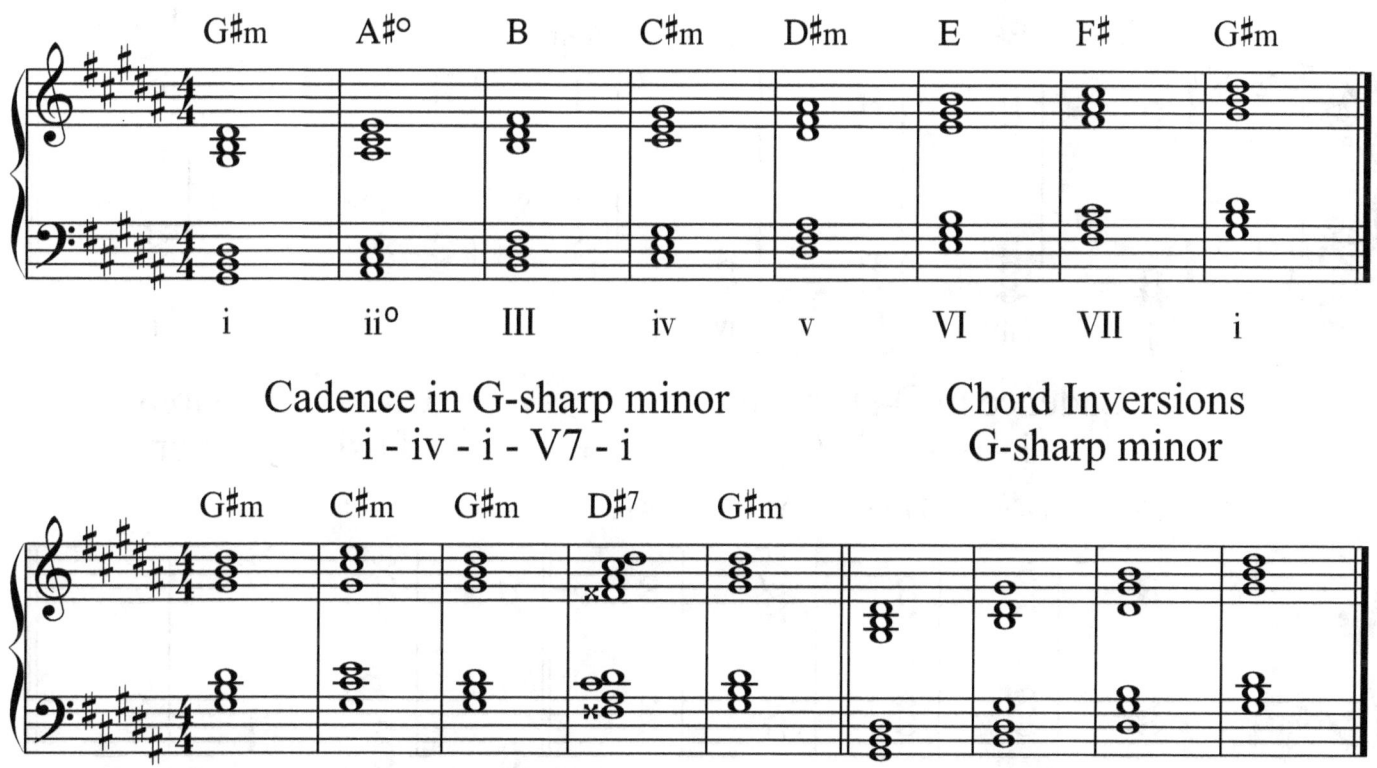

The scale-tone triads in the key of F-sharp major

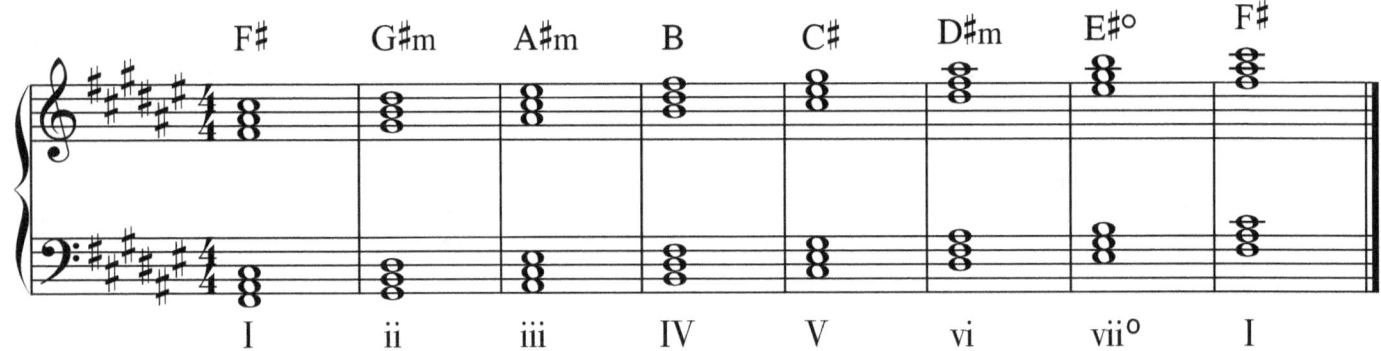

Cadence in F-sharp major
I - IV - I - V7 - I

Chord Inversions
F-sharp major

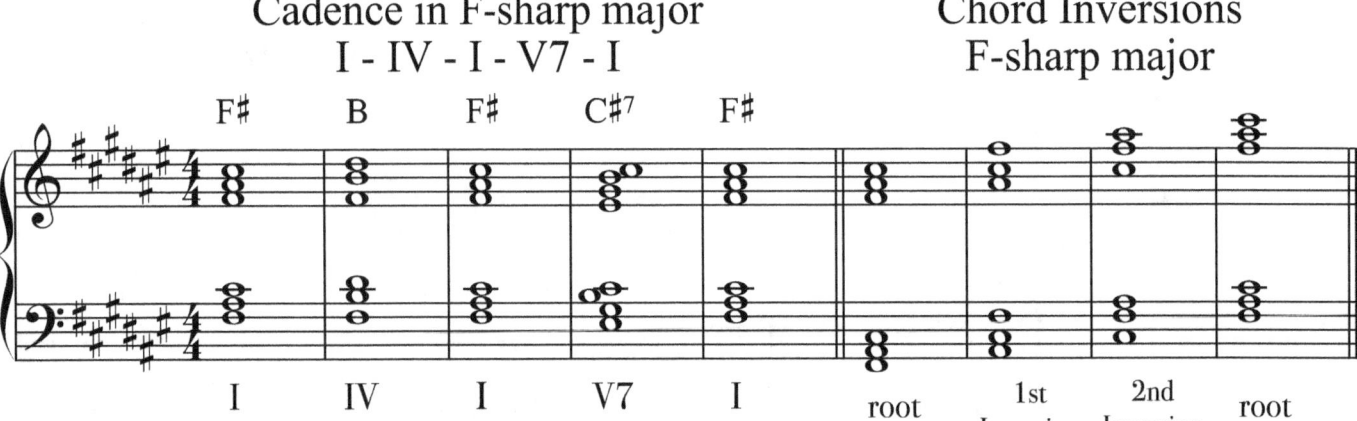

Scale-tone triads in the key of D-sharp minor

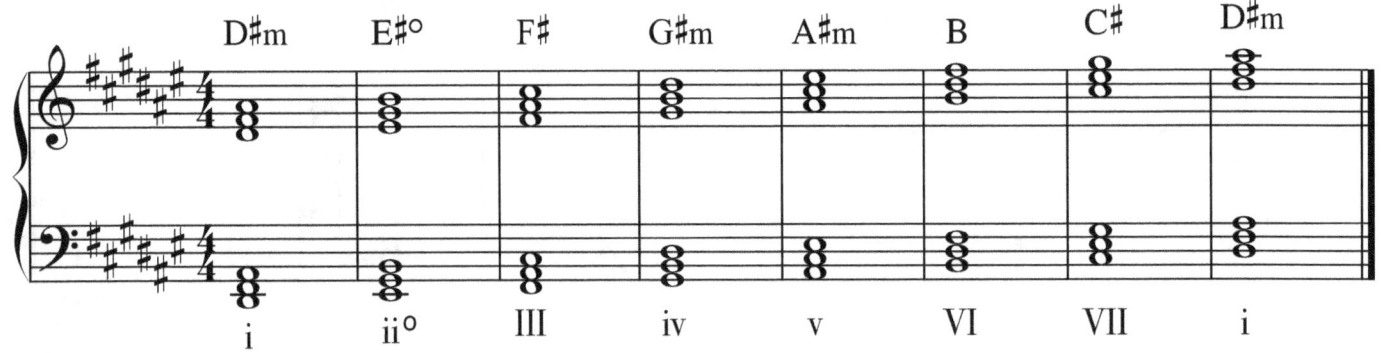

Cadence in D-sharp minor
i - iv - i - V7 - i

Chord Inversions
D-sharp minor

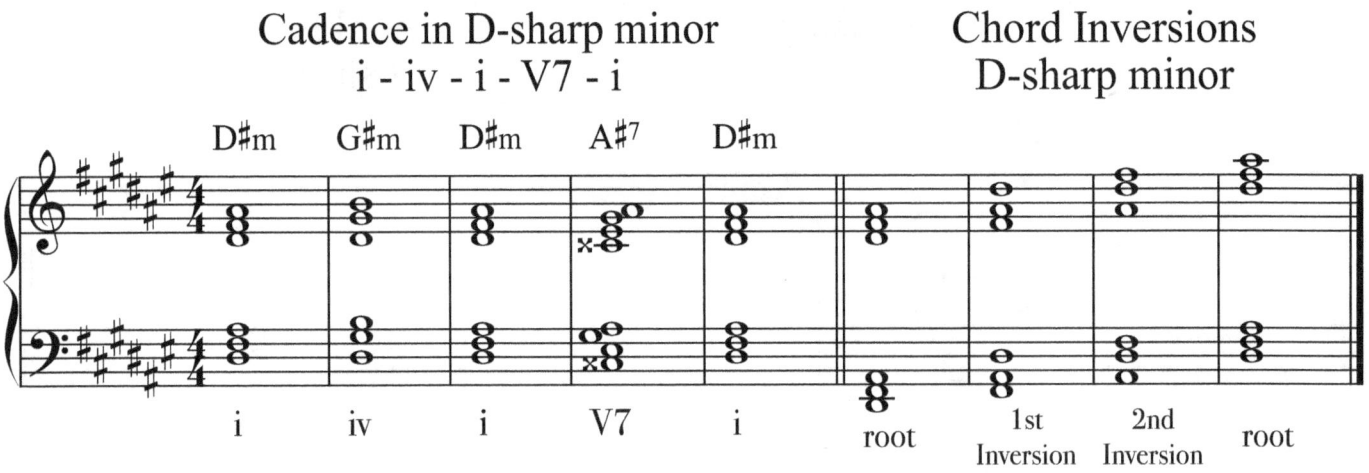

Scale-tone triads in the key of C-sharp major

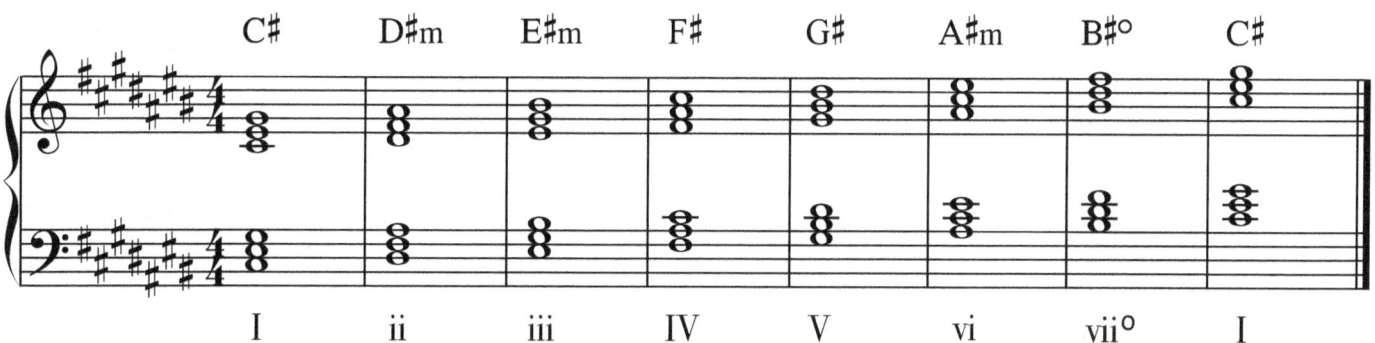

Cadence in C-sharp major
I - IV - I - V7 - I

Chord Inversions
C-sharp major

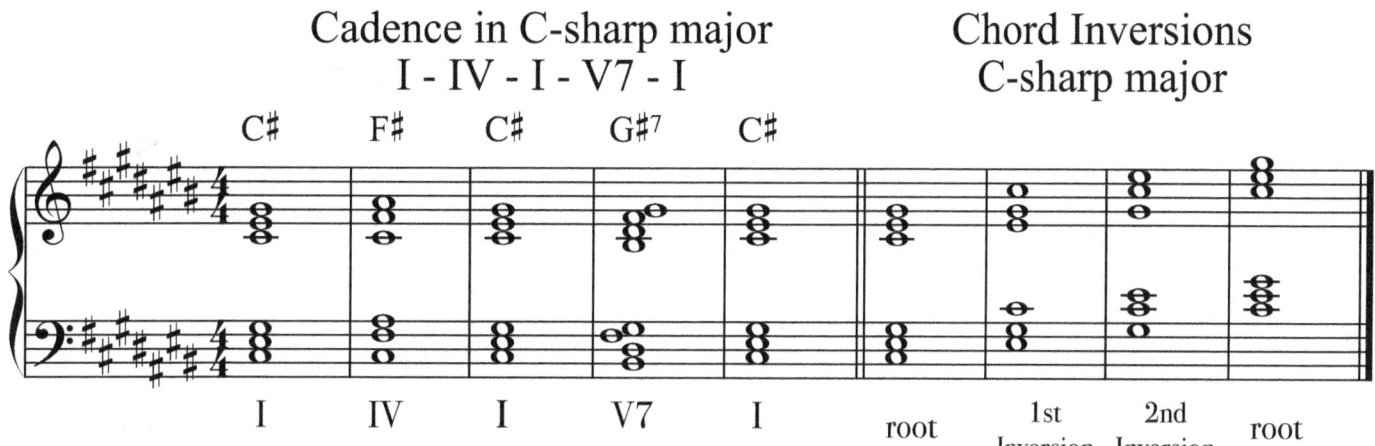

Scale-tone triads in the key of A-sharp minor

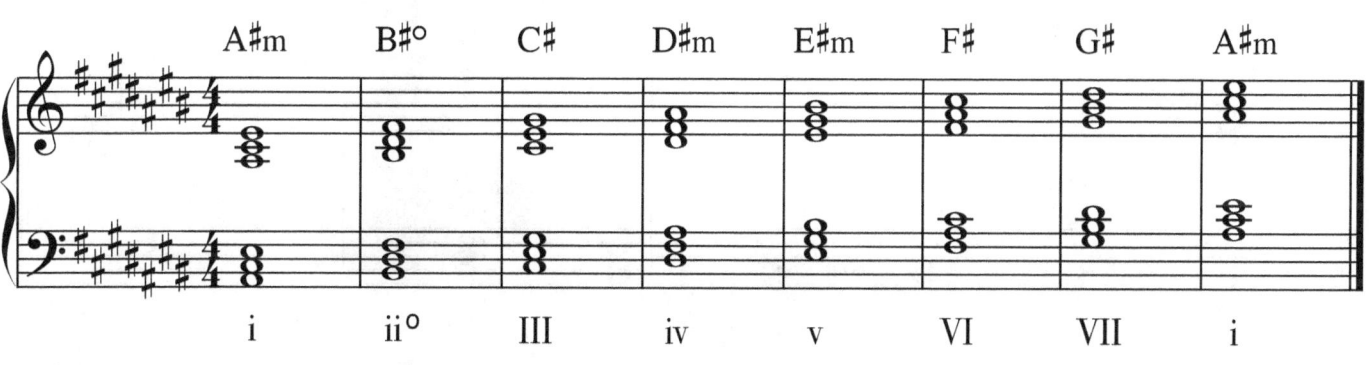

Cadence in A-sharp minor
i - iv - i - V7 - i

Chord Inversions
A-sharp minor

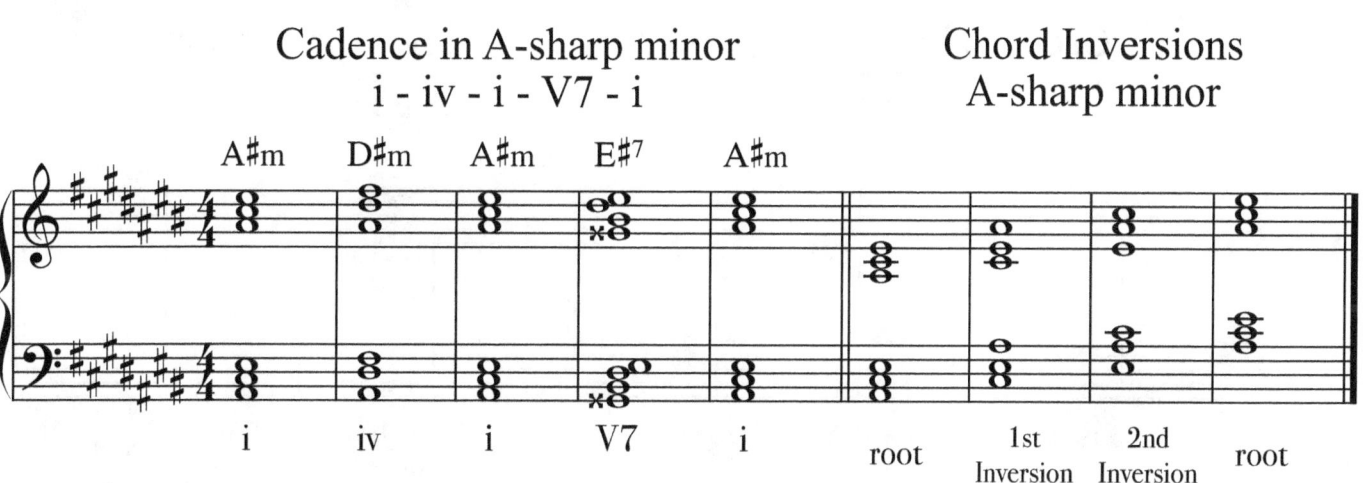

Scale-tone triads in the key of F major

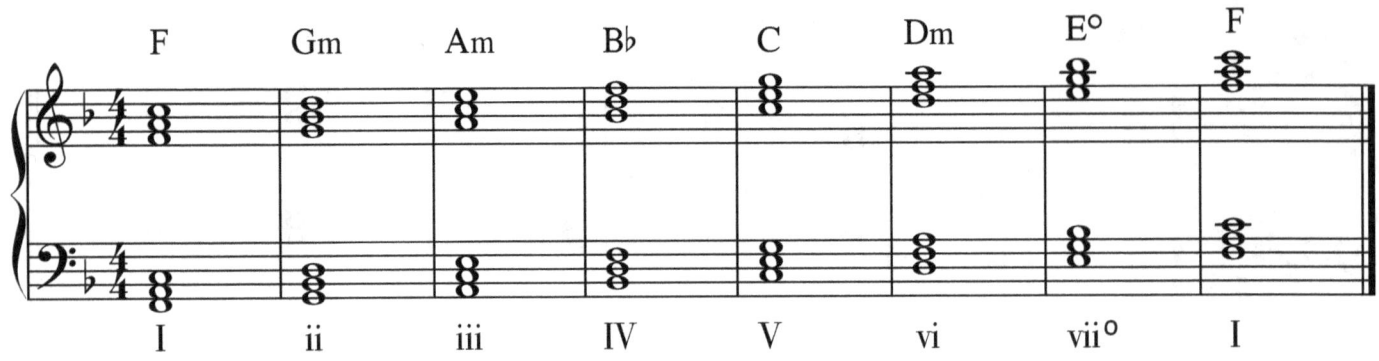

Cadence in F major
I - IV - I - V7 - I

Chord Inversions
F major

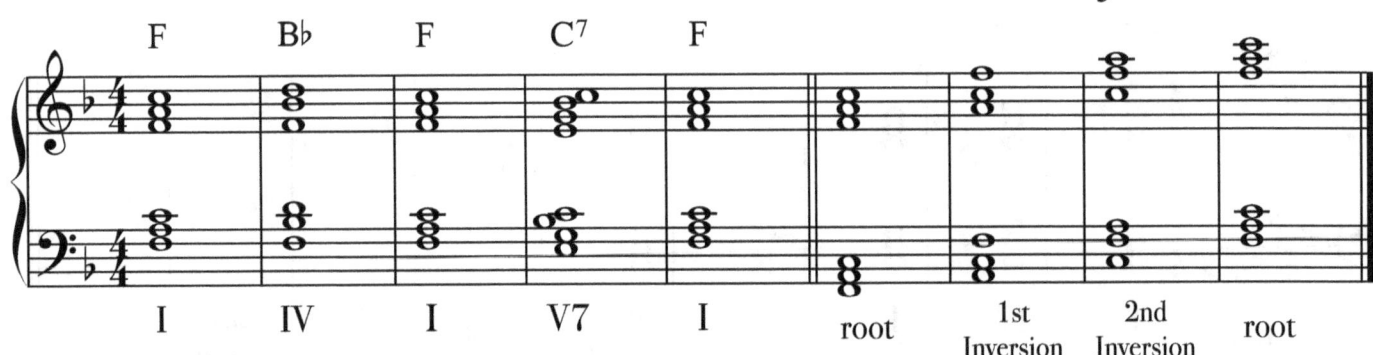

Scale-tone triads in the key of D minor

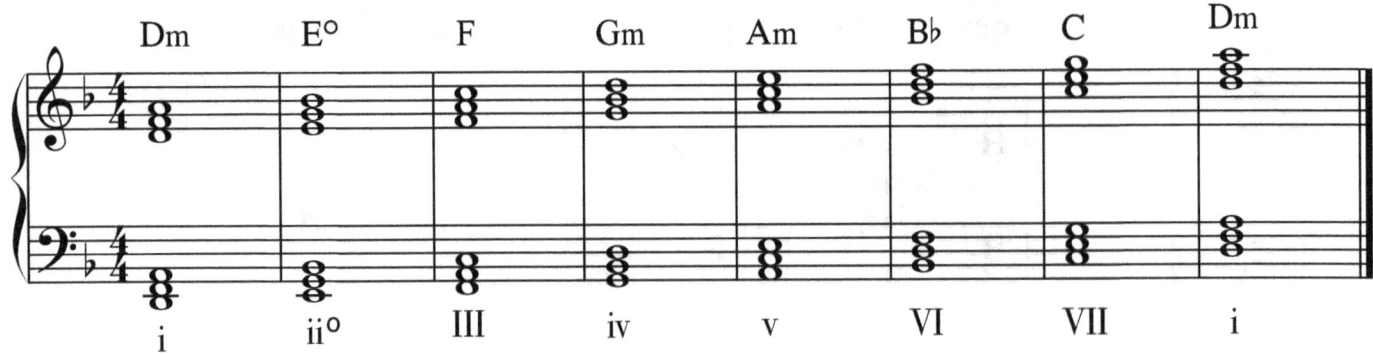

Cadence in D minor
i - iv - i - V7 - i

Chord Inversions
D minor

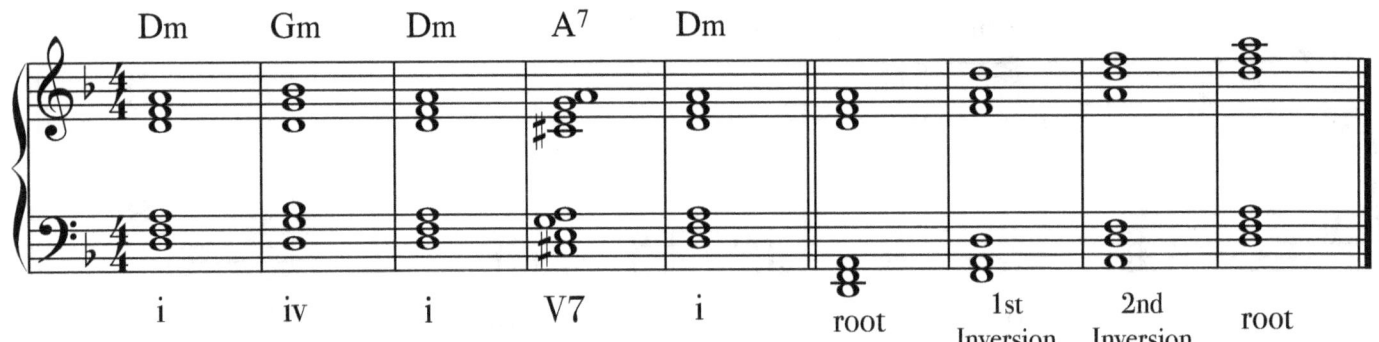

Scale-tone triads in the key of B-flat major

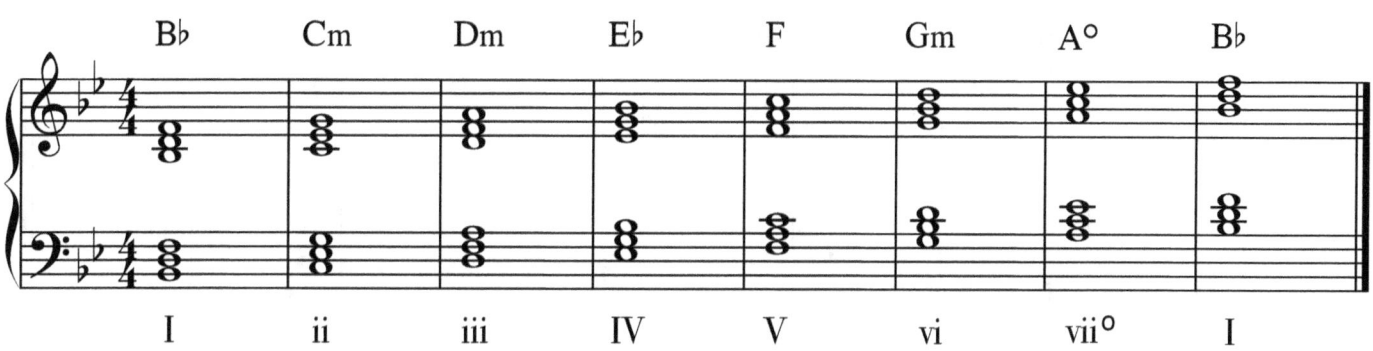

Cadence in B-flat major
I - IV - I - V7 - I

Chord Inversions
B-flat major

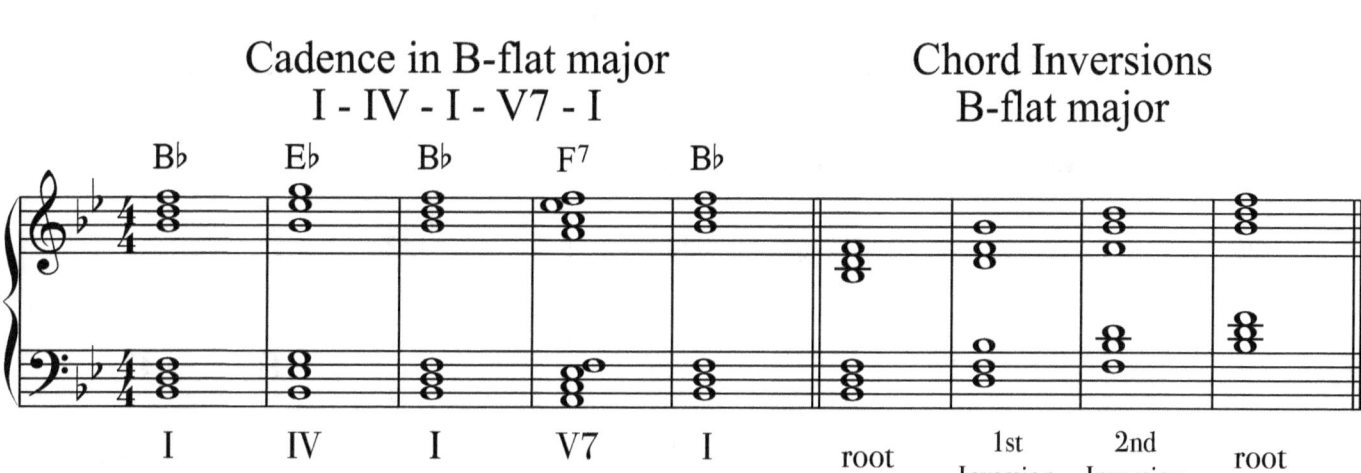

Scale-tone triads in the key of G minor

Cadence in G minor
i - iv - i - V7 - i

Chord Inversions
G minor

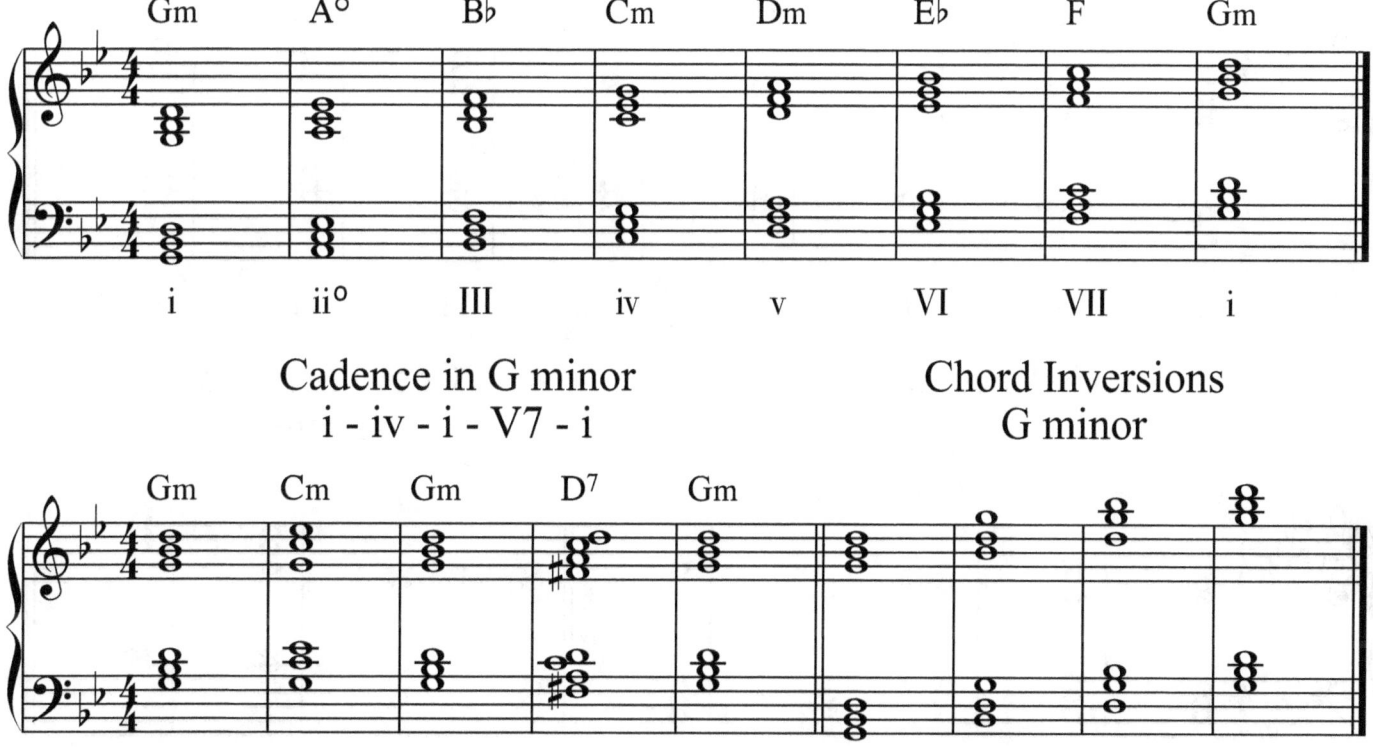

Scale-tone triads in the key of E-flat major

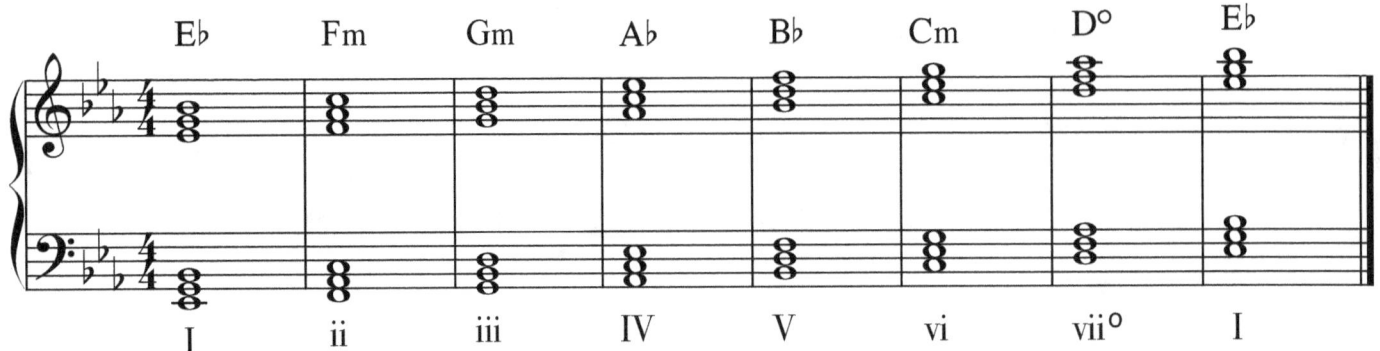

Cadence in E-flat major
I - IV - I - V7 - I

Chord Inversions
E-flat major

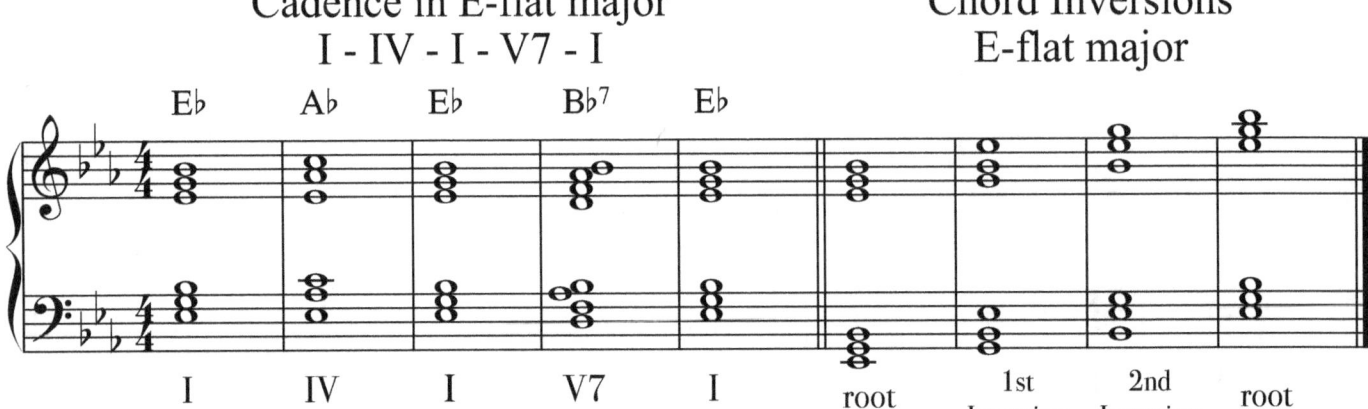

Scale-tone triads in the key of C minor

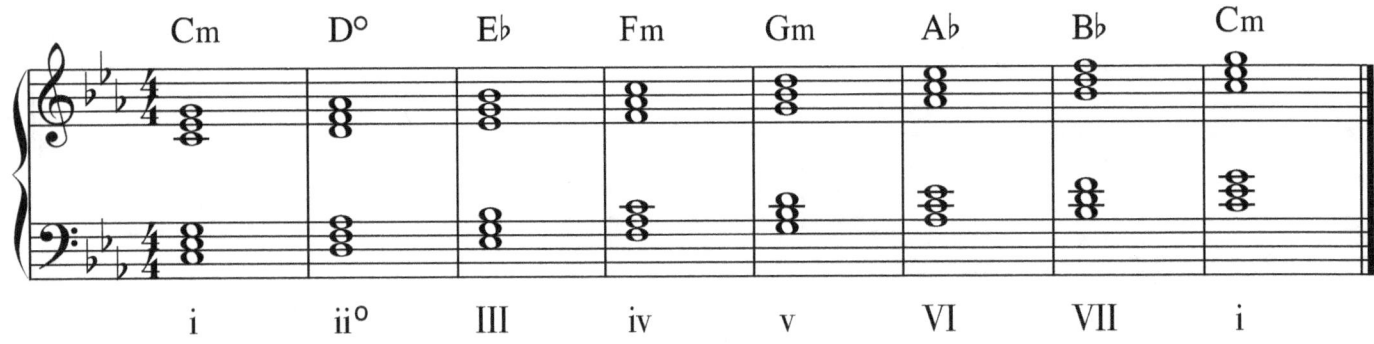

Cadence in C minor
i - iv - i - V7 - i

Chord Inversions
C minor

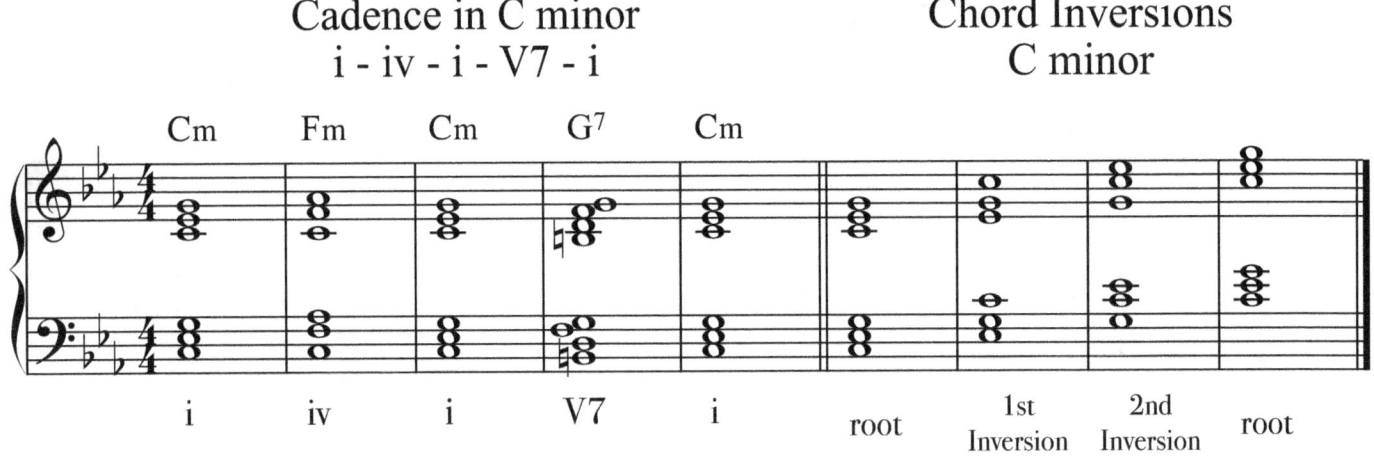

Scale-tone triads in the key of A-flat major

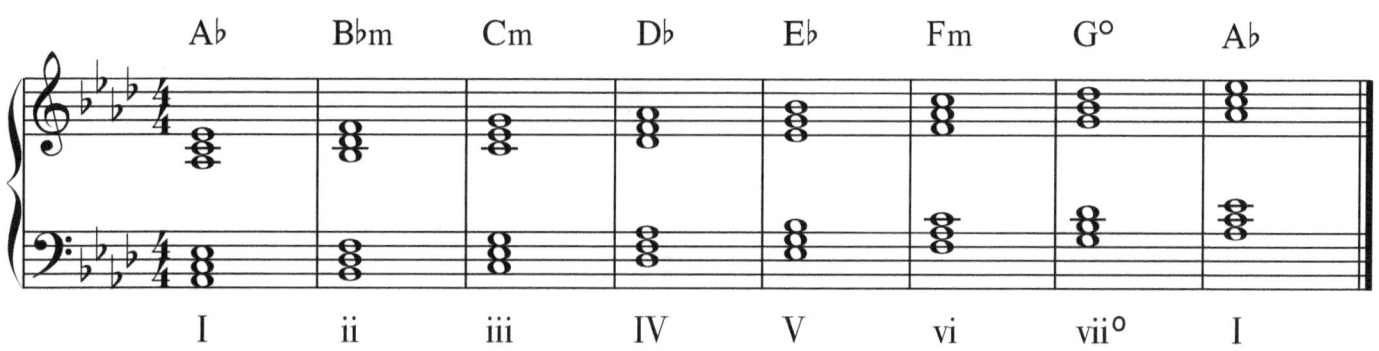

Cadence in A-flat major
I - IV - I - V7 - I

Chord Inversions
A-flat major

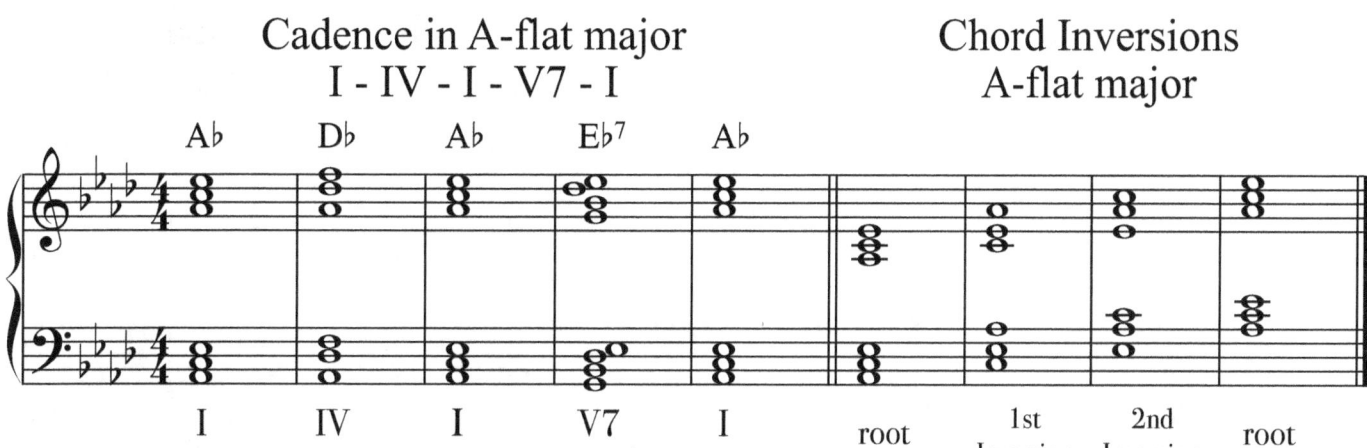

Scale-tone triads in the key of F minor

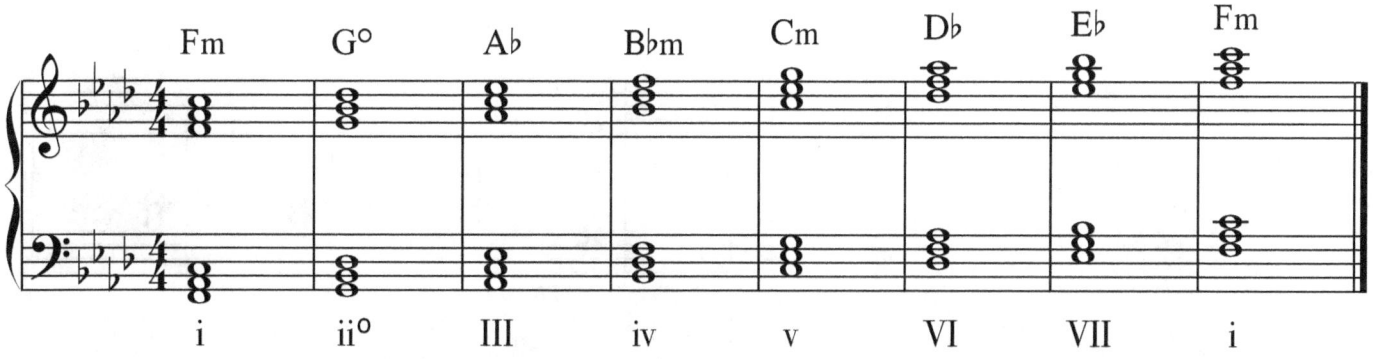

Cadence in F minor
i - iv - i - V7 - i

Chord Inversions
F minor

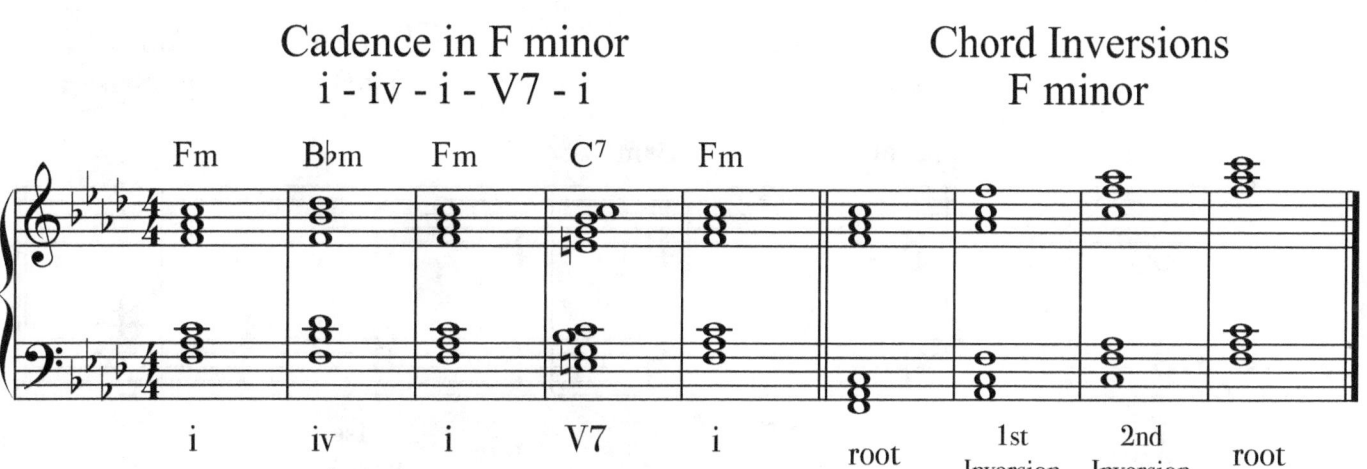

Scale-tone triads in the key of D-flat major

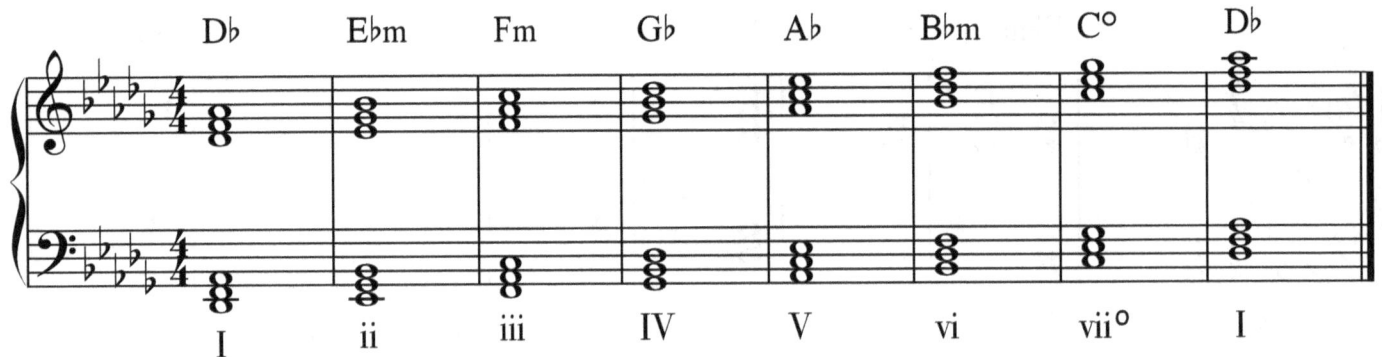

Cadence in D-flat major
I - IV - I - V7 - I

Chord Inversions
D-flat major

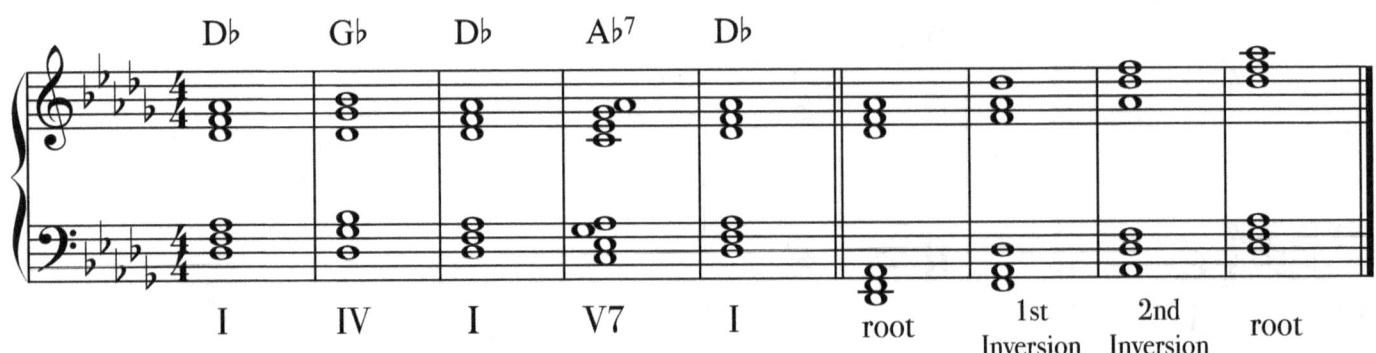

Scale-tone triads in the key of B-flat minor

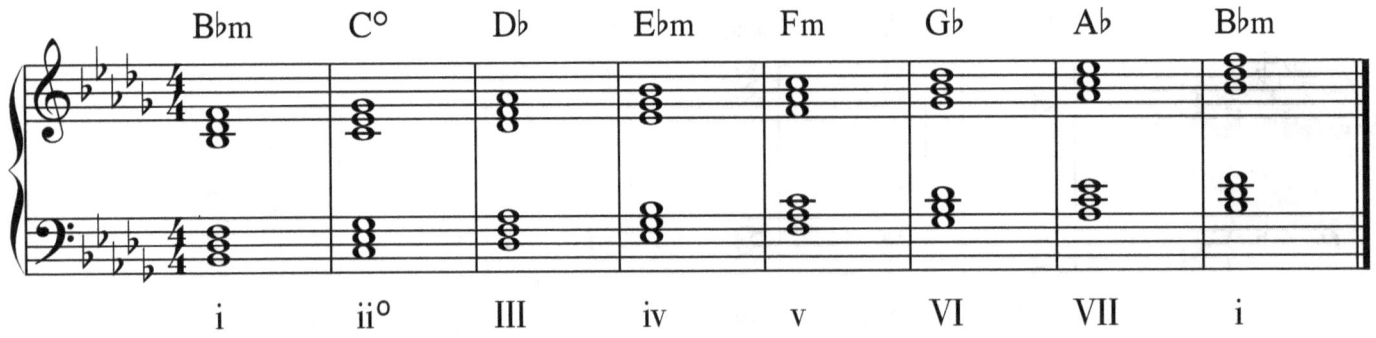

Cadence in B-flat minor
i - iv - i - V7 - i

Chord Inversions
B-flat minor

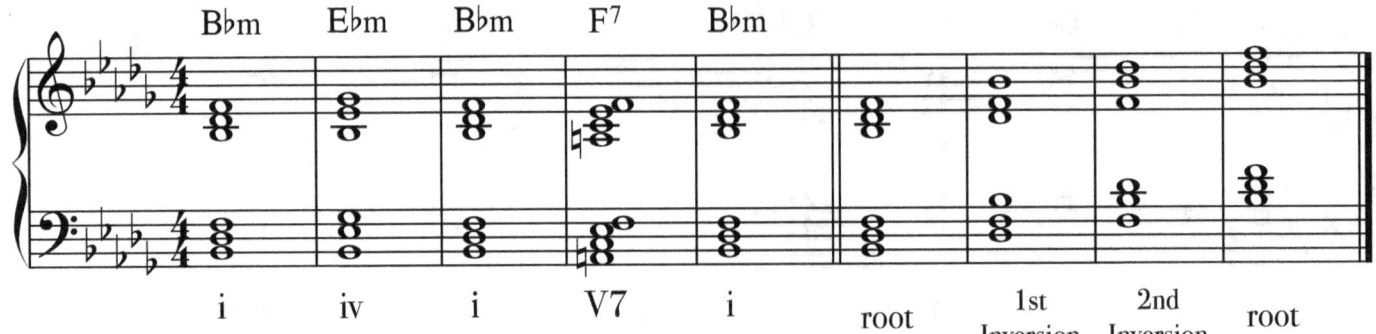

Scale-tone triads in the key of G-flat major

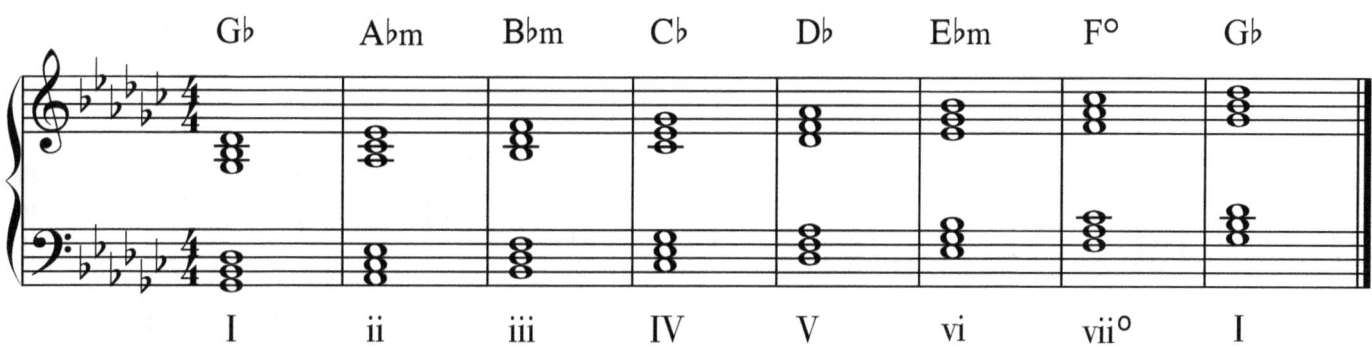

Cadence in G-flat major
I - IV - I - V7 - I

Chord Inversions
D-flat major

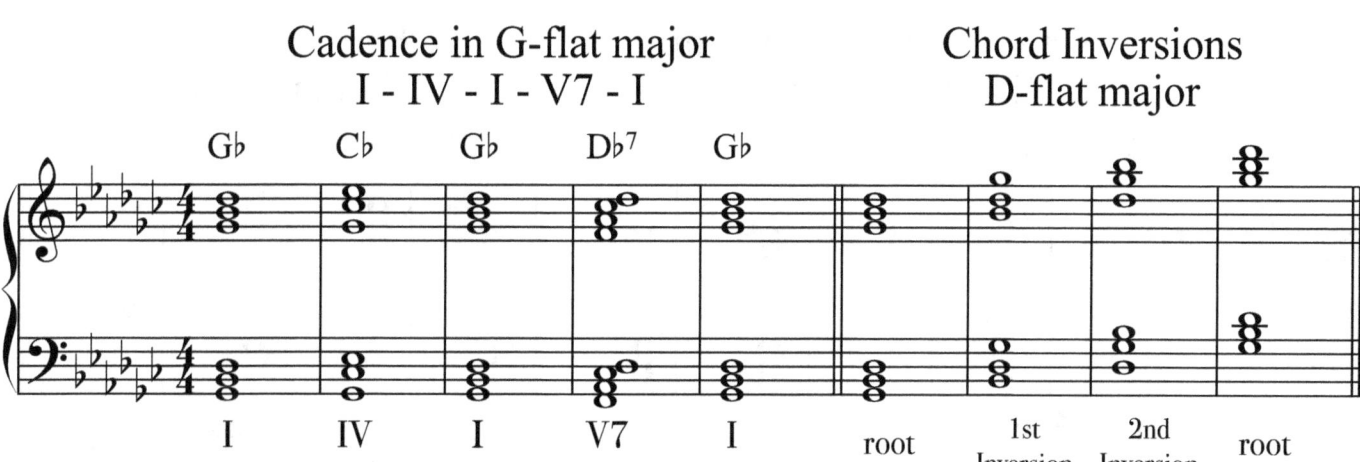

Scale-tone triads in the key of E-flat minor

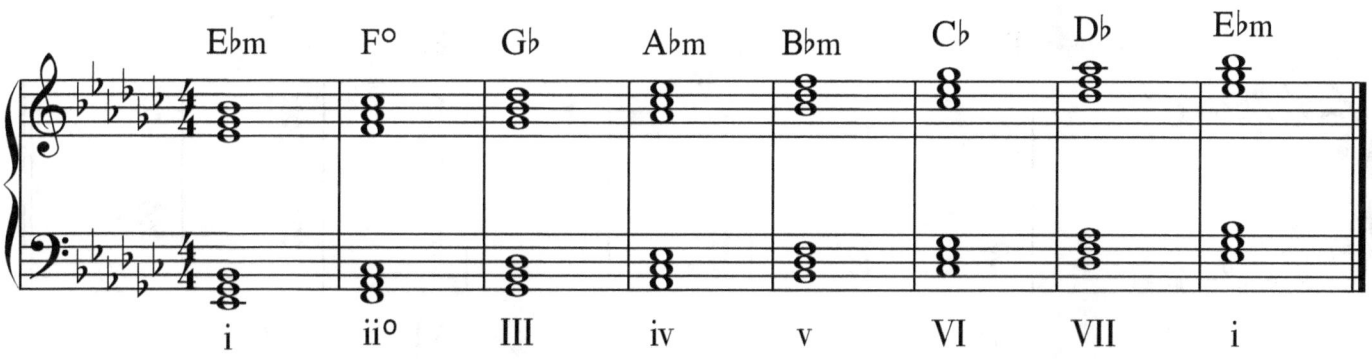

Cadence in E-flat minor
i - iv - i - V7 - i

Chord Inversions
E-flat minor

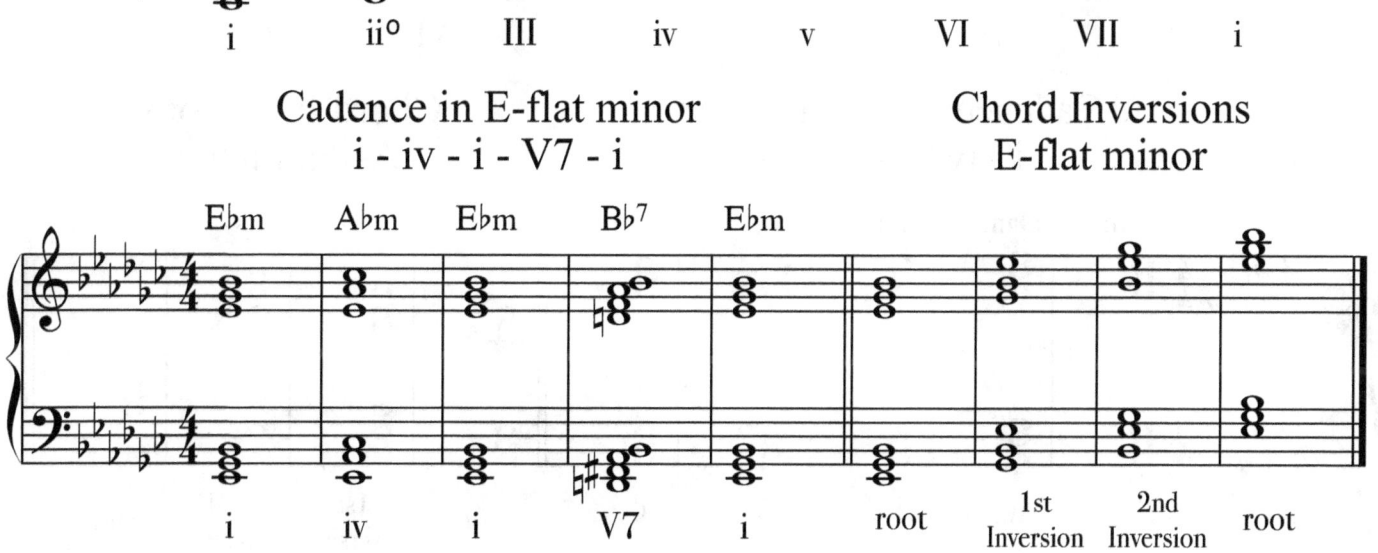

Scale-tone triads in the key of C-flat major

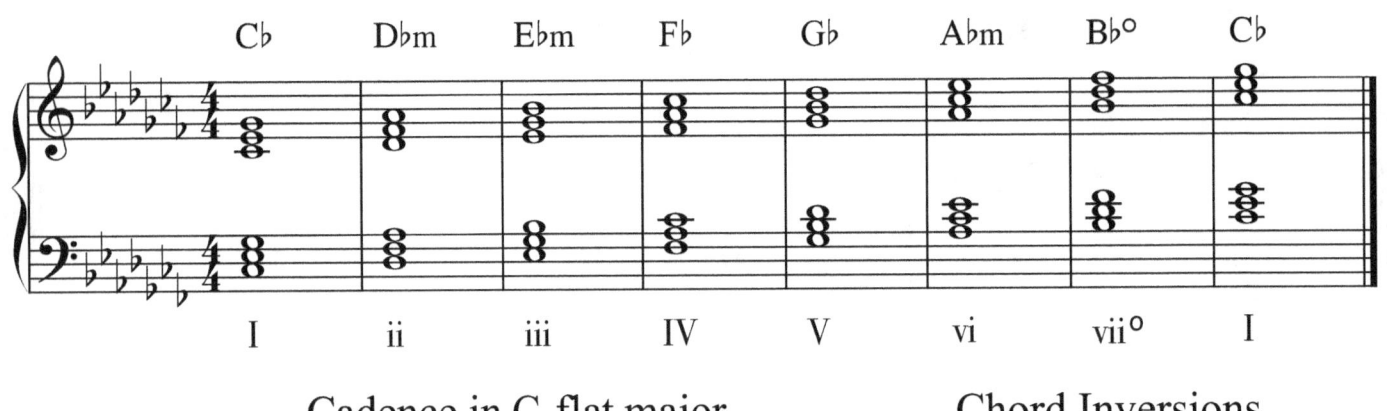

Cadence in C-flat major
I - IV - I - V7 - I

Chord Inversions
G-flat major

Scale-tone triads in the key of A-flat minor

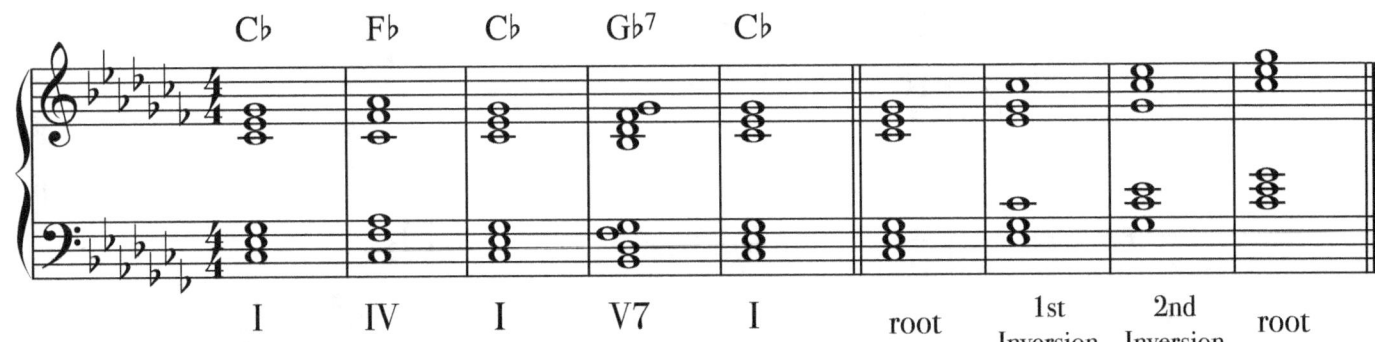

Cadence in A-flat minor
i - iv - i - V7 - i

Chord Inversions
A-flat minor

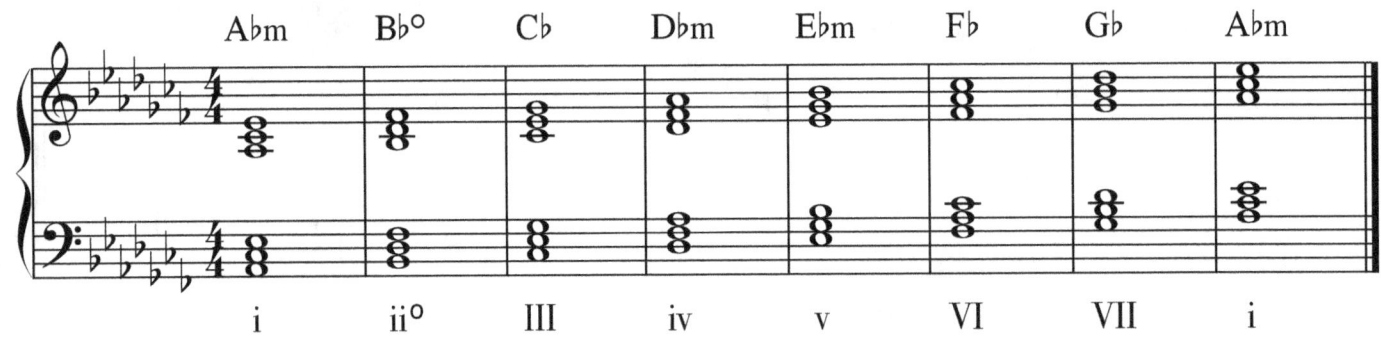

Chords with a root note of C

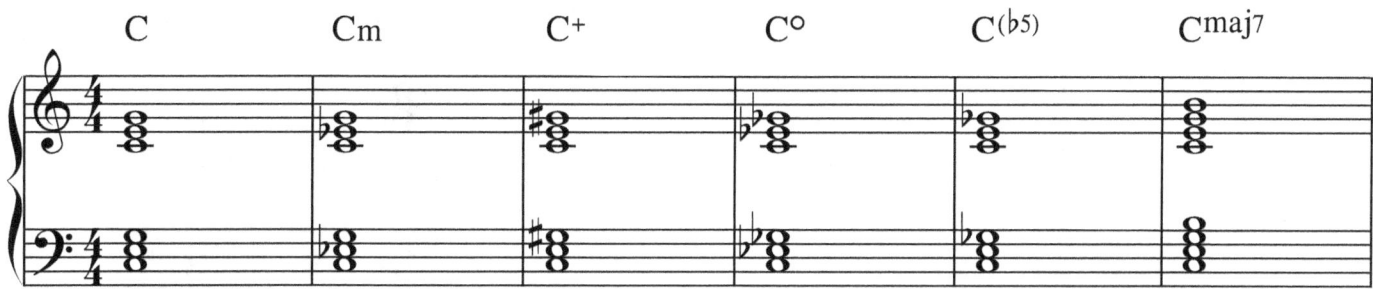

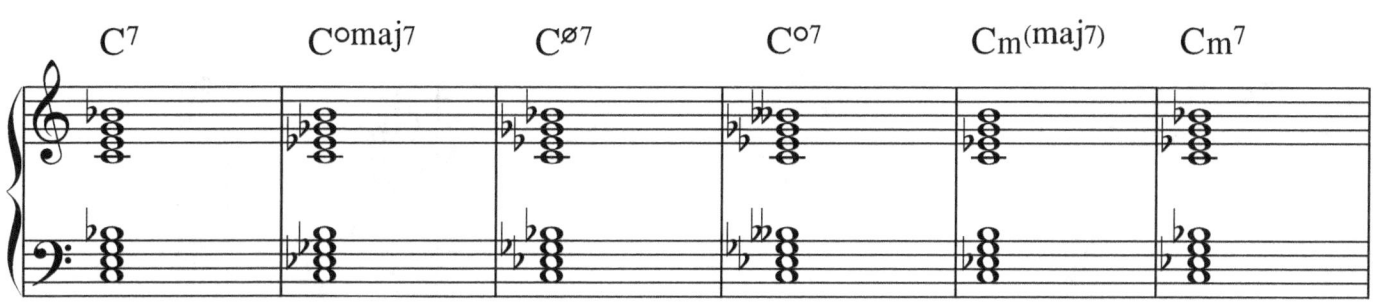

Note: For a detailed explanation of these 24 chords, see *Appendix B*, pages *iii - vi*

Chords with a root note of G

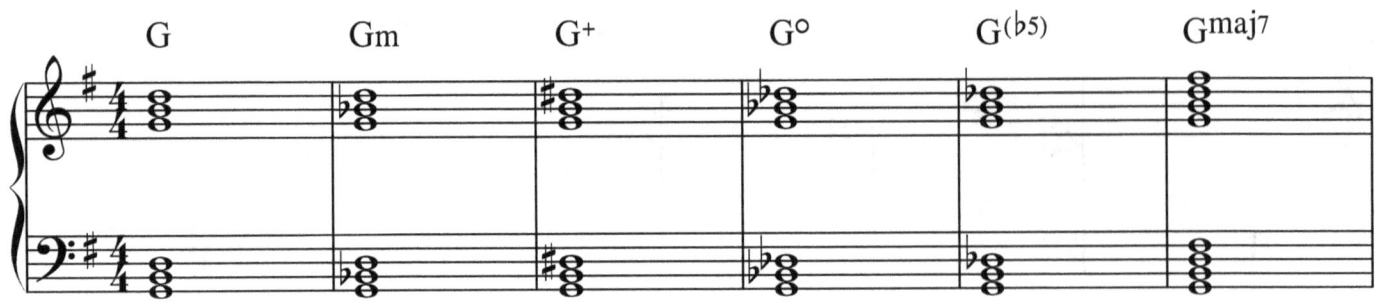
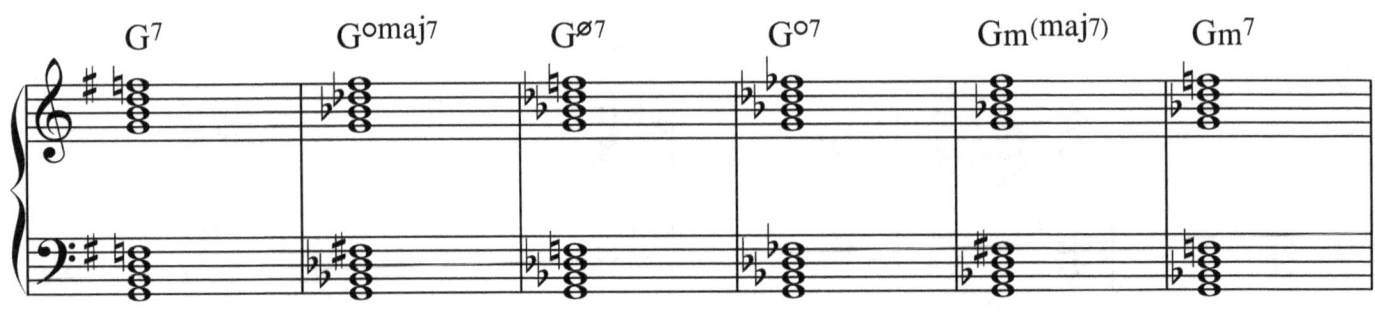
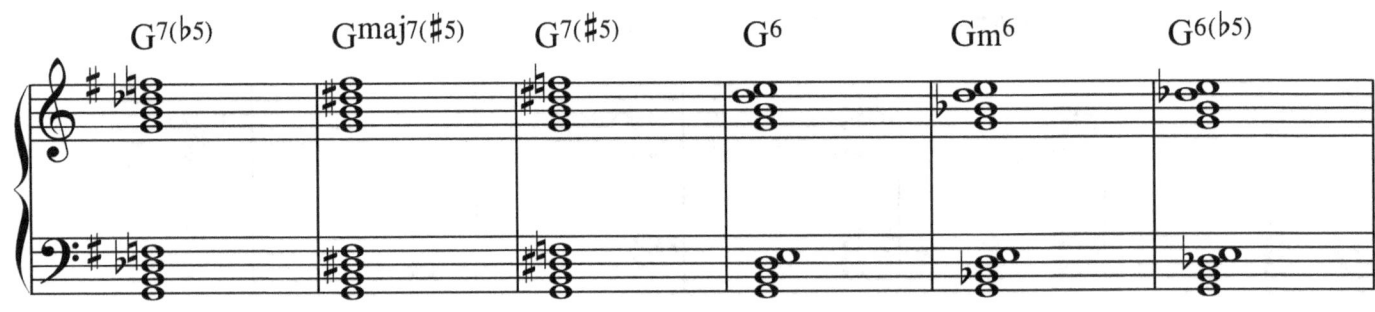

Chords with a root note D

Chords with a root note of A

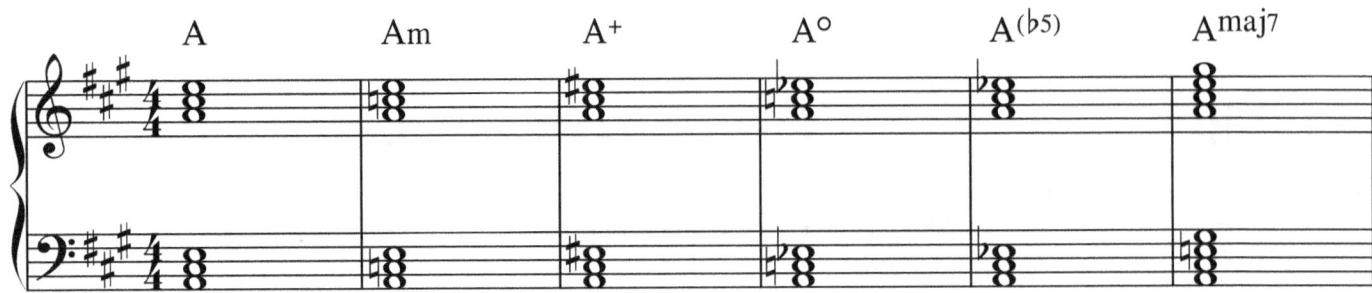

Chords with a root note of E

Chords with a root note of B

Chords with a root note of F-sharp

Chords with a root note of C-sharp

Chords with a root note of F

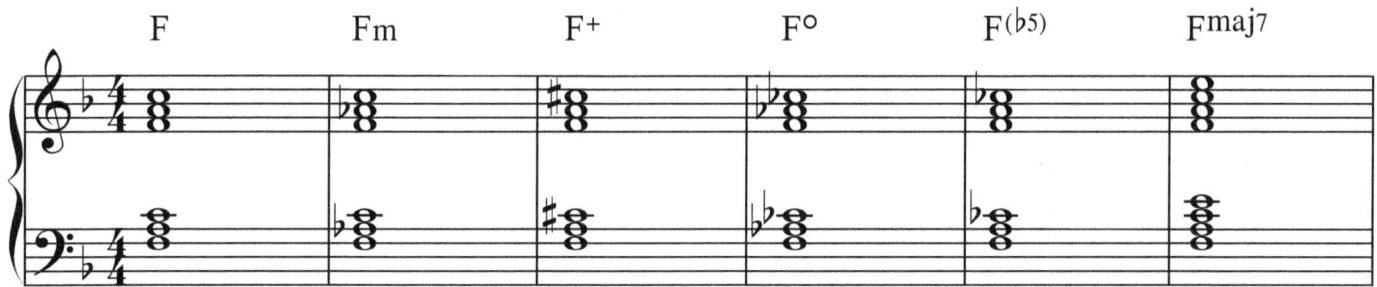
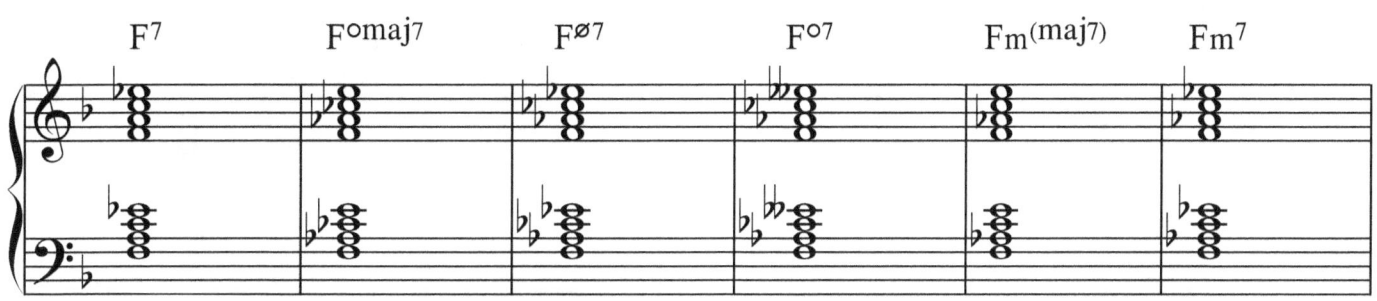

Chords with a root note of B-flat

Chords with a root note of E-flat

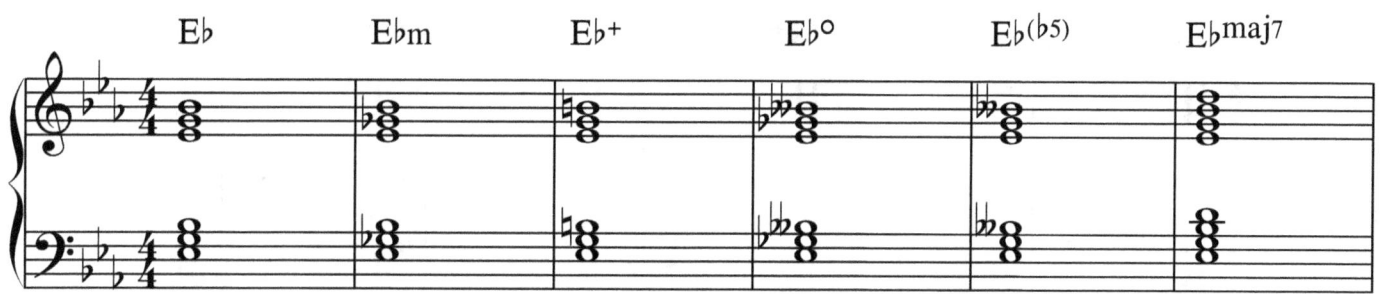
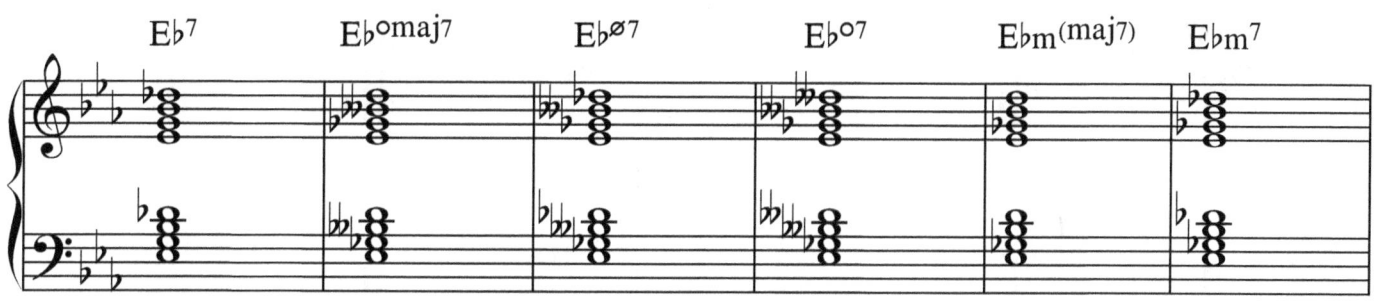
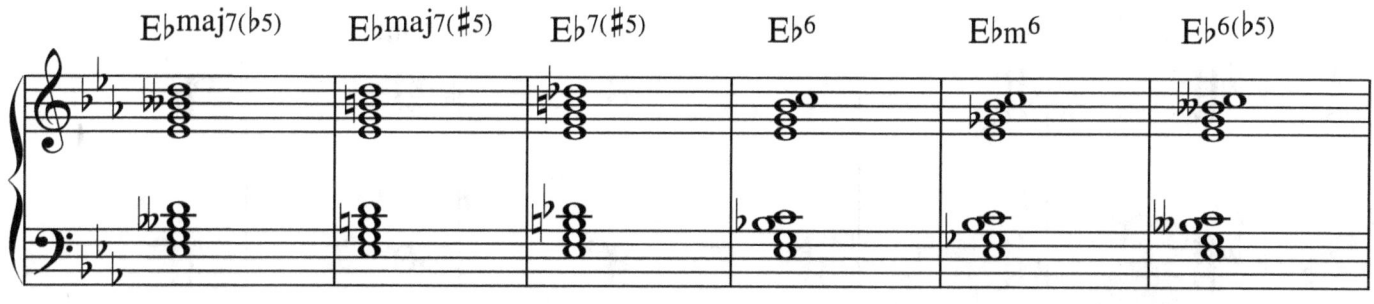

Chords with a root note of A-flat

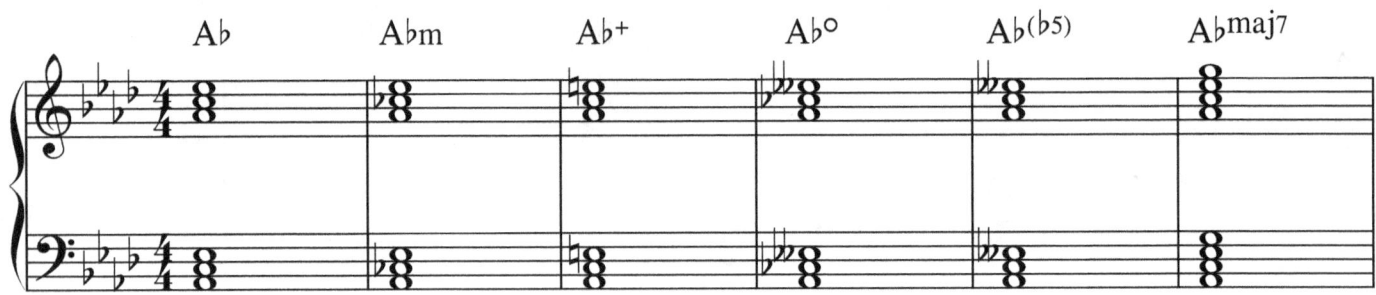

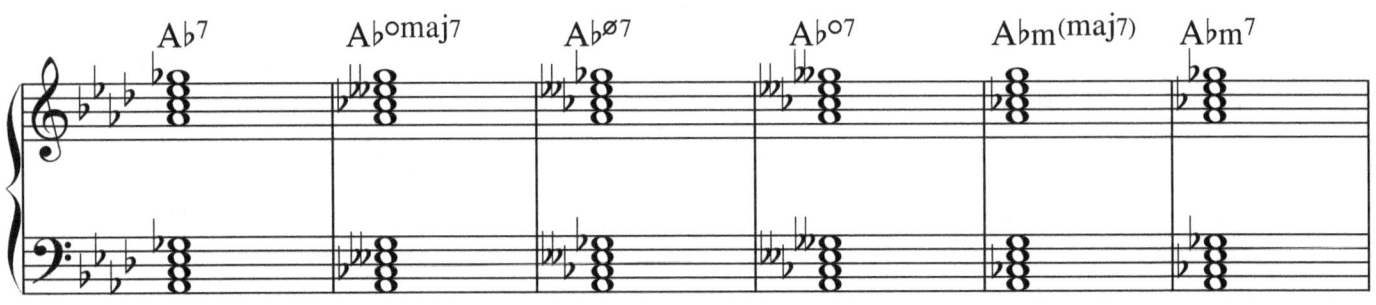

Chords with a root note of D-flat

Chords with a root note of G-flat

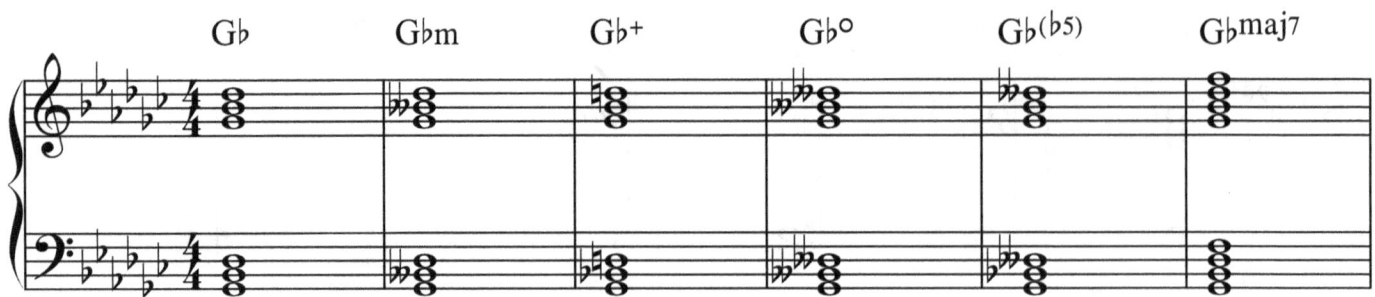

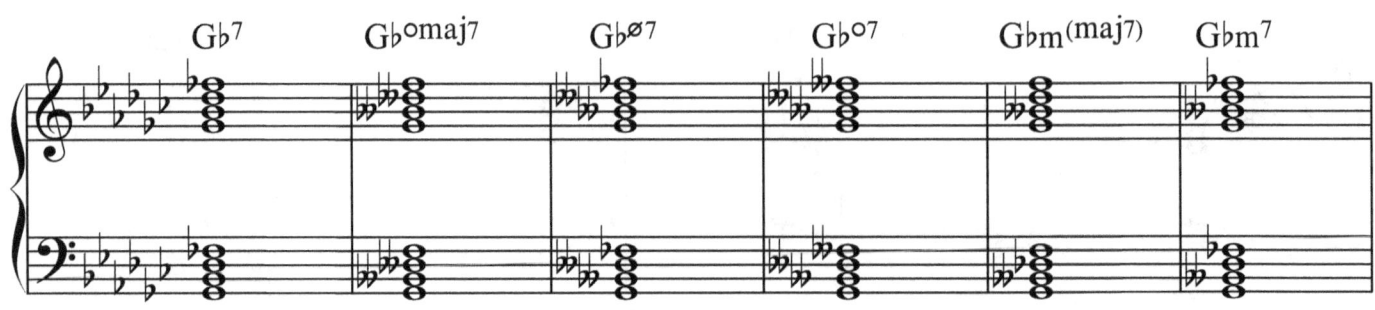

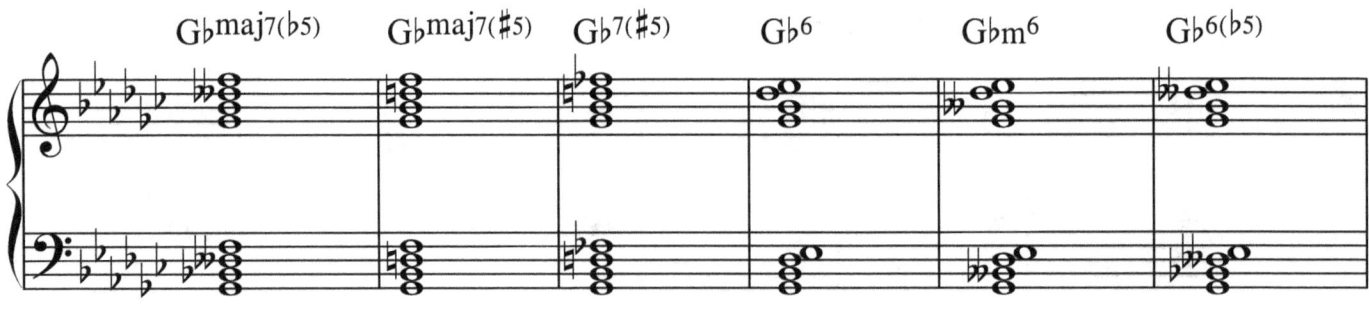

Chords with a root note of C-flat

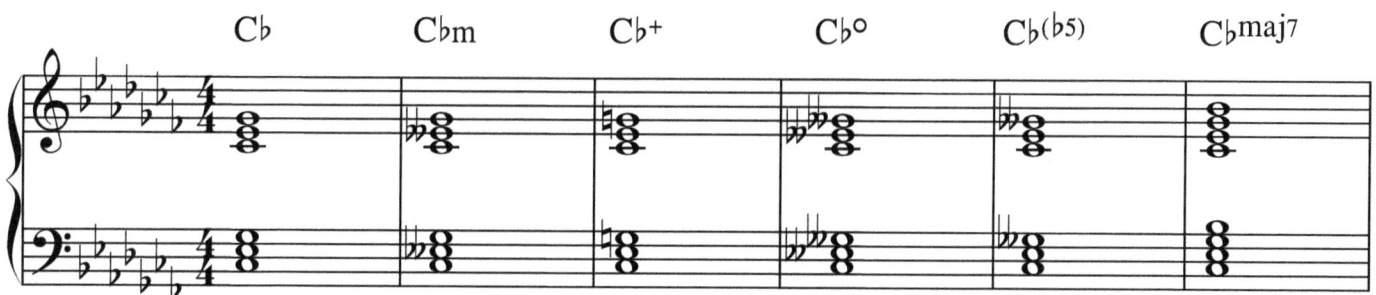
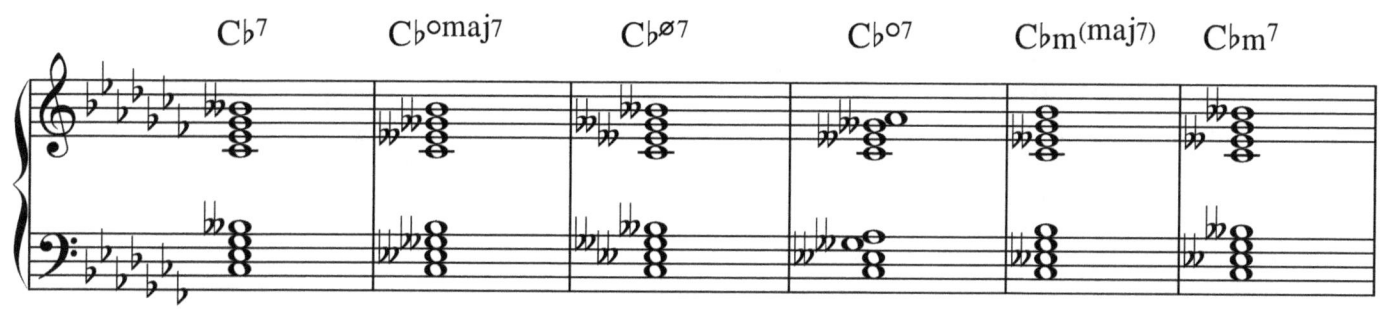
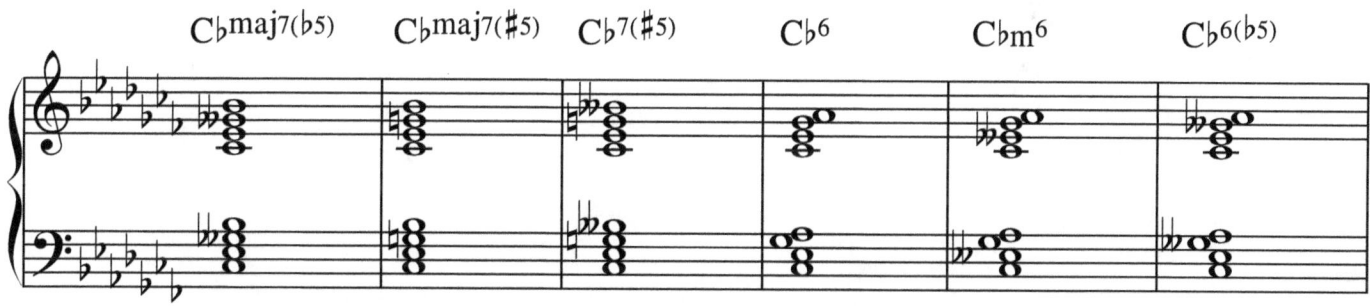

Circle of Fifths

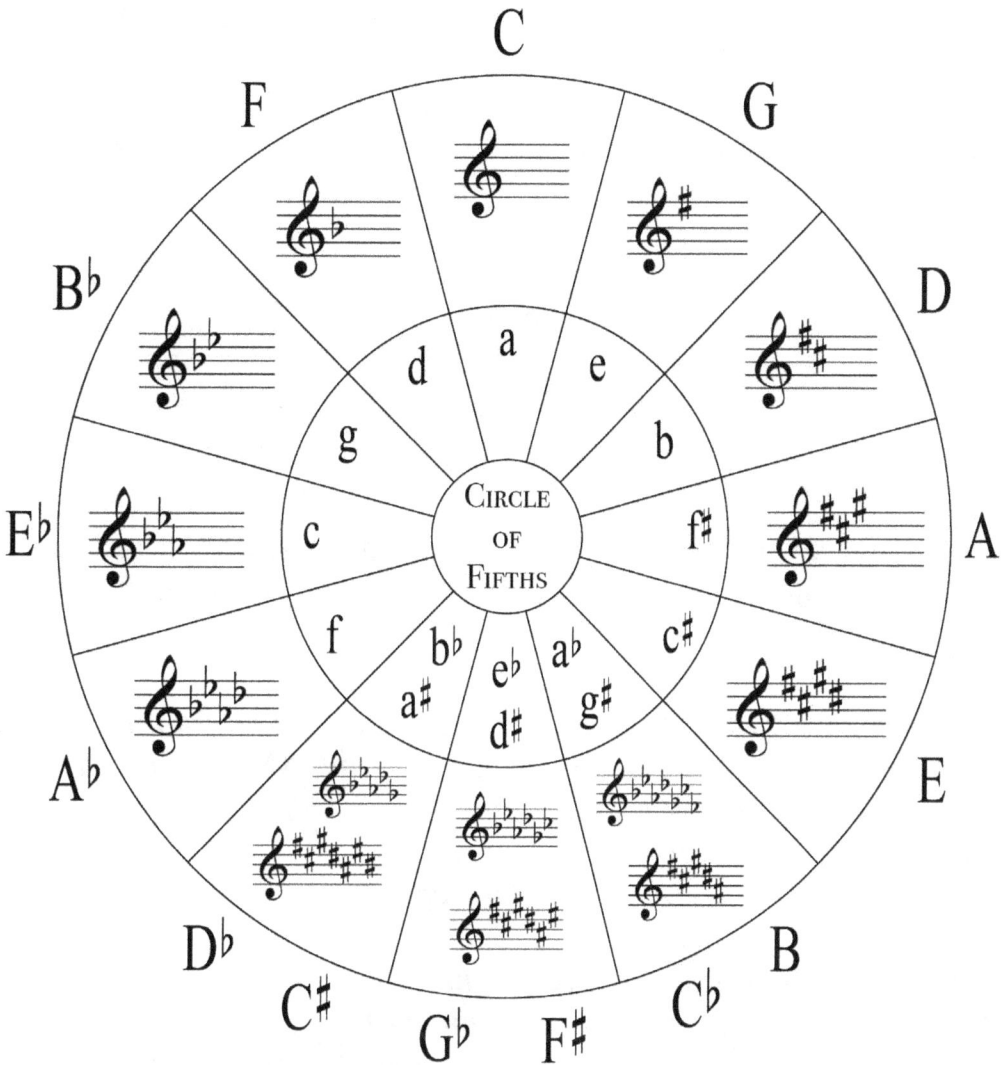

Order of Sharps: Travel clockwise around the circle ascending a perfect fifth.
    F♯, C♯, G♯, D♯, A♯, E♯, B♯
Order of Flats: Travel counter-clockwise around the circle descending a perfect fifth.
    B♭, E♭, A♭, D♭, G♭, C♭, F♭
Letters represent key signatures:
    The letters outside the outer circle represent major keys: **C** is **C major**.
    The letters inside the inner circle represent minor keys: **a** is **a minor**.
Enharmonic Equivalent Keys: Keys that sound the same, played the same but written differently.

The three **major** enharmonic pairs:	The three **minor** enharmonic pairs:
B - 5 sharps and **C♭** - 7 flats	**G♯** - 5 sharps and **A♭** - 7 flats
F♯ - 6 sharps and **G♭** - 6 flats	**D♯** - 6 sharps and **E♭** - 6 flats
C♯ - 7 sharps and **D♭** - 5 flats	**A♯** - 7 sharps and **B♭** - 5 flats

Appendix B

Arpeggios

An arpeggio is a type of broken chord in which the notes that make up that chord are played individually in succession either ascending or descending. For example: a one octave ascending and descending arpeggio of a C major chord would be the notes (C, E, G, C, G, E, C). The arpeggios contained in this book (pages 139-153) are four octaves, ascending and descending, and consist of the following four chords: **major**, **minor**, **dominant 7th** and **diminished 7th**.

Chords

A **chord** is any harmonic set of pitches consisting of three or more notes that are heard simultaneously. A **cadence** is a chord progression of at least two chords that ends a musical phrase. This book illustrates a **I - IV - I - V⁷ - I** major key cadence (chord progression) and a **i - iv - i - V⁷ - i** minor key cadence (chord progression). A **scale-tone triad** is a three note chord created using the notes of a given scale. The cadences and scale-tone triads in this book are based on all fifteen major and fifteen natural minor scales (pages 154-168).

- **Major key scale-tone triads** are created using the notes of a **major** scale. All major key scale-tone triads follow the pattern: **M - m - m - M - M - m - dim - M**.
  - I chord - **Major** - Scale Degree: *Tonic*
  - ii chord - **minor** - Scale Degree: *Supertonic*
  - iii chord - **minor** - Scale Degree: *Mediant*
  - IV chord - **Major** - Scale Degree: *Subdominant*
  - V chord - **Major** - Scale Degree: *Dominant*
  - vi chord - **minor** - Scale Degree: *Submediant*
  - vii° chord - **diminished** - Scale Degree: *Leading Tone*
  - VIII chord - **Major** - Scale Degree: *Tonic*

- **Natural minor key scale-tone triads** are created using the notes of a **natural minor** scale. All natural minor key scale-tone triads follow the pattern: **m - dim - M - m - m - M - M - m**.
  - i chord - **minor** - Scale Degree: *Tonic*
  - ii° chord - **diminished** - Scale Degree: *Supertonic*
  - III chord - **Major** - Scale Degree: *Mediant*
  - iv chord - **minor** - Scale Degree: *Subdominant*
  - v chord* - **minor** - Scale Degree: *Dominant*
  - VI chord - **Major** - Scale Degree: *Submediant*
  - VII chord - **Major** - Scale Degree: *Subtonic*
  - viii chord - **minor** - Scale Degree: *Tonic*

* **Note:** When a v chord is used in a minor key to return to, or resolve to the tonic, a **V⁷**

Appendix B

chord or **Dominant 7ᵗʰ** is used. When a **v** chord is used to pass to another chord in the minor key the **v** chord or **Minor** is used.
- **Example:** In the key of **A minor**, the fifth note of the scale is **E**. If a chord beginning on **E** is used to go back to the tonic, **A**, the **Dominant 7th** would be used: **E, G♯, B, D**. If a chord beginning on **E** does not return to the tonic, **A**, then the minor chord: **E, G, B** would be used.

This book presents **24** three and four note chords for each root note (pages 169-183). Below is a list of the chords that are presented in this book. Examples will use a root note of C.

- **Major:** A chord that contains the 1st, 3rd, and 5th notes of a major scale. There are 3 half steps between the first two notes, an interval of a major third. There are 2 half steps between the second two notes, an interval of a minor third.
    - Example: **C major** or **C** is made with the notes **C, E, G**.
- **Minor:** A chord that contains the 1st, lowered 3rd and 5th notes of a major scale. There are 2 half steps between the first two notes, an interval of a minor third. There are 3 half steps between the second two notes, an interval of a major third.
    - Example: **C minor** or **Cm** is made with the notes **C, E♭, G**.
- **Augmented:** A chord that contains the 1st, 3rd, and raised 5th notes of a major scale. There are 3 half steps between the first two notes, an interval of a major third. There are also 3 half steps between the second two notes, an interval of a major third.
    - Example: **C augmented** or **C⁺** is made with the notes **C, E, G♯**.
- **Diminished:** A chord that contains the 1st, lowered 3rd, and lowered 5th notes of a major scale. There are 2 half steps between the first two notes, an interval of a minor third. There are also 2 half steps between the second two notes, an interval of a minor third.
    - Example: **C diminished** or **C°** is made with the notes **C, E♭, G♭**.
- **Major, flat the 5th:** A chord that contains the 1st, 3rd, and lowered 5th notes of a major scale. There are 3 half steps between the first two notes, an interval of a major third. There is 1 half step between the second two notes, an interval of a major second.
    - Example: **C major, flat the fifth** or **C⁽♭⁵⁾** is made with the notes **C, E, G♭**.
- **Major 7th:** A chord that contains the 1st, 3rd, 5th, and 7th notes of a major scale. There are 3 half steps between the first two notes, an interval of a major third. There are 2 half steps between the second two notes, an interval of a minor third. Finally, there are 3 half steps between the third and fourth notes, an interval of a major third.
    - Example: **C major 7th** or **Cᵐᵃʲ⁷** is made with the notes **C, E, G, B**.
- **Dominant 7th:** A chord that contains the 1st, 3rd, 5th, and lowered 7th notes of a major scale. There are 3 half steps between the first two notes, an interval of a major third. There are 2 half steps between the second two notes, an interval of a minor third. Finally, there are 2 half steps between the third and fourth notes, an interval of a minor third.
    - Example: **C dominant 7th** or **C⁷** is made with the notes **C, E, G, B♭**.

Appendix B

- **Diminished major 7th:** A chord that contains the 1st, lowered 3rd, lowered 5th, and 7th notes of a major scale. There are 2 half steps between the first two notes, an interval of a minor third. There are 2 half steps between the second two notes, an interval of a minor third. Finally, there are 4 half steps between the third and fourth notes, an interval of a perfect fourth.
  - Example: **C diminished major 7th** or **C°maj7** is made with the notes **C, E♭, G♭, B**.
- **Half-diminished 7th:** A chord that contains the 1st, lowered 3rd, lowered 5th, and lowered 7th notes of a major scale. There are 2 half steps between the first two notes, an interval of a minor third. There are 2 half steps between the second two notes, an interval of a minor third. Finally, there are 3 half steps between the third and fourth notes, an interval of a major third.
  - Example: **C half-dimished 7th** or **C⌀7** is made with the notes **C, E♭, G♭, B♭**.
- **Diminished 7th:** A chord that contains the 1st, lowered 3rd, lowered 5th, and twice lowered 7th notes of a major scale. There are 2 half steps between the first two notes, an interval of a minor third. There are 2 half steps between the second two notes, an interval of a minor third. Finally, there are 2 half steps between the third and fourth notes, an interval of a minor third.
  - Example: **C diminished 7th** or **C°7** is made with the notes **C, E♭, G♭, B♭♭**.
- **Minor major 7th:** A chord that contains the 1st, lowered 3rd, 5th, and 7th notes of a major scale. There are 2 half steps between the first two notes, an interval of a minor third. There are 3 half steps between the second two notes, an interval of a major third. Finally, there are 3 half steps between the third and fourth notes, an interval of a major third.
  - Example: **C minor major 7th** or **Cm(maj7)** is made with the notes **C, E♭, G, B**.
- **Minor 7th:** A chord that contains the 1st, lowered 3rd, 5th, and lowered 7th notes of a major scale. There are 2 half steps between the first two notes, an interval of a minor third. There are 3 half steps between the second two notes, an interval of a major third. Finally, there are 2 half steps between the third and fourth notes, an interval of a minor third.
  - Example: **C minor 7th** or **Cm7** is made with the notes **C, E♭, G, B♭**.
- **Dominant 7th, flat the 5th:** A chord that contains the 1st, 3rd, lowered 5th, and lowered 7th notes of a major scale. There are 3 half steps between the first two notes, an interval of a major third. There is 1 half step between the second two notes, an interval of a major second. Finally, there are 3 half steps between the third and fourth notes, an interval of a major third.
  - Example: **C dominant 7th, flat the 5th** or **C7(♭5)** is made with notes **C, E, G♭, B♭**.
- **Major 7th, sharp the 5th:** A chord that contains the 1st, 3rd, raised 5th, and 7th notes of a major scale. There are 3 half steps between the first two notes, an interval of a major third. There are 3 half steps between the second two notes, an interval of a major third. Finally, there are 2 half steps between the third and fourth notes, an interval of a minor third.

Appendix B

- Example: **C major 7th, sharp the 5th** or **C**$^{\text{maj7(}\sharp\text{5)}}$ is made with the notes **C, E, G♯, B**.
- **Dominant 7th, sharp the 5th:** A chord the contains the 1st, 3rd, raised 5th, and lowered 7th notes of a major scale. There are 3 half steps between the first two notes, an interval of a major third. There are 3 half steps between the second two notes, an interval of a major third. Finally, there is 1 half step between the third and fourth notes, an interval of a major second.
  - Example: **C dominant 7th, sharp the fifth** or **C**$^{7(\sharp 5)}$ is made with the notes **C, E, G♯, B♭**.
- **Major 6th:** A chord that contains the 1st, 3rd, 5th, and 6th notes of a major scale. There are 3 half steps between the first two notes, an interval of a major third. There are 2 half steps between the second two notes, an interval of a minor third. Finally, there is 1 half step between the third and fourth notes, an interval of a major second.
  - Example: **C major 6th** or **C**^{6} is made with the notes **C, E, G, A**.
- **Minor 6th:** A chord that contains the 1st, lowered 3rd, 5th, and 6th notes of a major scale. There are 2 half steps between the first two notes, an interval of a minor third. There are 3 half steps between the second two notes, an interval of a major third. Finally, there is 1 half step between the third and fourth notes, an interval of a major second.
  - Example: **C minor 6th** or **Cm**^{6} is made with the notes **C, E♭, G, A**.
- **Major 6th, flat the 5th:** A chord that contains the 1st, 3rd, lowered 5th, and 6th notes of a major scale. There are 3 half steps between the first two notes, an interval of a major third. There is 1 half step between the second two notes, an interval of a major second. Finally, there are 2 half steps between the third and fourth notes, an interval of a minor third.
  - Example: **C major 6th, flat the 5th** or **C**$^{6(\flat 5)}$ is made with the notes **C, E, G♭, A**.
- **Major, suspended 4th**: A chord that contains the 1st, 4th, and 5th notes of a major scale. There are 4 half steps between the first two notes, an interval of a perfect fourth. There is 1 half step between the second two notes, an interval of a major second.
  - Example: **C major, suspended 4th** or **C**$^{(\text{sus4})}$ is made with the notes **C, F, G**.
- **Major, suspended 2nd:** A chord that contains the 1st, 2nd, and 5th notes of a major scale. There is 1 half step between the first two notes, an interval of a major 2nd. There are 4 half steps between the second two notes, an interval of a perfect fourth.
  - Example: **C major, suspended 2nd** or **C**$^{(\text{sus2})}$ is made with the notes **C, D, G**.
- **Major, add the 4th:** A chord that contains the 1st, 3rd, 4th, and 5th notes of a major scale. There are 3 half steps between the first and second notes, an interval of a major 3rd. There are 0 half steps between the second two notes, an interval of a minor second. Finally, there is 1 half step between the third and fourth notes, an interval of a major second.
  - Example: **C major, add the 4th** or **C**$^{(\text{add4})}$ is made with the notes **C, E, F, G**.
- **Major, add the 2nd:** A chord that contains the 1st, 2nd, 3rd, and 5th notes of a major scale. There is 1 half step between the first two notes, an interval of a major second. There is 1 half step between the second two notes, an interval of a major second.

Finally, there are 2 half steps between the third and fourth notes, an interval of a minor third.
- Example: **C major, add the 2nd** or **C(add2)** is made with the notes **C, D, E, G**.
- **Dominant 7th, suspended 4th:** A chord that contains the 1st, 4th, 5th and lowered 7th notes of a major scale. There are 4 half steps between the first two notes, an interval of a perfect fourth. There is 1 half step between the second two notes, an interval of a major second. Finally, there are 2 half steps between the third and fourth notes, an interval of a minor third.
  - Example: **C dominant 7th, suspended 4th** or **C7(sus 4)** is made with the notes **C, F, G, B♭**.
- **Major, suspended 9th:** A chord that contains the 1st, 5th, and 9th notes of a major scale. There are 6 half steps between the first two notes, an interval of a perfect fifth. There are 6 half steps between the second two notes, an interval of a perfect fifth.
  - Example: **C major, suspended 9th** or **C(sus 9)** is made with the notes **C, G, D**.

Circle of Fifths

The Circle of Fifths is a visual representation and a fundamental concept in music theory that helps musicians and composers understand the relationships between different key signatures, scales, and chords. It is a circular diagram that arranges the twelve unique pitch classes (notes) of the chromatic scale in a specific order, emphasizing the intervals of a perfect fifth between each successive note. See *Appendix A* for a visual representation of the Circle of Fifths. Here's how the Circle of Fifths works:

- **Note Arrangement:** Starting from the top (usually C major/A minor), the circle proceeds in a clockwise direction, adding one sharp to each successive key signature. This means that each new key is a perfect fifth higher than the previous key. Starting once again at the top and proceeding in a counter-clockwise direction, adds one flat to each successive key. This means that each new key is a perfect fifth lower than the previous key. These statements are true traveling either direction until one reaches either seven sharps or seven flats.
- **Sharps and Flats:** The key of C major and A minor, located at the top of the circle have no sharps or flats. Travel clockwise around the circle and keys gain sharps. Travel counter-clockwise around the circle and keys gain flats.
- **Order of Sharps:** The order in which sharps are added to key signatures follows a specific pattern: **F♯, C♯, G♯, D♯, A♯, E♯, B♯**. When traveling up the keyboard each sharp is a perfect fifth higher than the preceding sharp.
- **Order of Flats:** The order in which flats are added to key signatures also follows a specific patter: **B♭, E♭, A♭, D♭, G♭, C♭, F♭**. When traveling down the keyboard, each flat is a perfect fifth lower than the preceding flat.
- **Relative Keys:** The Circle of Fifths also helps musicians identify the relationship between a major key and its relative minor. The capital letters along the outside of the circle represent the major keys. The lower case letters of the inner circle are the relative

minor keys of the corresponding major key of the outer circle. A major key and its relative minor have the same number of sharps or flats. Examples:
- **C major** is the relative major of **A minor** (0 sharps or flats)
- **A minor** is the relative minor of **C major** (0 sharps or flats)
- **F major** is the relative major of **D minor** (1 flat)
- **D minor** is the relative minor of **F major** (1 flat)

- **Enharmonic Equivalent Key Signatures:** These are key signatures that have different names and are written differently that include **identical** pitches. Enharmonic equivalent key signatures are found at the bottom of the Circle of Fifths. These are the **major** and **minor** enharmonic equivalent key signatures:
  - **B major** (5 sharps) and **C♭ major** (7 flats)
  - **F♯ major** (6 sharps) and **G♭ major** (6 flats)
  - **C♯ major** (7 sharps) and **D♭ major** (5 flats)
  - **G♯ minor** (5 sharps) and **A♭ minor** (7 flats)
  - **D♯ minor** (6 sharps) and **E♭ minor** (6 flats)
  - **A♯ minor** (7 sharps) and **B♭ minor** (5 flats)

- **Circle of Fourths:** While the Circle of Fifths emphasizes either ascending or descending perfect fifths, one can also view the circle as a Circle of Fourths. Traveling counter-clockwise around the circle but ascending a perfect fourth results in adding one flat to each successive key signature. Additionally, traveling clockwise around the circle but descending a perfect fourth results in adding one sharp to each successive key signature. These statements are true traveling either direction until one reaches either seven sharps or seven flats.

In summary, the **Circle of Fifths/Circle of Fourths** is a powerful tool that aids musicians in grasping the complex relationship between keys, scales, chords, and harmonic progressions in music. It's an essential concept for understanding music theory, composition, and practical applications like transposing music or creating chord progressions.

Dynamic Markings

Dynamics are one part of what makes music interesting and refer to the loudness or softness of musical notes and phrases. Dynamics are relative and require the performer to make correct interpretations depending on the context of the music. The proper use of dynamics help musicians sustain interest in a piece of music and communicate a particular emotional state or feeling. Dynamic markings are generally placed in between the two staves of a grand staff. Below are listed the most common dynamic markings.

Basic Dynamic Markings:

- *pp* - pianissimo: Play very soft
- *p* - piano: Play soft
- *mp* - mezzo piano: Play moderately (medium) soft

- *mf* - mezzo forte: Play moderately (medium) loud
- *f* - forte: Play loud
- *ff* - fortissimo: Play very loud

Additional Dynamic Markings

- **Accent:** Dynamic marking generally placed above or below the note head to indicate a stronger (louder) attack to a given note. Indicated with this symbol: >
- **Crescendo:** To gradually get louder. (Abbreviated: *cresc.*)
- **Decrescendo:** To gradually get softer. (Abbreviated: *decresc.*)
- **Diminuendo:** Same as decrescendo. To gradually get softer. (Abbreviated: *dim.*)
- **Sforzando:** Suddenly with force. More emphasis than an accent. (Abbreviated: *sfz.*)

Intervals

In music theory, an interval is measurement or relationship between two pitches. Below is a list of the intervals found in one octave beginning with the root note C.

- **Minor 2nd:** C - C♯ (0 half steps between notes)
- **Major 2nd:** C - D (1 half step between notes)
- **Minor 3rd:** C - E♭ (2 half steps between notes)
- **Major 3rd:** C - E (3 half steps between notes)
- **Perfect 4th:** C - F (4 half steps between notes)
- **Tritone:** C - F♯ (5 half steps between notes, the midpoint of an octave)
- **Perfect 5th:** C - G (6 half steps between notes)
- **Minor 6th:** C - A♭ (7 half steps between notes)
- **Major 6th:** C - A (8 half steps between notes)
- **Minor 7th:** C - B♭ (9 half steps between notes)
- **Major 7th:** C - B (10 half steps between notes)
- **Octave:** C - C (11 half steps between notes)

Remember that intervals can start on any note. Think of the first note as the root note. Counting half steps begins with the root note. If the first note is **F**, the interval created will be based off the root note **F**. The interval **F - A** has 3 half steps between the two notes and is, therefore, a **major third**. The interval **F♯ - C♯** has 6 half steps between the two notes and is, therefore, a **perfect fifth**.

Scales

A scale is any ordered sequence of notes or intervals that divide an octave. In western music an octave is broken up into 12 half steps. From these 12 half steps are the various scales created. This book covers the major and the three minor (natural, melodic, and harmonic) scales, in addition to chromatic scales. Let's dive into the different types of scales.

- **Major Scale:** A major scale is like a happy cheerful ladder of notes. It has a specific pattern of whole steps (W) and half steps (H) between the notes. The pattern to create all major scales is as follows: **Tonic - W - W - H - W - W - W - H**. This pattern works for every starting point on the piano. Each note in a major scale has a name such as C, D, E, F, G, A, B, C, the notes of a C major scale. Each note also has a scale number or degree from one to eight (octave). C, the first note of the C major scale is 1. G is 5, etc. Each degree or number also has a name. They are:
    - 1st note of the scale: **Tonic**
    - 2nd note of the scale: **Supertonic**
    - 3rd note of the scale: **Mediant**
    - 4th note of the scale: **Subdominant**
    - 5th note of the scale: **Dominant**
    - 6th note of the scale: **Submediant**
    - 7th note of the scale: **Leading Tone**
    - 8th note of the scale: **Tonic**

- **Minor Scale:** Each minor key scale is based on the key of its relative major. While there is only one major scale for each major key, there are three minor scales for each minor key. They are the **natural, melodic** and **harmonic** minor scales. This book provides an opportunity to play all three minor scales in all fifteen minor keys.

    - **Natural Minor Scale:** The natural minor scale is a bit sad or mysterious. The natural minor scale uses the same notes as its relative major and follows a similar pattern of whole steps (W) and half steps (H). This pattern is used to create all natural minor scales and is as follows: **Tonic - W - H - W - W - H - W - W**.
        - Example: **A natural minor…A, B, C, D, E, F, G, A**.
        - The scale degrees for a natural minor scale are:
            - 1st note of the scale: **Tonic**
            - 2nd note of the scale: **Supertonic**
            - 3rd note of the scale: **Mediant**
            - 4th note of the scale: **Subdominant**
            - 5th note of the scale: **Dominant**
            - 6th note of the scale: **Submediant**
            - 7th note of the scale: **Subtonic**
            - 8th note of the scale: **Tonic**

    - **Melodic Minor Scale:** The melodic minor scale has two "faces" - one when you go up and another when you go down. When going up the melodic minor scale the 6th and 7th notes of the scale are raised one half step. When going down, the 6th and 7th notes are lowered to their original positions.
        - Example: **A melodic minor…A, B, C, D, E, F♯, G♯, A, G♮, F♮, E, D, C, B, A**.

- The scale degrees for a melodic minor scale are:
    - 1st note of the scale: **Tonic**
    - 2nd note of the scale: **Supertonic**
    - 3rd note of the scale: **Mediant**
    - 4th note of the scale: **Subdominant**
    - 5th note of the scale: **Dominant**
    - 6th note of the scale: **Submediant**
    - 7th note of the scale: **Leading Tone** (ascending), **Subtonic** (descending).
    - 8th note of the scale: **Tonic**

- **Harmonic Minor Scale:** The harmonic minor scale has a unique sound that's a bit exotic. It begins the same as the natural minor but raises the 7th note of the scale on the way up and on the way down.
    - Example: **A** harmonic minor…**A, B, C, D, E, F, G♯, A, G♯, F, E, D, C, B, A**.
    - The scale degrees for a harmonic minor scale are:
        - 1st note of the scale: **Tonic**
        - 2nd note of the scale: **Supertonic**
        - 3rd note of the scale: **Mediant**
        - 4th note of the scale: **Subdominant**
        - 5th note of the scale: **Dominant**
        - 6th note of the scale: **Submediant**
        - 7th note of the scale: **Leading Tone**
        - 8th note of the scale: **Tonic**

- **Chromatic Scale:** The chromatic scale is unique as it sequentially uses all the black and all the white notes in an octave. This book provides a great opportunity to play the chromatic scale in various intervals. An ascending chromatic scale from C - C contains the follow notes: **C, C♯/D♭, D, D♯/E♭, E, F, F♯/G♭, G, G♯/A♭, A, A♯/B♭, C**.

Tempo

Tempo is a term used to refer to the speed or pace of a piece of music. Below are some common terms found to describe the speed or pace of compositions. Notice, that many of the tempos listed below overlap one another. Additionally, tempo indications are more of a guideline than hard-fast-rules. It's up to the performer to interpret the indicators to create their desired performance. Instructions regarding tempo are generally placed above the upper staff.

- **Grave:** Very slow and solemn (24-40 bpm)
- **Largo:** Slow and broad (40-60 bpm)
- **Lento:** Very Slowly (40-60 bpm)
- **Adagio:** Slow and leisurely (60-76 bpm)
- **Andante:** Walking Pace (76-108 bpm)
- **Andante Moderato:** slightly faster than andante. Moderate walking pace (92-112 bpm)

- **Moderato:** Moderate speed (108-120 bpm)
- **Allegretto:** Moderately fast (112-120 bpm)
- **Allegro Moderato:** Close to but not quite allegro (112-124 bpm)
- **Allegro:** Fast and bright (120-156 bpm)
- **Molto Allegro:** At the fast end of Allegro. Quickly and swiftly. (132-160 bpm)
- **Vivace:** fast and lively (156-168 bpm)
- **Presto:** Even faster (168-200 bpm)

Additional Tempo Terms

- **A tempo:** return to current tempo
- **Accelerando:** gradually speeding up. (Abbreviation: *accel.*)
- **Molto:** a lot or much. Ex…molto ritardando (*molto rit.*) slow down a lot.
- **Poco:** a little. Ex…poco ritardando (*poco rit.*) slow down a little.
- **Rallentando:** freely slowing down, drifting away. (Abbreviation: *rall.*)
- **Ritardando:** a gradual slowing down (Abbreviation: *rit.*)
- **Tempo Giusto:** very strict tempo.
- **Tempo Primo:** return to the original tempo.
- **Tempo Rubato:** free adjustment of tempo for expressive purposes.

Other Books by Bill Walker Music Publishing

The Joy of Christmas
Published: 2023

Requiem Rising
Published: 2024

Reverie
Published: 2024

Visit my website
www.billwalkercomposer.com

Join my free Facebook group
www.facebook.com/groups/pianocomposers